THE CLASSICS OF WESTERN SPIRITUALITY

9. September, 2007

Dear George,

Thanks so much for your beautiful German liturgy. It was worth the wait!

May this book be a blessing to you. See p. 138 —

We are under a heaven of grace!

What do you make of the dialectic, p142?

LOVE JOY PEACE

Peter

THE CLASSICS OF WESTERN SPIRITUALITY
A Library of the Great Spiritual Masters

Luther's Spirituality

EDITED AND TRANSLATED BY
PHILIP D. W. KREY AND PETER D. S. KREY

PREFACE BY
TIMOTHY J. WENGERT

PAULIST PRESS
NEW YORK • MAHWAH

Cover Art: Painting of Martin Luther in Rydboholm Church, Sweden. Photograph by Nancy de Flon.

Cover and caseside design by A. Michael Velthaus
Book design by Lynn Else

Library of Congress Cataloging-in-Publication Data

Luther's spirituality / edited and translated by Philip D.W. Krey and Peter D.S. Krey.
    p.   cm.—(The Classics of Western spirituality)
  Includes bibliographical references and index.
  ISBN-13: 978-0-8091-0514-4 (cloth : alk. paper)
  ISBN-13: 978-0-8091-3949-1 (pbk. : alk. paper)
  1. Luther, Martin, 1483–1546. 2. Spirituality—History of doctrines—16th century. I. Krey, Philip D., 1950– II. Krey, Peter D.S.
BR333.5.S65L88 2007
248.092—dc22

2006029115

Published by Paulist Press
997 Macarthur Boulevard
Mahwah, New Jersey 07430

www.paulistpress.com

Printed and bound in the
United States of America

CONTENTS

Foreword...ix

Acknowledgments xi

Preface xiii

General Introduction xxi

Part I—Luther's Spirituality in a Late-Medieval Context

Editors' Introduction to Part I...1
Letter to George Spenlein: "Learn Christ,...the Crucified"..........3
Letter to the Elector, Frederick the Wise:
      Luther as Frederick's New Relic 6
Letter to Jerome Weller: On the Devil 8
Letter to Matthias Weller: The Mutual Consolation of the
      Faithful 11
Letter of Comfort to His Dying Father...13
Luther Counsels Weller: The Greater the Saint before God,
      the Greater the Temptations 16
About Fleeing into Solitude...18
Commentary on Psalm 82: Secular Saviors..................................19
An Admonishment to Pastors to Preach against Usury:
      How One Should Give, Lend, and Suffer 34
Preface to the Revelation of St. John (1522)................................46
Preface to the Revelation of St. John (1530 and 1546)..............48

Part II—Teaching the New Spirituality

Editors' Introduction to Part II 57
Scholia on Psalm 5: On Hope...59
The Freedom of a Christian 69
The Magnificat Put into German and Explained 91

CONTENTS

Preface to the Epistle to the Romans 104
Preface to the German Writings 119
Psalm 117: The Art That Cannot Be Mastered.........................125
Sermon at Coburg on Cross and Suffering................................151
Lectures on Galatians 3:6—"Thus Abraham Believed God" 161
On Jacob's Ladder 172

Part III—A New Path to Prayer

Editors' Introduction to Part III..183
The Large Catechism: Preface and First Commandment..........185
The Large Catechism: The Lord's Prayer 198
Commentary on Psalm 118—The Beautiful Thanksgiving 203
A Simple Way to Pray, for Master Peter the Barber 217
The Ten Commandments (Long Version).................................235
The Ten Commandments (Short Version)..................................237
The Lord's Prayer, Briefly Interpreted and Brought to Song 238
Christ Jesus to the Jordan Came..240
God Be Exalted! Sing God's Praise in Chorus...........................243
Were God Not with Us at This Time (Psalm 124)...................245
Lord God, I Cry from Deepest Need (Psalm 130)....................246
Jesus Christ, Our Lord and Savior 248
We Praise You, Jesus, That You've Come 250
Concerning the Temptation in Predestination to
    Doubt One's Own Election 252

Notes..253

Bibliography...283

Index...292

FOREWORD

The purpose of this book is to introduce the reader to Martin Luther's spirituality. This involves both his critique of the late-medieval spiritualities that he inherited and his various constructive proposals. The book is designed for the reader to discover the rich complex of issues that Luther contributes to the discussion of spirituality. We have attempted to footnote the text lightly, except where we felt some explanation necessary or to lead the reader to the ever-growing body of literature on Luther's spirituality that would not have been imagined a generation ago. The Classics in Western Spirituality series has had a profound influence on Lutheran scholarship in this regard.

The book is organized into three sections, representing different aspects of Luther's spirituality. At the request of Professor Bernard McGinn, Editor-in-Chief of the Classics in Western Spirituality series, Professor Heiko Oberman reviewed the selections and the contents of the book. The titles of each section and their organization are the result of his helpful suggestions, made not long before his death. We are honored to remember his contribution to Reformation scholarship by using his structure of the topic.

In addition to the preface and the general introduction, most individual texts are preceded by a brief editors' introduction to locate the piece and to suggest the reasons for its inclusion in a volume on Luther's spirituality. Since Part 3 includes Luther's songs and hymns, there is only one editors' introduction for the whole section.

We have attempted to use inclusive language throughout the volume. While some may find this a challenge at first, these translations have been used in three seminars, and the words of women in one class are assuring: "This was the first time we were able to read Luther and not quit because of the lack of inclusive language." We feel confident that our attempt is true to the spirit of Luther, who wrote the great treatise on translation ("On Translating: An Open Letter" [1530], in *Luther's Works*, ed. E. Theodore Bachmann [Philadelphia:

Muhlenberg Press, 1960], 35:175–202). We wish to thank our students for all they have taught us and for their rich insights. All biblical translations are from the New Revised Standard Version, except where Luther's use of the text required keeping a more direct translation of Luther's own words, and these places are noted.

It is an honor to thank those who have contributed to this volume. Our thanks to Professor Bernard McGinn for his invitation to prepare this volume. He has been instrumental in the project from its inception and enormously patient as careers changed and matured through the translation process. We are most grateful for his assent to Peter's joining the project when Philip became president of the Lutheran Theological Seminary at Philadelphia. This has fulfilled a dream of ours to work together on a project of mutual interest, and the experience has proved a delight. Additionally, we wish to thank Professor Timothy Wengert, Philip's colleague at LTSP, for writing the preface and for helping at the early stages to pick the selections that represent Luther's spirituality. We are also grateful to Professor Scott Hendrix, who made suggestions that were crucial for the contents of the book and whose own work in Luther's spirituality has been an invaluable guide along the way. We owe a debt of thanks to Professor Jane Strohl for her clear introduction, which is another example of the collaborative effort among scholars that this book represents. Philip wishes to thank the Lutheran Theological Seminary at Philadelphia for a timely sabbatical, during which the research was done for this volume at the Herzog August Bibliothek in Wolfenbüttel.

Our thanks to the editors at Paulist Press, Nancy de Flon and, earlier, Christopher M. Bellitto, for their expert guidance and advice. Particular thanks are due to René Diemer Krey, who spent countless hours editing the book according to the Paulist Press guidelines, and to Professor Gerald Christianson, Philip's teacher and Professor McGinn's student, for reading the manuscript and offering helpful corrections and comments. All errors of commission and omission are, of course, ours. A long project like this requires that sacrifices be made by families. Peter dedicates this book to his spouse, Nora, and their sons, Ashley, Joshua, and Mark. Philip dedicates this book to his spouse, René, and their children, Jessicah, Lindsay, Jordan, Noah, and Micah. To God be the glory.

ACKNOWLEDGMENTS

These are largely fresh translations, two of which appear for the first time in English, but it is with gratitude that we acknowledge the permissions granted by publishers for the use of critical editions and translations that we used as guides.

We did, however, use other critical editions and existing translations for particular texts, and we are grateful for the following permissions, listed according to the publisher:

The *Magnificat* from *Luther's Works*, vol. 21, c. 1956, 1984 Concordia Publishing House. Used with permission.

"On Jacob's Ladder" from *Luther's Works*, vol. 5, c. 1968, 1996 Concordia Publishing House. Used with permission.

"Commentary on Galatians 3:6" from *Luther's Works*, vol. 26, c. 1963, 1991 Concordia Publishing House. Used with permission.

"Commentary on Psalm 118" from *Luther's Works*, vol. 14, c. 1958, 1986 Concordia Publishing House. Used with permission.

"Preface to the Epistle of St. Paul to the Romans" from *Luther's Works*, vol. 35, ed. E. Theodore Bachmann, c. 1960 Fortress Press. Used with permission of Augsburg Fortress.

"Preface to the Revelation of St. John (1522)" from *Luther's Works*, vol. 35, ed. E. Theodore Bachmann, c. 1960 Fortress Press. Used with permission of Augsburg Fortress.

"Preface to the Revelation of St. John (1530 and 1546)" from *Luther's Works*, vol. 35, ed. E. Theodore Bachmann, c. 1960 Fortress Press. Used with permission of Augsburg Fortress.

"Sermon on Cross and Suffering, Preached at Coburg the Saturday before Easter, Based on the Passion History, April 16, 1530" from *Luther's Works*, vol. 51, ed. John W. Doberstein, c. 1959 Fortress Press. Used with permission of Augsburg Fortress.

"Scholia on Psalm 5: On Hope." The text for the translation in this volume, the first in English, is from a Vatican manuscript of John Aurifabers in *Martin Luther: Evangelium und Leben*, vol. 4 of *Martin Luther Taschenausgabe*, eds. Horst Beintke, Helmar Junghans, and Hubert Kirchner, c. 1983 Evangelische Verlagsanstalt. Used by permission of Evangelische Verlagsanstalt.

The text used in this volume for "The Magnificat" is in Martin Luther, *Studienausgabe*, vol. 1, ed. Hans-Ulrich Delius, c. 1979 Evangelische Verlagsanstalt. Used with permission of Evangelische Verlagsanstalt.

The text used in this volume for "The Preface to the Epistle to the Romans" is in Martin Luther, *Studienausgabe*, vol. 1, ed. Hans-Ulrich Delius, c. 1979 Evangelische Verlagsanstalt. Used with permission of Evangelische Verlagsanstalt.

The text used in this volume for "Preface to the Revelation of St. John (1530 and 1546)" is in Martin Luther, *Studienausgabe*, vol. 1, ed. Hans-Ulrich Delius, c. 1979 Evangelische Verlagsanstalt. Used with permission of Evangelische Verlagsanstalt.

The text for the translation in this volume of the German version of "The Freedom of a Christian" is in Martin Luther, *Studienausgabe*, vol. 2, ed. Hans-Ulrich Delius, c. 1982 Evangelische Verlagsanstalt. Used with permission of Evangelische Verlagsanstalt.

The text for the translation of the "Preface to the German Writings" and "Psalm 117" is in the Weimar Edition (D. Martin Luthers Werke. Kritische Gesamtausgabe; Weimar, 1883–), Hermann Böhlaus Nachfolger Weimar GmbH & Co. Used with permission.

The text for the translation in this volume of "The German Catechism: Preface and First Commandment" is in *Die Bekenntnisschriften der Evangelischen Lutherischen Kirche*, 10th edition, c. 1986, and is used with permission of Vandenhoeck & Ruprecht.

The text for the translation in this volume of "The Lord's Prayer" is in *Die Bekenntnisschriften der Evangelischen Lutherischen Kirche*, 10th edition, c. 1986, and is used with permission of Vandenhoeck & Ruprecht.

Except where otherwise noted above, the text for these translations was Dr. Martin Luthers Sämmtliche Schriften, 25 vols., ed. Johann Georg Walch, 1880–1910, Concordia Publishing House.

Whenever other texts, such as pamphlets, were used for minor improvements to these texts, we have identified them in the notes. Every reasonable attempt has been made to obtain and to credit the necessary permissions to reproduce copyrighted work and translations included in this volume.

PREFACE

Martin Luther did not want his literary output preserved for future generations—or so he said. Following Renaissance humanist conventions (and Augustinian humility), Luther granted that only two of his works (the Catechism and his attack on Erasmus, *De servo arbitrio [On the Bound Choice]*) should be preserved for posterity. No one today takes Luther at his word, as a glance at the over one hundred volumes of the critical edition of his works, the Weimarer Ausgabe— to say nothing of the fifty-five volume English edition—proves. But even in Luther's day, no one took him seriously, as is shown by the fact that his editors forced him to provide prefaces to the first volumes of his German works (1539) and his Latin writings (1545).

The more "spiritual" of the two prefaces, the one from 1539, may be found in this collection. However, it may well be that only by reading the two prefaces side by side may we gain the true measure of Luther's spirituality. In 1539 Luther called upon his monastic roots and "St. David," who (he assumed) wrote Psalm 119, to give readers an introduction not so much to his works as to his theological and exegetical method. As Luther doubtless knew, the monastic encounter with biblical texts took place through a three-fold *oratio, meditatio, et illuminatio seu contemplatio* (prayer, meditation, and illumination or contemplation). Luther, too, began with prayer *(oratio)*—not because he was pious, but because the biblical text overthrows all human reason and forces the reader to call upon the Holy Spirit for help. As he would occasionally blurt out during theological disputations held in Wittenberg during the 1530s and 1540s, "The Holy Spirit uses a different grammar and logic!" The biblical text makes no reasonable sense. Thus, throughout Psalm 119, David prayed for God's help to understand the law and the word. Any approach apart from such prayer reduces God's word to the level of Aesop's fables, an ancient text Luther loved but knew was not inspired.

Still in line with medieval monastic models, Luther proceeded to meditation *(meditatio)*, by which he meant nothing less than a close reading of the text, asking what the Holy Spirit was up to by using the words and phrases one found there. Again, the writer of Psalm 119 demonstrated the same commitment to such close encounters with the text of Torah.

The third step in Luther's spiritual encounter with God's word runs counter to medieval expectation and practice. Neither illumination nor contemplation but rather spiritual attack *(tentatio)* concluded Luther's engagement with scripture. For him, when the Holy Spirit breaks our reason and reveals to us the true intention of God's word, we are not drawn into some sort of heavenly realm or closer contact to the divine by our effort. Instead, all hell breaks loose. The flesh, the world, the devil and any other anti-spiritual power attempt to wrest from the believer the comfort of God's unconditional grace and mercy. No wonder the psalmist cried out for deliverance from his enemies in Psalm 119!

The 1539 preface brings us to the heart of Luther's "spirituality" (if a Latin word first encountered in Pelagian writings properly names Luther's brand of piety). Here we discover that Luther's encounter with God leaves God as the only subject of the theological sentence—by grace alone—and forces humankind to become the object of God's favor. Here, "faith alone" is not a codeword for "deciding for Christ" (an Aristotelian category imposed upon the biblical message), but is precisely the result of an encounter with God's word mediated through the Holy Spirit. Likewise, "word alone" is never an excuse for either modern biblicism or historical modernism but defines an address from God that does what it says by putting to death and bringing to life.

However noble Luther's words here may seem, they still lack one thing, crucial to the life of the theologian: experience. Although Luther asserts in the 1539 preface that "experience makes a theologian," it is first in 1545 that he proves it on the basis of his own life. The 1545 preface to the Latin works (LW 34:323–43), often misused by Luther scholars simply as a primary source for a description of his "breakthrough" to an evangelical understanding of God's righteousness, actually shows students precisely how the biblical text drove Luther himself to prayer, meditation, and struggle.

PREFACE

Without prayer and the Holy Spirit, Romans 1:16–17 ("Through [the gospel] the righteousness of God is revealed, as it written, 'The just shall live by faith'") could only function in Luther's experience as law, driving him to hate the righteous God who punishes the unrighteous. However, by "meditating day and night" (a reference to both Psalm 1 and monastic *meditatio)* and by the mercy of God, Luther discovered a new face to the text: that God declares the unrighteous sinner righteous according to the mercy of Christ alone. Suddenly, God's Holy Spirit transformed the law's judgment into sheer grace and a gate to paradise. Yet this entire exposition of Romans 1 comes in the middle of Luther's account of his publication of the 95 Theses and the subsequent persecution and abuse by his Roman opponents, that is, in the middle of *tentatio*, struggle (German: *Anfechtung*). Thus, in the 1545 preface, Luther used his own life as an example of Christian piety, tracing the movement from prayer to meditation to struggle.

This selection of Luther's spiritual writings demonstrates the heart of Luther's practical, experiential piety as an encounter with God's word. In this connection one must read Luther both as a late medieval thinker and as a reformer. Luther's "down-to-earth approach to the gospel," to borrow the words of the subtitle to Gerhard Forde's book *Where God Meets Man* (Minneapolis: Augsburg, 1972), meant that at Luther's hands medieval piety not only received criticism but also found a new home. Thus, the careful reader will recognize Luther's debt to late medieval nominalism, mysticism, and biblical humanism. However, none of these strains in Luther's thought fully expressed his theology—not simply because he rejected papal authority (which he surely did by 1521) but because his encounter with God's word demanded that he both use theological language with which he was most familiar and, at crucial places, break it open in favor of the theology of the cross, defined as God's revelation in precisely the last place anyone would reasonably look, that is, in the gracious, faith-creating promise of the Crucified.

Thus, in the first section of readings here, Luther's letter to his fellow monk George Spenlein reveals the Christocentric heart of his spirituality. Yet, the same "Know Christ and him crucified" comes to expression in his almost insulting letter to Frederick the

Wise from the Wartburg, where he goads the elector to accept a new, real cross, namely, Martin Luther himself, who had departed from his prince's protective custody, publicly preaching again in Wittenberg. Luther's "letters of spiritual counsel," to borrow the title of Theodore Tappert's apt collection of Luther's down-to-earth spiritual advice, allow us to see a late medieval man and evangelical reformer at work, using all of the tools at his disposal to deliver God's mercy to his flock and even to his family. Nowhere is the practicality of Luther's spiritual center better proven than in his interpretation of Psalm 82 and his comments on usury. The Christian exists only in this world, sent back to it through prayer and meditation to encounter the attacks implicit in God's saving word. Put another way, because justification by grace through faith frees believers from worry about their relation to God, they are freed to serve the neighbor, especially the poor. Thus, service to neighbor is one of the most striking results of Luther's spirituality.

Luther also marked life in the Spirit by a profound sensitivity to the end of all things. The attacks on his proclamation of the gospel that he experienced convinced him by 1530 that the Book of Revelation, far from being the unrevealing book he took it to be in 1522, was far more: a divine elucidation of the nearing eschaton. This apocalyptic sensitivity, while never issuing in speculation about the "day and hour," nevertheless left Luther convinced of the finality of the spiritual attacks he suffered. On occasion, as Heiko Oberman has shown in his biography *Luther: Man Between God and the Devil* (New Haven, CT: Yale University, 1989), Luther's apocalyptic certainty could lead him to a kind of triumphalism that placed Jews, Turks, and Papists on one side of the eschatological equation and himself and other like-minded believers on the other. More often, however, it left him at the mercy of God.

Luther's breakthrough to a completely new, evangelical spirituality shows itself even more clearly in the second major section of this book, where we discover a Luther teaching his "dear Germans," as he often called them (although he also used other, less complimentary names to designate his compatriots), the insights of God's gracious encounter with them. From the beginning of his evangelical experience of God's word to the end, the reader discovers a Luther whose single-minded struggle with God in the biblical text leads first to judgment of spiritual business-as-usual but finally ushers in a relation to God based on a faith created by God's promise of unbounded grace. We hear echoes of Luther in the classroom, carefully describing the spiritual power of Psalms 5 (on hope) and 117. Then we hear the earthy tones of the German version of his famous tract from 1520, *The Freedom of a Christian*. His Marian piety and theology of the cross come to expression in another exegetical tour de force, his interpretation of the Magnificat. The preface to Paul's Letter to the Romans, written for his translation of the New Testament and first published in 1522, contains one of Luther's most succinct meditations on Pauline theology. His moving sermon at the Castle Coburg, delivered to Elector John of Saxony and his entourage as they were about to depart for the 1530 Diet of Augsburg, shows Luther's homiletical sensitivity to the spiritual plight of his listeners, who are about to embark upon a "venture of which they cannot see the ending." Excerpts from his two greatest commentaries (on Galatians and Genesis) again show Luther as the spiritual professor, allowing the biblical text to force him to profess Christ.

Luther not only taught this new approach to the Christian life, he also prayed it, as the third section of this book makes clear. This too is part of the experience of the theologian: to begin and end with prayer. Here excerpts from his Large Catechism, as later generations of Lutherans have titled it, demonstrate both the centrality of faith (the first commandment) and the significance of faith's breath (prayer). Luther's meditative, prayerful side also comes to expression in comments on the thanksgiving of Psalm 118 and in his delightful introduction to prayer written for his star-crossed barber, Master Peter. Nine hymns selected from the many Luther wrote show us the unique blend of pedagogy and piety that stimulated Christians of various traditions to express their faith in song. Where modern writers separate scholarship and spirituality, Luther consciously combines school and Spirit, allowing him to sing even the catechism (here represented by hymns on the Ten Commandments, the Lord's Prayer, baptism, and the Lord's Supper).

Taken together, this book elucidates the central aspects of Protestant spiritual life: catholic (universal) to the end; rooted in God's justifying, faith-creating word of grace; expressed always in the actual event of hearing and believing, dying and rising with Christ. A fine summary of the spiritual, Christocentric core of Luther's thought comes not from Luther but from Elizabeth von Merseburg, one of the nuns who escaped her cloister to come to Wittenberg (where she married Luther's student Caspar Cruciger, Sr., and later died tragically in childbirth). She wrote a hymn included in the first "Protestant" hymnbook from 1524 and in Lutheran hymnbooks down to the present (here in my own translation).

> Christ comes from God, forever
> The Father's only Son,
> From God's heart, ceasing never,
> As prophets long have sung:
> "He is the Star of Morning,
> Whose beams afar are soaring
> Above all other lights."
>
> Now, at the end of ages,
> He comes a human born,
> The poor receive God's wages:
> Sin's judgment from us torn.
> Now death for us is broken;
> And heaven's portals open
> Life blossoms forth again.
>
> Let us, from your love drinking,
> Of Wisdom take our fill,
> Remain in faith, ne'er shrinking,
> And serve the Spirit's will:
> Our hearts, now having tasted
> Your sweetness, never wasted,
> Will thirst alone for you.
>
> O Maker of all creatures,
> Come with a parent's hand;
> Forever rule o'er nature,
> In strength, come take your stand:

PREFACE

Our hearts you will be moving,
    Your love our senses proving
    That from you we not stray.

Oh, slay us through your goodness;
    Awaken us through grace.
Bring to the old such sickness,
    That we new life embrace.
Then we, on earth now dwelling,
    Your praises will be telling
    With mind and sense and tongue.

—Timothy J. Wengert

GENERAL INTRODUCTION

In the early 1530s Luther's friend Michael Stiefel tried to predict the second coming of the Lord. On the basis of a mathematical reckoning that involved numerical equivalents for the letters of scripture, he proposed a number of dates before finally settling on Sunday, October 19, 1533, at 8:00 a.m. Stiefel was incensed by Luther's skepticism at his calculations. News of Stiefel's irritation reached the reformer in Wittenberg, who wrote him in amicable tones on June 24, 1533, beseeching him not to throw over their old friendship for a difference of opinion involving nonessentials. He assured Stiefel that about the heart of the matter they were in agreement, since Luther, though he regarded such calculations as a devilish temptation to be rejected, did believe that the last times were at hand.

Eschatology

One must understand Luther's spirituality within the context of this urgent eschatological expectation. The church of Luther's day held out the possibility of justification at the bar of divine judgment. Through grace one might bring forth the love and good works needed to be deemed righteous. Although the prospect for steady progress from grace to grace to ultimate justification was presented as hopeful, Luther was not unique in his fear of *the jungsten Tag*, the day of final reckoning when Christ would return to judge the world. It seemed all too possible that one's best efforts in cooperation with grace would prove inadequate. In his darkest moments Luther felt the cause was inevitably a lost one. No one could love God as required when one knew that God stood ready to condemn and destroy at the last, making grace a cruel mockery of the miserable sinner.

xxi

Wrestling with this fear of judgment, Luther came to an understanding of the righteousness of God that made justification not just a future possibility for the believer but a present reality. Salvation is given not to a complex of faith cooperating with grace, formed by love and manifested in good works, but is lodged wholly in Christ and appropriated by trust in the divine promises that join the sinful body to its merciful Head. The believer has in essence already received God's favorable verdict. Now, as at the future judgment, he or she stands clothed only in the righteousness of Christ and for his sake is assured of life. Thus, the fear of condemnation disappeared for Luther, and, instead of holding out the return of Christ as an object of terror, he could exhort his parishioners to pray for the speedy arrival of the *lieben jungsten Tag*, the dear last day, when the riches of divine grace, invisible to the eye and accessible only to faith in this world, would be revealed in the kingdom of God.

Luther identified the gospel as the dynamic of all history. Nations and epochs, like individuals, are judged by their response to it. For Luther, the word always remains its own master, emerging when and where God wills but never abandoning its hiddenness to become the property of the church. Thus, the growing magnificence and power of the Church of Rome over the centuries was not necessarily evidence of God's blessing. Indeed, experience confirmed Luther's suspicion that by the criterion of the gospel, the church that had formed him stood condemned for unbelief. Luther's assertion that only the advent of Christ could right the wrongs of the age resulted not just from a dire assessment of contemporary social conditions. The article of justification dictated it. At the last, as at the beginning, redemption is the work of Christ alone. Luther's confidence in the lovingkindness of the returning Lord coexisted over the years of public strife with bitter frustration at the world's unwillingness to hear and repent.

Luther was a wounded man. He felt that the church had abused him by its failure to proclaim the gospel faithfully and by its insistence on good works, which created a false confidence in believers. The eschatological horizon of Luther's spirituality is evident again in his focus on the hour of death. Here was the ultimate test of the truthfulness of the church's proclamation and practice. Had it prepared its children to face confidently their final hour?

They could take nothing with them, and a fine résumé of good works in obedience to the church would never deflect the whisperings and mockery of the devil. As Luther liked to point out, the thief on the cross who turned to Jesus, beseeching his mercy, had no opportunity to perform good works. Yet the Lord promised that he would dwell that day in paradise. At the end it was faith alone that mattered.

One could describe Luther's career as the mounting of a life-long pastoral malpractice suit against the church's authority at every level of the hierarchy. He was determined to preserve the gospel at any cost, so that no member of Christ's flock would perish in despair. Earthly life was like boot camp. With the regular exercise of faith, absolute reliance on Christ was to become second nature. One was strengthened through bitter trials and temptations (what Luther called *Anfechtungen*) as one learned how to fight them and how to recover in the wake of defeat. Through prayer and repentance the believer would endure until the end came.

The cost of such evangelical ferocity was high. Luther moved readily from disagreement to judgment, often violating his own understanding of the ambiguity of history. God works in the world through masks; one cannot read ultimate divine judgments from historical events. Yet Luther demonized his opponents. They were flat-out enemies of the gospel, with whom there should be no compromise and to whom no mercy was due. So Luther could dismiss the Roman Church, once he was convinced that its authorities understood the evangelical message but deliberately rejected it in order to preserve their power. He was implacable toward other Protestant movements that challenged his sacramental teaching. He saw the Turk as a scourge from God, merely an instrument in God's disciplining of Christendom. Most notoriously, when the Jews rejected the gospel, even in its purified evangelical form, Luther viciously attacked them. He presumed to find in the circumstances of their exile proof that God had abandoned the Jewish people in disgust at their pride and obstinacy. And Luther expected this judgment to have consequences in the political realm. He advised the civil authorities to adopt a scorched-earth policy that would have effectively destroyed Jewish communities.

Daily Living

When Luther's daughter Magdalena died, he was at first virtu-ally speechless with grief. Yet with time he was able to accept that she was well out of this world. If the gospel had emerged in power and clarity unparalleled since the time of the apostles, the forces of evil had to go on high alert. The world was a desperately dangerous place, full of temptation and deceit. To hold on to the gospel had never been more urgent or more difficult. Death was a kindly deliv-erance, putting one beyond the reach of evil and temptation.

There was, however, another side to Luther's view of the world. Long attributed to him has been the saying, "If I knew the world would end tomorrow, I would go out and plant an apple tree today." Luther was criticized for neglecting good works in his the-ology, indeed for going so far as to denigrate them as potentially dangerous to one's salvation. Yet he insisted that the gospel did not free Christians from good works but rather from false understand-ings of good works. Justifying faith was the creation of God in the believer, but once this new relationship was established, the believer then had a righteousness of his or her own. Faith was to be a busy, active thing, abounding in good works for one's neighbors. Believers liberated in Christ are no longer turned in upon themselves but gifted with eyes to see and ears to hear the needs of the world. Now one is both the perfectly free lord of all and the perfectly bound ser-vant of all.

Luther levels the wall between a higher spiritual estate apart from the world and the commonplace realities of earthly life. By baptism a person enters the priesthood of all believers, rising from the water priest, bishop, and pope, as Luther famously claimed. The tasks of discipleship are now clear. Christians are to exercise their priestly office in behalf of others. They are to proclaim the gospel in deeds of mercy as well as in confession of the faith, so that others might hear and believe. They are to pray. They are empowered to speak the word of absolution to the troubled conscience of sinners.

In tandem with Luther's understanding of the priesthood of all believers is his emphasis on vocation. Luther eventually rejected monastic practice because of what he judged to be its false and dan-gerous claims. To be bound by vows of poverty, chastity, and obedience as a higher and meritorious service to God was inimical to the teaching of free justification. The superior value accorded this estate was a human calculation, not a divine one. Luther deplored the fact that young people were pressured into taking vows before they were mature enough to understand the lifelong implications of these commitments. Celibacy was a charism and should not be imposed. After all, God commanded Adam and Eve to be fruitful and multiply, whereas the church defied God's will with its requirement of monastic and priestly celibacy. Such a decision about one's state in life should be free. One can either marry or not as one sees fit. One can even make the choice to live under vows if one feels called to do so, as long as it is understood that this is a way of living out the grace God has given rather than a means of securing that grace.

Luther advocated spiritual disciplines. He knew that the passions and pride of believers constantly need to be broken to the bridle of godliness. Christians have to attend to the mastery of their sinful impulses so that they can serve their neighbors effectively. Luther approached the issue of sanctification with some reserve for fear that his generation, so recently weaned from the idea of good works as a means to grace rather than the fruit thereof, would fall back into the old patterns of thought. Still, one has only to read his explication of the Ten Commandments in the Large Catechism to see that Luther expected the recipients of grace to live with their neighbors in a new way, with a generosity and an honesty that could well transform the world. Everyday relationships and duties prove the greatest spiritual discipline of all. As partner and parent, son or daughter, friend, craftsman, employer or servant, soldier or diplomat, pastor or layperson, one encountered neighbors to serve and gave glory to God in doing so. It was not one's prerogative to seek a discipleship that circumvented this common realm or to choose what sacrifices one would make in following Christ. Luther felt there was no need to design one's own crosses when life would bring a generous supply on its own.

Luther placed special emphasis on family life as the preeminent setting for discipleship. There was no neighbor closer than the young ones dependent on the older generation for care. Parents were responsible for having their children baptized (Luther was a passionate proponent of infant baptism) and for nurturing them in the true faith. The reformer prepared the Small Catechism to help them with this task, and schooling the household by means of this primer in the evangelical teaching was an important part of the priesthood of all believers.

Parents were also responsible for their children's social welfare. They were to provide for their education so that the children in turn might become productive and pious citizens. (It is striking that the catechism also concerns itself with issues of good citizenship and obedience.) Luther was appalled by the anti-intellectualism of his compatriots. He sought to prevent families from using their children solely for their own self-aggrandizement, cutting short their schooling to involve them in the family business, for example. The world had need of competent civil servants and informed pastors. Consequently, the community had a greater claim on promising young men than did their families when it came to determining the best use of their abilities. Although women did not fill positions of public leadership, education was important to prepare them for their domestic duties as wives and mothers and their particular responsibility for the religious life of the family. The last of the four major parental tasks, according to Luther, was to help children contract a suitable marriage at the appropriate time, that is, before lust drove them into sin or neglect forced them to make their own, potentially unsatisfactory, arrangements.

In these familial and communal matters, Luther's despairing view of the world and expectation of its imminent end seem to recede. Parents, rulers, and the wider community make provision for the future. Acting out of the conviction that another will take their place, they plant their own apple trees with determination and faithfulness. Though, according to Luther, God's rule through the law and God's rule through the gospel are to be sharply distinguished, they both have God's cherished world and its concerns as their objects.

The Practices of Faith

One could describe Luther's spirituality as a quadrilateral, the four sides of which are the terror of the conscience, faith, repentance, and assurance. Trial and temptation are the initial means of spiritual formation. Through them the Christian is stripped time and time again of presumption and the delusions of righteousness. One is thrust into a kind of existential free fall with nothing to break the descent into darkness, nothing to hold onto but Jesus the Christ. If one is full of one's own works, there is no room for grace. The life of discipleship is a constant process of emptying so that the believer may be filled with Christ's gifts. All that Christ has becomes ours, and the weight of our sinfulness and mortality become his. Faith creates this new relationship by fulfilling the first commandment. It takes God at God's word, relying solely on God's faithfulness as it grasps the promise of forgiveness and new life in Christ.

We have already discussed service to the neighbor as one of the foundations of discipleship. There are three others: confession, prayer, and the sacraments. By grace one boldly dares to acknowledge one's sin before God and to receive with confidence the word of absolution. God commands people to pray, and Luther exhorts them to do as they are told. But prayer is more than a matter of obedience. It is also the enactment of faith. Once again, the believer takes God at God's word, that the one he addresses hears him and will respond as a loving parent, not an implacable judge. The Christian rises from the waters of baptism *simul iustus et peccator*, simultaneously saint and sinner, wholly clothed in the righteousness of Christ and still the willing agent of sin. Here once again Luther's eschatology comes into play. This *simul* condition is an untenable position over the long haul. It drives relentlessly toward the resolution that only the coming of the Lord can effect. The question arises: If baptism leaves us sinners, what difference does it make? For Luther, it makes all the difference in the world that one is now Christ's sinner, armed to fight the enemy with the power of confession and prayer.

Luther found in the sacraments clear and undeniable assurance of the graciousness of God for which he so desperately longed. Luther supported infant baptism because it embodied the gospel so perfectly. A baby can do nothing to prepare for baptism and does not even comprehend what is being done to it. Acting through the pastor, God claims the child by name, attaches the promise of salvation to this particular individual and places the infant where his or her faith can find nourishment. Baptism brings a child into the body of Christ, the church, where he or she can hear the gospel proclaimed, join with the Savior in the supper, and be strengthened through the mutual consolation of brothers and sisters in Christ. No matter what the age or cognitive development of the recipient, the power of the sacrament comes from God's promise and command. The subjective experience of faith does not validate the sacrament, nor does the experience of doubt render it void. For Luther, the objective nature of baptism, the concrete fact of its having occurred, of its being witnessed by others, means that it can be neither doubted nor denied. This gives the believer great assurance. This one thing he or she knows to be true: "I am baptized." And thus the meaning of the believer's life is secured.

Luther did not finally include confession as a sacrament because there was no material element involved (unlike the water of baptism and the bread and wine of the Lord's Supper). Yet he regarded confession as a key way of living out one's baptism. It was the path by which one returned daily to the water to drown the old Adam and raise up the new. Luther made regular use of the practice of private confession and rejoiced in it as a gift from God rather than an onerous obligation. To speak truthfully of one's condition, to hear the word of absolution, to receive hope for the amendment of life, who would not eagerly seize such an opportunity? (Despite Luther's enthusiasm for the practice, it was and has remained a hard sell among Lutherans.)

Participation in the Lord's Supper is also part of living out one's baptism and is characterized by the same reassuring objectivity. Its power has nothing to do with the participant's state of mind and everything to do with Christ's presence. One encounters Christ throughout the creation, says Luther, but the troubled conscience experiences him as its judge and flees in terror. In the supper, however, the believer meets the Lord unequivocally as the savior who lays his life down *for me* ("This is the body of Christ given for you; the blood of Christ shed for you"). There is no escaping Christ's single-minded intention. He proclaims his love to each and every participant and asks only that they take him at his word.

To understand the nature of Luther's spirituality, it is helpful to look at biblical figures he regards as models of discipleship. Peter betrays Jesus three times, yet, says Luther, in contrast to Judas Iscariot, Peter does not despair but turns back to the merciful Christ for forgiveness and restoration. In the courtyard after Jesus' arrest he claimed not to know the man, but in his penitence Peter shows that he knows the Lord very well. Another exemplary figure for Luther is the Canaanite woman (Matt 15:21–28) who seeks healing for her daughter. Relying on the good word she has heard about Jesus, she travels to him. When confronted by the hostility of the disciples and the apparent indifference of Jesus, she perseveres. The disheartening circumstances do not quench her faith, and finally, Jesus does not fail her. She believes in a powerful and merciful Lord, and as she believes, so she ultimately finds him to be.

Conclusion

Luther insisted that no one could believe for someone else or die for them. Confessing the Lord in life and in death was the responsibility of each individual. Luther was under no illusion that faith was easy. In the sermon he preached to the elector of Saxony and his party on the eve of their departure for the Diet of Augsburg in 1530 (included in this volume), Luther reminds them of the experience of St. Christopher. Christopher set out to ford a river, carrying the infant Christ to the other side. The task began easily enough, but, as he continued, Christopher found that the child became painfully heavy and the current swift and deep. So, said Luther, was the experience of many in the faith. When they first heard the proclamation of the evangelical gospel, people responded with ardor and enthusiasm. As time passed, however, many faltered under its challenges and experienced the freedom it created as frightening and burdensome. Yet, as for Christopher, there is only one option—to press forward, holding on to the good, stout promises of God to draw one safely to the other shore.

The journey, however, is not a solitary one. Each of us is called into the presence of God, and we must claim the place created for us when God names us individually in our baptism and gives himself to us, person by person, in communion. Yet this happens within the community of the church. As the Reformation scholar Eric Gritsch has said, "It takes two to gospel," at the very least. We cannot proclaim Christ's promises to ourselves; we cannot store them away safely on a computer disk or in a safety deposit box for later reference. We need the word to come from outside of us so that it may reign over us. Someone must wash us, someone must feed us, someone must speak an inescapable and unconditional word of absolution, and in doing so these someones become Christ for us. The worldly spirituality of Luther with its emphasis on vocation and service to the neighbor is also a thoroughly churchly spirituality. We are called to venture forth on our individual paths of discipleship as members of a redeemed people, the very body of Christ.

—Jane E. Strohl

PART I

Luther's Spirituality in a Late-Medieval Context

Editors' Introduction to Part I: Martin Luther is frequently portrayed as the great reformer who suddenly strides across the world stage to stand as a religious genius before emperor and princes. By protesting the repression of a conscience subject to the word of God and reason, he thus launches the Reformation and the beginning of the modern era. At the same time, Luther, the former monk, is frequently depicted as a beer-drinking, boisterous, irreverent, and sometimes harsh critic of medieval piety and practice.[1] Both images have some truth to them, as the letters and selections in Part I and throughout this volume show. With a public spirituality Luther speaks the truth to political and ecclesiastical power in his context, exemplified in his commentary on Psalm 82 and his denunciation of nascent capitalism. The letters that follow demonstrate his critique of late medieval piety. Note, for example, his attack on the spiritual benefits of solitude in this section.

There are other images of Luther and his spirituality presented in Part I.[2] There is Luther, the pastor and consoler of those in temptation and despair.[3] There is Luther, the monk who took monasticism to its extremes and continued to struggle mightily with temptation, despair, and attacks of the devil after he left it. In the letters that follow, he consoles others who experience similar attacks. As Heiko Oberman has shown, Luther had a lively doctrine of the devil that could not be construed as modern in the least.[4] He also demonstrated an apocalyptic spirituality that was at once both late medieval and innovative.[5] Luther truly believed that the gospel was being preached by the reformation movement in the face of a

1

critical conflict between Christ and the devil as the world was coming to an end.

Part I emphasizes Luther's spirituality in his late-medieval context. It represents a break from and a critique of the spirituality of his contemporaries but is also derived from it.[6] Except for the letters and table talks, which are quite brief, each separate entry has a short editors' introduction.

LETTER TO GEORGE SPENLEIN: "LEARN CHRIST,... THE CRUCIFIED"

Wittenberg, April 8th, 1516
To the devoted and upright Brother George Spenlein,[1] Augustinian Hermit at the Memmingen Convent, from his friend whom he accepts in the Lord.[2]

Jesus Christ

Grace and peace be with you from God our Father and the Lord Jesus Christ. Dearest Brother George, I would like to let you know that, from the sale of your things, I have gotten three-and-a-half gulden together; namely, one for your garment from Brussels, a half gulden for the larger work of [Trutvetter][3] from Eisenach, a gulden for the habit, and several other things. Now only a few things remain, like the poetry book of Baptista[4] and your collection, for which, sadly, we will have to take a loss when it is sold, for up to now we have not been able to sell it. For that reason we have handed three-and-a-half gulden over to the honorable vicar-general for you.[5] As for the last half gulden that you owe him, you should take care to pay it back or receive a remission of your debt. I believe, however, that the honorable father, because he is partial to you, will not make an issue of relieving you of the payment that remains.

Anyway, I would gladly know how things are with your soul. Have you finally become sick and tired of your own righteousness and taken a deep breath of the righteousness of Christ and learned to trust in it? For in these days the temptation of presumption glowers in many people and especially in those who want with all their strength to be good and righteous. They do not know the righteousness of God, which in Christ is given us freely as a gift so richly overflowing,

3

and they attempt to do good until they at last have the confidence to stand before God, garlanded at once with their virtues and merits. This, of course, must be impossible. You also lived among us with this opinion (or rather, this error), and I also believed it. Yes, and I still fight against this craziness and have not yet finished the fight.

Therefore, my dear brother, learn Christ, specifically, the Crucified. Learn to sing him and in your despair at yourself to say to him, "You, Lord Jesus, are my righteousness; I, on the other hand, am your sin. You have taken upon yourself what is mine and given me as a present what is yours.[6] You took upon yourself what you were not and gave me the gift of what I was not." Watch out for yourself that you do not one day strive for such purity that you do not even see yourself as a sinner, nor even want to be one. For Christ dwells only in sinners. That is why, of course, Christ descended from heaven—where he dwelt with the righteous—so that he might also dwell in sinners. Always remember this love of Christ, and you will experience the sweetest divine comfort of all. For if we had to achieve a cheerful conscience through our own worry and sorrow, then for what purpose did Christ die? Therefore, you will find peace in Christ only through a confident despair in yourself and your works. Then, in addition, learn from Christ himself how in accepting you he has made your sins his and also made his righteousness to be yours.

When you believe that firmly, as you must (because one who does not believe it is cursed), then you also accept those who are disobedient and still erring and bear with them patiently. Make their sins your own, and, if there is something good about yourself, then let it belong to them. For this is what the Apostle teaches: "Welcome one another, just as Christ has welcomed you, for the glory of God" (Rom 15:7); and once again, "Let the same mind be in you that was in Christ Jesus, who, though he was in the form of God, did not exploit it, etc." (Phil 2:5f.). So also, if you consider yourself to be better, do not exploit it, as if it belongs to you alone, but empty yourself (Phil 2:7); forget who you are and be like one of them, so that you bear them up.

Unholy, however, is the righteousness of those who, thinking others worse than themselves, will not tolerate them but think to run away and draw back into solitude, though one should, of course, remain with them patiently and be helpful to them by prayer and example. This is burying the talent of the Lord (Matt 25:18); it does not give one's fellow servants what is owed them (Matt 18:28). So, if you are a lily and a rose of Christ, know that your walk through life goes through thorns (Song 2:2). Take care that, through impatience, easy judgments, and secret pride, you do not yourself become a thorn. The kingdom of Christ is in the midst of its enemies, as the psalm says (Ps 110:2), so what do you imagine surrounding yourself with friends will do for you?

If you lack anything, then cast it at the feet of the Lord Jesus and ask him for it. He will teach you everything—just take note of what he has done for you and for everyone, so that you also learn what you are obligated to do for others. If Christ had wanted to live only among the good and had wanted to die only for his friends, then for whom could he possibly have died, or with whom could he have ever lived?

Follow that, my dear brother, and pray for me, and the Lord be with you. Farewell in the Lord. Wittenberg on Tuesday after *Misericordias Domini* 1516.

Your Brother, Martin Luther, Augustinian

LETTER TO THE ELECTOR, FREDERICK THE WISE: LUTHER AS FREDERICK'S NEW RELIC

[Wartburg, February 24, 1522.][1]
My most gracious Lord, Duke Frederick,[2] Elector of Saxony (for his own hands).

Jesus

Grace and blessings from God the Father for your new relic! I send you this greeting now in writing, my most gracious Lord, in place of my reverence. For these many years your electoral Grace has let relics be collected and purchased in every country, but now God has heard your Grace and answered the desire of your Grace's heart and, without any cost or trouble, has sent home to you a whole cross, complete with nails, spears, and whips. Again I say, grace and blessings from God for your new relic! Just don't take fright, your Grace. No, just stretch out your arms with confidence, and let the nails penetrate deeply; yes, give thanks and be happy! For whenever one desires to have God's word, not only will Annas and Caiaphas happen to be there to throw tantrums, but also a Judas among the apostles, and Satan among the children of God. Now your Grace has to be clever and wise and not judge according to reason and natural appearances; only, don't be fainthearted, because it has not gone as far as Satan wants it to go. Let your Grace believe the fool [Luther] just a little,[3] for I know these and similar holds of Satan and am, therefore, not afraid, and that hurts him. It is all still the beginning. Let the world scream and judge; let fall who falls, even St. Peter and the apostles! They will certainly return on the third day when Christ rises again. That must also still be fulfilled in us (2 Cor 6:4f.: *Exhibeamus nos in seditionibus* [Let us commend ourselves in dissension], etc.). May your Grace reckon this good. For it

6

is with great haste this quill had to dash. I do not have any more time, and I will, if God wills, soon be there with you myself. Your Grace should not assume responsibility for me.

Your Grace's humble servant, Martin Luther

Letter to Jerome Weller: On the Devil

July 1530[1] from the fortress at Coburg
Grace and peace in Christ.

My dear Jerome:[2]

You must believe that this temptation of yours is from the devil,[3] who vexes you thus because you believe in Christ. For you see how secure and happy he permits the worst enemies of the gospel to be. Just think of Eck, Zwingli, and others. It is necessary for all of us who are Christians to have the devil as an adversary and as an enemy. As Peter says, "Your adversary the devil prowls around," etc. (1 Pet 5:8).

Excellent Jerome, you ought to rejoice in this temptation by the devil, because it is a certain sign that God is favorable and merciful to you. You say that the temptation is heavier than you can bear, and you fear that it will break and oppress you so that you will fall into despair and blasphemy. I know this trick of the devil. If he cannot break a person on the first attack, he perseveres in trying to wear out and weaken that one until the person falls and confesses defeat. Whenever this temptation comes to you, avoid arguing with the devil or dwelling on those deadly thoughts. For to do so is just to yield and succumb to the devil. You must work as hard as you can to spurn these thoughts introduced by the devil. In this kind of temptation and fight, contempt is the best and easiest method to conquer the devil. Mock your adversary, and ask with whom you are conversing. Flee solitude in any way you can, for he can best lie in wait and capture you when you are alone. The devil is conquered by mocking and despising him, not by resisting and arguing with him. Therefore, my Jerome, join in jokes and games with my wife and the rest, and in this way you will cheat those diabolical thoughts and take good courage.

This temptation is more important to you than food and drink. Let me remind you what happened to me when I was your age. When I first entered the monastery, it came to pass that I was sad and downcast, and I could not lay aside my melancholy. On this account I made confession to and took counsel with Doctor Staupitz, a person I gladly remember, and opened to him what horrible and terrible thoughts I had. Then he said, "Don't you know, Martin, that this temptation is useful and necessary to you? Do not fear; God does not occupy you thus, you will see, except to use you as a servant to accomplish great things." And so it happened. I was made a great doctor (it is proper for me to proclaim this about myself), even though then, when I was suffering that temptation, I would never have believed it would come about. And I have no doubt that this will happen to you too. You will become a great man. Just see to it that you are of good courage in the meantime, and be persuaded that such sayings, especially those which proceed from learned and great persons, are not without prophetic quality.

I remember that a certain man whom I once comforted on the loss of his son said to me, "Wait and see, Martin; you will become a great man."[4] I have often thought of these words, for, as I have said, such sayings have something of a prophetic quality. Be strong and of good courage, and by all means throw aside these monstrous thoughts. Whenever the devil vexes you with these thoughts, seek the company of others, or drink more, joke, make nonsense, or engage in some other form of merriment. Sometimes one must drink more, play, or make nonsense, and even commit some sin in defiance and contempt of the devil in order not to give him an opportunity to make us scrupulous about trifles. We shall be conquered if we worry too much about falling into some sin.

Thus, if the devil should say, "Do not drink!" you should reply to him thus, "On this very account, because you forbid it, I shall drink, and, what is more, I shall drink a generous amount." Thus one must always do precisely what Satan forbids. What do you think is my reason for drinking undiluted wine, talking freely, and eating more often, if not to torment and vex the devil, who decided to vex and toy with me? If only I could designate some token of sin to deceive the devil, so that he might understand that I acknowledge no sin and am not conscious of any sin with respect to myself. When the devil seeks and vexes us thus, I say, we must set aside the whole Decalogue from the body and the soul. But when the devil throws our sins up to us and declares that we deserve death and hell, then we ought to say, "Indeed, I confess that I deserve death and hell, but what afterward? Will I therefore be condemned eternally? By no means. For I know a certain one, who suffered and made satisfaction for me, and he is called Jesus Christ, the son of God. Where he is, there I shall be also."

Yours,
Martin Luther

Letter to Matthias Weller: The Mutual Consolation of the Faithful

7th of October 1534[1]
Grace and peace in Christ! Honorable and gracious friend!

Your dear brother informed me that you are quite distraught and suffer from attacks of depression.[2] Now what I discussed with him he will probably also report to you. My dear Matthias, do not pursue your own thoughts; listen instead to what other people say to you! God has commanded that one person should comfort another and also desires that one who is troubled should believe such comfort as God's own voice. For thus [God] speaks through St. Paul, "Comfort the sorrowful" (1 Thess 5:14), and in Isaiah 40:1f., "Comfort, O comfort my people, and speak tenderly," and in another place, "It is not my will that a person be sorrowful, but you shall serve me cheerfully and offer no sacrifice with sadness" (Deut 28:47), just as Moses and the prophets often preach. Therefore, [Christ] too commanded that we should not worry, but cast our cares on him, for he worries and will care for us. (Cf. Ps 55:22; Matt 6:25; Phil 4:6; 1 Pet 5:7.)

Since God wills that one comfort the other and each one believe the comfort, let your thoughts go, and know that the one plaguing you with them is the devil, who does not want us to have a cheerful thought.

So now listen to what we, in God's name, say to you, namely, that you should be happy in Christ, who is your gracious Lord. Cast your anxieties on him, and he will care for you [cf. 1 Pet 5:7], even if you do not yet have what you would like to have. Christ still lives, and so expect the best from him, for that pleases him and the scriptures

11

say that is the very best offering (cf. Ps 4:5). For there is no lovelier offering than a cheerful heart.

Therefore, if you are sad and your [sorrows] try to take the upper hand, then say aloud, "I have to play a song for my Lord Christ on the keyboard[3] (perhaps it could be the *Te Deum laudamus* or the *Benedictus*), because the scriptures teach me that God likes to hear cheerful singing and the lyre."[4] Then run your fingers over the keys, and sing to the tones until your thoughts go away, as David and Elisha did (2 Kgs 3:15). If the devil comes and gives you thoughts or pours worries into your mind, then defend yourself afresh. Say: "Get out, devil. Right now I have to sing and play for my Lord Christ."

In this way you truly have to learn to oppose him and not allow him to give you thoughts. For when you allow one thought to enter and listen to it, then he indeed drives in ten more behind it, until he has overcome you. There is thus nothing better to do than immediately to smack him in the mouth first. It is like the husband in a marriage who, when his wife began to nag and bite, took a flute out from under his belt and played cheerfully; in the end she became too tired and left him in peace. In the same way let your fingers run over the keys of the piano, or take a few good fellows and sing in opposition, until you learn to mock him.

For if you could believe that such thoughts belong to the devil, then you would already have won. However, because you are still weak in faith, hear us, who know, and steady yourself on our staff, until you learn to walk yourself. And when good people comfort you, my dear Matthias, then learn to believe that it is God saying these things to you. Follow, and do not doubt that it is certainly God's word that, according to the command, is comforting you through people.

And the same Lord, who called me to do in obedience to God what I had to do, give you the faith to believe it all, and [may God] say all these things in your heart, which I hereby speak into your ear. Amen.

At Wittenberg, Wednesday, the day after St. Francis, 1534.

D. M. Luther

LETTER OF COMFORT TO HIS DYING FATHER

15th of February, 1530[1]
To my dear father, Hans Luther, Citizen of Mansfeld in the Dale.
Grace and peace in Christ Jesus, our Lord and Savior. Amen.

Dear Father,

My brother, James, wrote me that you were dangerously ill. For as there is now treacherous air about and many other dangers besides,[2] and because of the time, I feel moved to care for you. For while God has given and sustained a firm and hard body for you up to now, your present age now fills my thoughts with concern. Indeed, despite this, we can never be sure of the hour, nor should we be. It is for that reason that I would have been glad beyond all measure to be able to come myself to be with you physically, but good friends of mine advised me against it and talked me out of it. And I myself must also consider that I should not tempt God by daring to risk danger, for you know the "favor" the lords and peasants feel for me. But it would be such a great delight for me, if it were possible, if you and my mother let yourselves be driven over here to us. My Kate also yearns tearfully for that, as do we all. I hope we are able to take good care of you. To that end I prepared Cyriac to take this trip to you to see if, in view of your weakness, it might be possible.[3] For whatever happens to you, according to the divine will, in this or the next life, I would gladly from my heart do what is right, according to the fourth commandment, and be with you in person and prove my gratitude to you with childlike faithfulness and service.

With that I pray to the Father, who created you and gave you to me as my father, from the bottom of my heart, that God's unfathomable goodness will strengthen, illuminate, and sustain you with the divine Spirit, so that you come to know with joy and thanksgiving the blessed teaching of Jesus Christ, God's son, our Lord, to whom you now through grace have also been called and have come out of the gruesome earlier darkness and error. And I hope that the divine grace that gave you this knowledge and thereby started the divine work in you (Phil 1:6) will bring it to an end in the next life and save and perfect it until the joyful coming again of our Lord Jesus Christ. Amen.

For God has already sealed in you this teaching and faith and confirmed it with marks and signs (Gal 6:17), namely, that for it you have suffered on my account much slander, shame, scorn, ridicule, rejection, hate, hostility, and danger, as did we all. These are the true marks and signs, which we have to have equally or similarly to our Lord Christ, as St. Paul says, so that we will also share equally in Christ's future glory (cf. Rom 8:17).

So now in your weakness let your heart be fresh and confident, for we have a sure and true advocate with God, Jesus Christ, who for us strangled death, along with our sins, and now sits together with the angels watching over us and waiting for us, so that, when we have our homecoming, we need not worry or be afraid that we will sink or fall into the abyss. Christ has such great power over death and sin that they can do nothing to us. The heart of Christ is also so faithful and blessed that he cannot leave us, nor does he want to, except that we have to yearn for it without doubt.

For Christ has said it, given his word, and promised, and he most certainly does not lie to us or deceive us. "Ask," says Christ, "and it will be given you; search and you shall find; knock, and the door will be opened for you" (Matt 7:7). And in another place, "Everyone who calls on the name of the Lord shall be saved" (Acts 2:21). And the whole psalter is full of such comforting promises, especially Psalm 91, which is very good to read to the sick.

I wanted to speak with you about such things in writing, being concerned about your illness (because we do not know the hour), so that I might participate in your faith, struggle, comfort, and gratitude toward God for the divine holy word, which Christ gave us at this time so richly, mightily, and with such rich grace.

If it is God's will, however, that you shall have to wait somewhat longer for that better life and continue to suffer together with us, see and hear misfortune in this distressing and unholy vale of tears, or, rather, with all Christians help to bear and overcome it, then God will also provide the grace to accept all such things willingly and obediently. For this accursed life is indeed nothing but a real vale of tears, in which the longer one lives, the more sin, arrogance, plague, and misfortune one sees and experiences. And it all does not stop or decrease until the sound of the shovels filling our graves, where it must finally leave us in peace and allow us to sleep peacefully in the rest of Christ, until he comes again and with happy rejoicing wakes us up. Amen.

Herewith I commit you to the one who loves you more than you do yourself and proved this love by taking your sins upon himself and paying with his blood. God declares this to you through the gospel and then through the Spirit gives you the gift to believe such things and has prepared and sealed them with utmost certainty. Thus you no longer have to worry or be afraid; only remain steadfast and confident in God's word and faith. When that happens, then let Christ worry; he will act (Ps 37:5). Indeed, Christ has already done everything well, more than we can even comprehend. The same dear Lord and Savior be with you and by you, and may God grant, whether it happens here or there, that we may joyfully see each other again. For our faith is certain, and we do not doubt that we will again see each other shortly in the presence of Christ, since the departure from this life for God is far less significant than if I were to move from here to Mansfeld or you moved from Mansfeld to Wittenberg. It is most certainly true that it is only a little hour's sleep, and then it will be different.

Although I now hope your pastor and preacher will in such things richly prove their faithful service, so that you have little need for my chatter, still I ask your forgiveness for my physical absence, which, God knows, pains my heart.

Greetings to you, and also faithful prayers for you from my Kate, little Hans, little Lehne, Aunt Lehne, and the whole house. Greet my dear mother and all the relatives. God's grace and strength be and remain with you eternally. Amen.

Wittenberg, February 15, 1530.

Your dear son, Martin Luther

LUTHER COUNSELS WELLER: THE GREATER THE SAINT BEFORE GOD, THE GREATER THE TEMPTATIONS

March 29, 1538[1]

Then Doctor J. Weller arrived,[2] greatly depressed and faint-hearted. Luther consoled him and bid him lift up his heart in the Lord and seek the company of people. He then asked him if he was raging against God, against Luther, or against himself.

He replied, "I confess I am murmuring against God."

Luther countered, "God does not care at all about that. I have also often worshiped God in the same way. Instead of offering a sweet-smelling fragrance, I bring the stinking pitch and devil's dirt of murmuring and impatience. If we did not have the article of forgiveness of sins, which God certainly promises and delivers, then we would be in bad shape."

Weller said, "The devil is masterful at finding the place where you hurt the most."

"Yes, the devil does not learn that from us; he is quite apt. Just as he did not exempt the patriarchs, prophets, and Christ, the prince of the prophets, he will not let it pass over us."

"The devil can devise the most extraordinary arguments: 'You sinned. God is enraged against sinners. Therefore, despair!' In this matter, it is necessary for us to proceed from the law to the gospel and grasp the article concerning the forgiveness of sins. You are not the only one, my brother, who has suffered such anguish. For Peter also admonishes us not to be surprised when the same suffering is required of us in the community of the brothers and sisters [1 Pet 4:12; 5:9]. Moses, David, Isaiah suffered much and often. What

16

kind of anguish do you suppose David may have felt, when he composed the psalm, 'O Lord, rebuke me not in your anger, etc.' [Ps 6:1]. He would much rather have died by the sword than experience these hard feelings against God and those of God against him. I believe that the confessors suffer more than the martyrs, for day after day they see idolatries, scandals, sins, the prosperity and security of the godless, and the anguish of the godly, who are accounted as sheep for the slaughter" (Ps 44:22; Rom 8:36).

About Fleeing into Solitude[1]

The papists and Anabaptists teach that if you wish to know Christ and keep your heart pure, then make it your preference to be alone. Do not wish to relate to people, but separate yourself, like a Nicolaitan brother.[2] This idea is a devilish counsel that fights against the first and second tables [of the Ten Commandments]. The first table requires faith and awe, which in the other commandments is to be preached and glorified for the people and to be proclaimed among the people. We are not to be fleeing and crawling into corners, but socializing with others. Thus the second table teaches us to benefit the neighbor, with whom we are to associate and not isolate ourselves. So [isolation] militates against marriage, the household, statecraft, and the life of Christ, who did not always want to be alone. His life was filled with what most resembles a riot, for the people were always crowding around Christ. He was never alone, except when he prayed. So away with those who teach, "Be glad to remain alone, and your heart will be pure."

COMMENTARY ON PSALM 82:
SECULAR SAVIORS

Editors' Introduction: This commentary demonstrates Luther's public spirituality.[1] It seems to have been written in Wittenberg, possibly just before Luther left for the Coburg Castle on April 3, 1530. It was prompted by the visitation of the churches of Saxony.[2] With a free-flowing exposition and attention to current events, Luther proclaims that, contrary to some prior medieval ecclesial views, temporal rulers are accorded their own legitimacy by God.[3] In the words of Psalm 82, he calls the rulers "gods," though this does not render them unaccountable. A non-Christian prince can rule by reason, following the examples of the great poets and philosophers.[4] The Christian prince is accountable to God and reason.[5] As a guide for the business of society and government, reason is surpassed by nothing.[6]

Luther regards the Christian prince as a secular savior, making it safe for the gospel to be proclaimed. The prince ensures the peace and the just laws that enable households and commerce to conduct their vocations. The prince also protects the poor and weak from the powerful. It is not the powerful who need government, but the poor. For Luther, Christian instruction cannot occur at home without good government. All community is a gift of God. Thus a just and effective government does not depend upon the spirituality of the home; rather, Christian family values depend upon a well-ordered and just government that protects everyone and preserves the peace. The prince is a secular savior, redeeming the people from war, violence, and injustice. When the prince does not fulfill this role, it is the responsibility not of the private citizen but of the priest or preacher to stand in the assembly and publicly rebuke the prince.

Preface

Once upon a time popes, bishops, priests, and monks had such authority that with their little letters of excommunication they could compel and drive kings and princes wherever they wished, without resistance or defense. In fact, kings and princes could not ruffle the hair of any monk or priest, no matter how insignificant the worm was. They had to put up with it when a rude jackass in the pulpit would vilify kings or princes and make fun of them whenever he felt like it. It was called preaching, and no one dared make a stir against it. The temporal rulers were completely subject to these spiritual giants and tyrants, and these dissolute and rude people walked all over them. The single canon, *si quis suadente*,[7] was that powerful. Besides, there was no understanding or teaching as to what temporal authority was and how necessary it was to distinguish it from the spiritual authority. Therefore, the temporal rulers did not know how to avenge themselves against the spiritual authorities, except that they were regularly hostile to them, spoke evil of them, and, wherever they could, played secret tricks and quietly permitted what others did against them.

Now, however, the gospel has come to light, and there is a clear distinction between the temporal and spiritual estates.[8] Moreover, the gospel teaches that the temporal estate has a divine ordinance that everyone should obey and honor. Now they rejoice in their freedom, and the spiritual tyrants need to pull in their pipes, and the tables are turned. Now popes, bishops, priests, and monks have to fear and honor the princes and lords and nobles, give them gifts and presents, keep the fasts and the feasts, and worship at their feet as though they were their gods. This tickles them so that they do not know how to abuse this grace and liberty wantonly enough. Meanwhile, they are persecuting the gospel, by means of which they have become gods and lords over the clergy, under the pretense of protecting and defending the spiritual estate. But, alas, the protection that the clergy get for such a price may hurt them in life and limb—though, to be sure, it serves them right!

Nevertheless, [far from] showing their gratitude to the gospel, they will not suffer its rebuke of their injustice and wickedness. They have now made a new proclamation, stating that whoever reprimands them is rebellious, resists the authority ordained by

God, and defames their honor. Therefore, because they are free from spiritual tyranny and cannot be reprimanded by the clergy, they now want to be rid of the gospel that made them free in the first place. Their goal is to do whatever they wish without shame or fear, without being hindered or reprimanded, but with honor and glory. Thus they may become that noble, praiseworthy folk of whom St. Peter says (2 Pet 3:3), "In the last days scoffers will come, scoffing and indulging their own lusts." And this is done by force.

There were such little squires among the people, too, as this Eighty-second Psalm shows. They have before them the saying of Moses (Exod 22:9), in which he calls the overlords and judges gods, saying, "If a case cannot be decided, both parties are to be brought before the gods, that is, the judges." They made of this passage a cloak for their shame and a defense of their iniquity against the preachers and prophets; they would not be reprimanded by them, puffed themselves up against their reprimands and their preaching, and struck them on the head with this, saying: "Will you reprimand us and teach us? Do you not know that Moses calls us gods? You are a rebel; you are speaking against God's ordinance, and your preaching insults our honor. You must listen to us, learn from us, and let yourself be reprimanded by us. Hold your tongue, or you must burn!" That is just what these same junkers [squires] say (Ps 12:4): "Our lips are our own; who is our master?" And again (Ps 11:3), "What can the righteous do to us?" And again (Ps 4:6), "O that we might see some good!" There are many such passages. It is as if they were saying, "We endure no master who reprimands. We are the gods; they must hear us."

* * *

Against these squires the psalm is written. It says, "God stands in the assembly of God and is judge among the gods."[9]

The psalmist confesses and does not deny that they are gods. He will not be rebellious or demean their honor or power, as the disobedient, rebellious people or the mad saints, heretics, and enthusiasts do. Nevertheless, he makes a clear distinction between God's power and theirs. He will let them be gods over people, but not over God, as if to say, "It is true, you are gods over us all, but not over the God of us all. God established you as gods but certainly wills to be an exception and will not subject God's divinity to your divinity. God

21

does not allow you to be gods and thereby cease to remain God. God wills to be the supreme God, the one who judges all the gods."

Moses calls them gods because all the offices of government, from the least to the highest, are by God's command, as St. Paul teaches (Rom 13:1); and King Jehoshaphat tells his officials (2 Chr 19:6), "Consider what you are doing, for you judge…on the Lord's behalf." Now, this is not a matter of human will or devising, but God appoints and preserves all authority. If God no longer sustained it, it would all fall down, even if the whole world clung to it. Therefore, it is truly called a godly thing, a divine ordinance. Such persons are rightly called divine, godlike, or gods, especially when their establishment is the result of God's word and command, as is true for the people of Israel, whose priests, rulers, and kings were established by the oral command and word of God.

Thus we see how God wills to have rulers held in honor and esteem, and that people ought to obey them as God's officers and be subject to them with all fear and reverence, as if to God. For they resist God if they are disobedient or despise those who are called by God's own name, being called gods. Moreover, whoever despises, disobeys, or resists those to whom God attaches God's own honor thereby despises, disobeys, and resists the true supreme God, who is in them, speaks and judges through them, and calls their judgment God's judgment. St. Paul shows what they gain by it (Rom 13:4), and it is abundantly shown by experience.

All this is written because it is God's will to establish and maintain peace among Adam's children for their own good. As Paul says (Rom 13:4), "For [governing authority] is God's servant for your good." For where there is no government and wherever it is not honored, there also can be no peace. Where there is no peace, there can be no livelihood, and no one can keep one's life and goods safe from another's violence, theft, robbery, force, and wickedness. Thus, one will be much less able to teach God's word and raise children in the fear and discipline of God (Eph 6:4).[10] God does not wish to have the world uninhabited and void but has created the world that we may live in it, cultivate it, and fill it, as is written in Genesis 1:28–30. Since none of this can happen without peace, God is compelled as creator to uphold God's own creatures, works, and ordinances by instituting and preserving government and to commit to it the sword and laws....

Just as, on the one side, God prevents the disorder of the rabble and subjects it to the sword and the laws, on the other side, he prevents the government from arbitrarily misusing its majesty and power. God ensures that governments use it for that which God established and sustained them, namely, for peace. Nevertheless, God does not wish the members of the rabble to raise their fists against the government or to reach for the sword to punish or to judge the rulers.[11] No, they should leave that alone; God has not committed this to them. Thus they should not be their own rulers; nor should they avenge themselves or resort to outrage and violence. God will punish wicked rulers and impose statutes and laws upon them and will be the judge and master over them. God will bring their injustices into the open, better than anyone else can, as has been done since the beginning of the world.

This is what this first verse says: "God stands in the assembly of God and is judge among the gods." In other words, let no one undertake to judge the gods, punish them, or correct them, but be quiet, keep the peace, be obedient, and suffer.[12] Neither are the gods to be proud and self-willed. For they are not gods over the people and lords over the assembly in order that they may have this position all to themselves and do as they like. Not so! God is there also and will judge, punish, and correct them. If they do not obey, they will not escape. "God stands in the assembly," because the assembly belongs to God. Furthermore, "God judges the gods," because the government belongs to God. Because both are God's, it is right for God to take the side of both. God wants to be respected and feared by both, so that the assembly may be obedient to the rulers for God's sake, and the rulers may administer justice and peace, likewise for God's sake. Thus the things of this life will go along well in the fear and obedience of God. But if one party or the other does not do its duty, if the assembly is disobedient and the rulers self-willed, then both are worthy of death in God's sight. And both are punished—the assembly by the government and the rulers by God, who can bring down the powerful from their thrones (Luke 1:52) and tear them up by their roots, destroying their name and their memory, as the illustrations show.[13]

Note that all communities or organized assemblies are called "the assembly of God,"[14] because they are God's own and God accepts them as God's own work, just as God calls Nineveh "a city of God" (Jonah 3:3).[15] For God has created and makes all communities and still brings them together, feeds them, lets them grow, blesses and preserves them, gives them fields and meadows, cattle, water, air, sun and moon, and everything they have, even body and life, as it is written (Gen 1:29). For what does the whole world have or we have that we have not received unceasingly from God [1 Cor 4:7]?[16] Even though we ought to learn this from experience, God must say it in plain words and openly proclaim and boast that all communities are God's own. For mad reason, in its shrewdness, and all the worldly wise do not understand that a community is God's creation and ordinance. They think only that it has come into being by accident, through people coming together and living side by side, in the same way murderers and robbers and other wicked bands gather to disturb the peace and God's order; these are the devil's communities. Only believers know the article about creation from Genesis 1, although they believe inadequately and many of them never think of it or speak of it. David knows it very well when he says (Ps 24:1–2), "The earth is the Lord's and all that is in it, the world and those who live in it, for God has founded it on the seas and established it on the rivers." His son Solomon says (Ps 127:1), "Unless the Lord guards both house and city, the builder and the guard build and watch in vain." What could the worldly wise know of heavenly things, when they do not even know the things among which they live now (John 3:12)?

Since such communities are God's work, and since God creates, increases, and nourishes them daily so that they can be at home, have children and educate them, etc., this word is above all a great and sweet comfort to all who find themselves in such a community. They are certain that God accepts them as God's own work and creation, cares for them, protects them, and nourishes them, as one can see with one's own eyes. For who could have or keep a cow or a heifer if God did not give it and help and guard it? Therefore, we should admonish ourselves with this glorious freedom, more willingly be obedient to all that the government asks of us, and be joyful to be worthy to eat bread and live in such a community. For this word, "assembly of God," is a

24

precious word; and anyone who is part of it ought to be ten times happier than to be counted as a Roman citizen, which was once a great honor on earth. Reason, however, does not consider this.

Moreover, it is a terrible and threatening word against the wicked, self-willed rulers, for it tells them that they are set, not over wood and stone, or pigs and dogs (about which God has given no commandments), but over the "assembly of God." They ought to fear, lest the wrong they do be done against God. For the communities do not belong to them, as do the pigs and dogs that God has freely given them. God wishes to be among them and calls them God's own assembly. On either side, then, when there is fear of God and humility, everything will go well. Subjects will have regard for God and gladly be obedient for God's sake, and rulers will also have regard for God and, for God's sake, will do justice and keep the peace....

Now, in order that these proud gods may be deprived of their defiant boastfulness, whereby they think that no one can judge them or reprimand them without being called a rebel, they are brought down a peg or two, and a stick is laid beside the dog. Thus they are properly reprimanded and spoken to boldly, sharply, and hard. As this psalm says, "God stands in the assembly and judges the gods," that is, God reprimands them. For God holds the upper hand and has the right to judge them. God does not, in making them gods, abolish God's own sovereignty and let them do as they please, as if they alone were gods. On the contrary, it is God's will that they be subject to the word and either listen to it or suffer all misfortune. It is enough that they rule over everything else; they are not to rule over God's word. For God's word appoints them, makes them gods, and subjects everything to them. Therefore, they are not to despise it, for it established them and appoints them, but they are to be subject to it and allow themselves to be judged, reprimanded, and corrected by it.

Where then is God? Or how can we be sure that there is a God who thus reprimands? Answer: You hear in this [psalm] that "God stands in the assembly." Where God's assembly is, there you will find God. For God has appointed there priests and preachers, to whom God has committed the duty of teaching, exhorting, reprimanding, comforting, in a word, of preaching the word of God. How it has been commanded to preach the word of God and how it has been commanded to preach the word of God in every place and in all the world I cannot tell here. I think everyone sees the churches and pulpits; they all rest on this one foundation (Matt 28:19–20): "Go...and make disciples of all the nations,...teaching them to obey everything that I have commanded you." Would God that only faithful preachers had this office and administered it faithfully and purely, and that it were not abused so shamefully and hatefully! Nevertheless, abuse does not destroy the office; the office is true, exactly as temporal rule is a true and good office, even though a knave has it and abuses it.

Observe, however, that a preacher by whom God reprimands the gods is to "stand in the assembly." The preacher is to "stand," that is, the preacher is to be firm and confident and deal uprightly and honestly with it; and "in the assembly," that is, openly and boldly before God and humans. Thereby two sins are prevented. The first is unfaithfulness. There are many bishops and preachers in the ministry, but they do not "stand" and serve God faithfully. On the contrary, they lie down or otherwise play with their office. These are the lazy and worthless preachers who do not confront the princes and lords with their sins. In some cases they do not notice the sins. They lie down and snore in their office and do nothing that pertains to it, except that, like pigs, they take up the space where good preachers should stand. These form the great majority. Others, however, play the hypocrite and flatter the wicked gods, strengthening them in their self-will. Even now they are raging and raving against the gospel and are stirring up their princes and lords to blasphemy and murder. Still others fear for their skins and are afraid that they will lose life and goods. All these do not "stand" and are not faithful to Christ.

The other sin is called backbiting. Every corner of the world is full of preachers and laypersons who bandy evil words about their gods, that is, princes and lords, cursing them and calling them names, though not boldly in the open, but in corners and in their own sects. However, this results in just making the evil worse. It serves only to set a secret fire by which people are moved to disobedience, rebellion, breach of the peace, and contempt for their rulers. If you are in the ministry and are not willing to reprimand your gods openly and publicly, as your office demands, at least desist from private backbiting, name calling, criticizing, and complaining, or go hang. But if you are not in office, then leave off all reprimanding and criticizing, both public and private. Otherwise, the devil is already your abbot and does not need to become so, for in Matthew 7:1 God has forbidden secret judging or judging where there is no office. On the other hand, it is God's will that those who are in office and are called to do it shall reprimand and judge their gods boldly and openly.

So, then, this first verse teaches that reprimanding rulers is not seditious, provided it is done in the way here described, namely, by the office to which God has committed that duty, and through God's word, spoken publicly, boldly, and honestly. Reprimanding rulers in this way is, rather, a praiseworthy, noble, and rare virtue, and a particularly great service to God, as the psalm here proves. It is far more seditious for a preacher not to rebuke the sins of the rulers, for then the people become angry and sullen. Thus [the preacher] strengthens the wickedness of the tyrants, becomes a partaker in it, and bears responsibility for it, and God might become angry and send rebellion to plague them. On the other hand, when both the lords and the people are reprimanded equally, as the prophets did, neither side can blame the other, and they have to bear with one another, be satisfied, and be at peace with one another.

Those preachers who, like Müntzer, Carlstadt, and other fanatics,[17] take the one side and scold the lords in order to win over the people and flatter the peasants—or, on the other side, scold the peasants in order to flatter and serve the lords, as our opponents do—are poisonous and dangerous. The thing to do is to chop both parties up in one bowl and make one dish out of the two of them. For the office of the preacher is neither a servant at court nor a hired hand. The preacher is God's servant and farm hand and has a commission over lords and servants. As the psalm says, "God judges and reprimands the gods." This is the meaning of the word *judge*, namely, "by judgment and law."[18] The preacher is to do what is right and proper, not with a view to favor or disfavor, but according to law, that is, according to God's word, which knows no distinction or respect of persons.

"How long will you judge unjustly and show partiality to the wicked? Every prince should have these next three verses[19]—indeed the whole psalm—painted on the wall of his chamber, on his bed, over his table, and on his clothes. For here princes find what lofty, princely, and noble virtues their office can exercise, for, next to the preaching office, temporal government is the highest service to God and the most useful office on earth. This should surely comfort a lord and motivate him to exercise his office with joy and to practice these virtues. How can you praise them more than by calling them gods and saying that they are such? The works and virtues of their office are not merely princely or royal, or even angelic, but divine. On the other hand, they discover how ungodly, unprincely, and even inhuman and altogether devilish are the iniquities they perform, and how they are the most harmful persons on earth when they forsake the virtues of their office and do the opposite. Then they are not to be called gods but devils, and they no doubt are, even if they sit in the godly offices. They bear the name in vain.

Now let us see, one by one, what great virtues they can perform. The first is that they can provide justice for those who fear God and can repress those who are godless. As the psalmist says, "How long will you judge unjustly and show partiality to the wicked?" Who can count, however, the number of rich virtues and profits that come about from this first virtue? For where God's word is protected and supported so that it can be freely taught and learned, and if the sects and false teachers are not given license and not defended against those who fear God, what greater treasure can there be in the land? God must certainly live there, as if in God's own temple. Many kings and princes have established great and glorious churches and built temples, but, even if a king could build a church of solid gold or pure emeralds and rubies, how could even this great and glorious thing compare to an upright, god-fearing pastor or preacher? This same one can save a thousand souls, both in this life and in the life to come. For a pastor can bring them to God through the word and make of them able and accomplished people, obedient to God, honorable and wholesome and useful to the world. A church or a temple cannot benefit one this way. In fact, it cannot help one at all, but only stands there and lets itself be helped and decorated.

But who is this prince? Where are the eyes that may see such virtue in a lord or prince? Supporting and protecting a poor, upright pastor or preacher does not glitter or shine and appears as a nothing. But to build a marble church, give it golden ornaments, and serve dead stone and wood—that glitters and shines! That is considered royal and princely virtue. All right, let it shine; let it glitter. Meanwhile, my pastor, who does not glitter, is practicing the virtue that increases the reign of God, fills heaven with saints, harrows hell, robs the devil, wards off death, restrains sin, teaches and comforts all according to their stations in life, upholds peace and unity, raises fine young persons, and plants all kinds of virtue in the people. In short, the pastor creates a new world—not a temporary house, but an eternal and beautiful paradise in which God is pleased to dwell. An upright prince or lord who supports or protects such a pastor can have a role in all of this. Indeed, this whole work and all the fruits of it are his, as though he had done it all himself, because, without his protection and support, the pastor could not abide. Therefore, no silver or golden mountain in the land can be compared with this treasure. Blessed are the eyes that know this and the hands that can do this.

The second virtue of a prince is to help the poor, the orphans, and the widows to have justice and to defend their cause. Who can describe all the virtues that follow from this one? This virtue includes all the works of righteousness, for, when a prince, lord, or city has good laws and customs and everything is regulated and in order and when order is kept by people in all ranks, occupations, trades, businesses, services, and works, it is not said, "The people are without laws." Where there are no regulations, the poor, widows, and orphans are trodden down, because there is no peasant so low that he cannot practice extortion. This is equally true of buying, selling, inheriting, lending, paying, borrowing, and the like; it is only a matter of getting the better of another, robbing, stealing, and cheating one another. This happens most of all to the poor, the widows, and the orphans. Now who can count the alms that such a good prince bestows continuously? For so he supports not only the pastor about whom we spoke above, but also all the subjects that he has. He may well be called the father of them all, as in ancient times the heathen called such upright princes fathers and saviors of their country.[20]

See now what a hospital such a prince can build! He needs no stone, wood, or builders, and he does not need to give either endowment or income. To endow hospitals and help the poor is indeed a worthy and good work, but when such a hospital becomes so large that the whole land and especially the truly poor benefit from it, then it is a general, true, princely, indeed, a heavenly and divine hospital. The former hospitals benefit a few people and sometimes wicked persons who masquerade as beggars. The latter kind of hospital comes to the aid of the truly poor, widows, orphans, travelers, and other forgotten people. This hospital upholds the life and goods of each and every person, whether rich or poor, so that he or she does not have to become a beggar or poor. Where the law is not upheld no one can protect his or her goods from another, and all will become beggars and be ruined and destroyed. This lord is providing this hospital for the many who are not beggars and do not become beggars. Assisting someone not to become a beggar is just as much a good work, virtue, and almsgiving as giving to one who has already become a beggar....[21] Therefore, even the heathen say that righteousness is such a beautiful virtue that it outshines the sun, moon, and the morning star.

In sum, after the gospel and pastoral ministry there is no better purse or greater treasure on earth, or more generous alms, or a more beautiful endowment, or better good than a ruler who makes and upholds just laws. Such rulers are rightly called gods....That they can guard and protect against force and violence—in other words, that they can establish peace—is the third virtue. Thus the emperors themselves have divided their office into two parts when they say that an emperor or prince should be equipped with laws and arms. For this reason they are painted on their documents with a book in one hand and a sword in the other, as a sign that they administer law and peace. Because the law is wisdom, it should be the first of the two. To govern by force without wisdom cannot last. They also wear golden crowns so that they recognize that they are established as gods by God and not by themselves, and they should thus be God's helpers.

Now who can relate all the usefulness and benefits that come from this third virtue? First, one would have to relate what peace is good for and what damage the lack of peace does. Who on earth is so eloquent and clever as to begin to enumerate both? Through these gods God creates all the good that peace can do and all the harm that the absence of peace can cause. God defends us again through these gods. Through peace we have our body and life, spouse and children, house and home, and all our limbs—hands, feet—and eyes, health and freedom; and within these walls of peace we sit in safety. "Where there is peace, it is almost heaven."[22] On the other hand, even if you had the money and wealth of a Turk but were not at peace, all your wealth would do you so little good that you could not eat your bread or drink your water in peace. If things went well, there could be concern, fear, and danger all around; if things were worse, there would be only blood and fire and robbery and every kind of adversity. Thus, lack of peace may be counted as sheer hell, or hell's introduction and onset.

Nevertheless, peace can help you so that a piece of dry bread tastes like sugar and a sip of water like sweet wine. Why am I so foolish as to narrate the benefits of peace and the injuries of lack of peace? I might as well count the sands on the seashore or the leaves and the grass in the woods. Christ himself (Matt 5:9) compares peace to heaven and says, "The peacemakers...will be called children of God." But God's children do not belong in this world, much the less peace. See now these virtues lie in heaps in this estate, but they are not seen, for they do not glisten. Because of their goodness and their number they do not shine. Yet the empty, worthless, useless works, these make a show! These are held in high esteem.

I must remember here my monks and priests, who have the reputation of carrying heaven on their shoulders in their acts of worship....What are they all, compared with one who inhabits this divine office?...I think they are about as useful in the world as the rust on the iron; for they are as good to the world or to this divine office as the rust on the tools of a carpenter. Nay, I shall name the very best of them—the hermits, like Hilary, Jerome, and the rest, who have their great reputation because of the holy hermits' life they led. If wishing could do it, I would rather be an upright secretary or tax collector for one of these "gods" than twice a Hilary or a Jerome among the angels. Even though my little pen or miserable penny would count for less in the world's eyes than their gray beards and

31

wrinkled skin, I would not worry about that, if only I were a partaker of all those divine virtues of government of which I have spoken.

So now what an imperial, what a heavenly stronghold such a prince can build for the protection of the subjects. It is indeed a splendid and needful thing to build strong cities and castles against one's enemies, but that is nothing when compared with the work of a prince who builds a stronghold of peace, that is, who loves peace and administers it. Even the Romans, the greatest warriors on earth, had a saying that to make war without necessity was to go fishing with a golden net: if it was lost, the fishing could not pay for it; if it caught anything, the cost was too much greater than the profit.[23] One must not initiate a war or work for it; it comes unbidden all too soon. One must keep peace as long as one can, even if one must buy it with all the money that would be spent on the war or won by the war. Victory never makes up for what is lost by war.

These then are the three main virtues of the gods treated in these three verses, and each in a special way can fill the world with good and salvation. The first verse commends the first virtue, namely, that the gods or the princes and lords should honor the word of God above all things and further the teaching of it. It says, "How long will you judge unjustly and show partiality to the wicked?" The godless and the false teachers always have a great reputation in the eyes of reason and the world. They know, too, how to make a fine appearance before both lords and people, and thus to spread their poisonous errors....

The next verse teaches the second virtue, namely, that they are to make and administer just laws so that the poor, the suffering, widows, and orphans are not oppressed but have rights and can keep them. It says, "Give justice to the weak and the orphan; maintain the right of the lowly and the destitute." By saying that "they are to help them to justice," it helps us understand that, while there are certainly judges and courts, things go by favor or friendship, out of envy or revenge, so that often the one who is put in the right is really in the wrong.

The third virtue is taught by the third verse. They are to defend against force and harm and prevent violence, punish the rascals, and use the sword against the wicked so that peace will be upheld in the land. It says, "Rescue the weak and the needy; deliver them from the hand of the wicked."[24] The preceding verse speaks of "justice," this verse of "the hand," to show that there it was speaking of wrong and here of violence. For these two, wrong and violence, go together in the world. As we say, "He is doing me violence and injustice." Injustice is done by the mind or with the mouth; violence, with the fist and with wickedness. A prince and lord should suppress both....

To conclude these three virtues: such a prince should bear with honor the three divine offices and names. In this way the prince should help, sustain, and save and therefore be called a savior, father, deliverer. By the first virtue the word of God is furthered, and many are helped to blessedness so that they may be redeemed from sin and death and obtain salvation. Through the next virtue just laws are upheld, and the prince sustains subjects as a father provides for his children. As it is said, where the law is not upheld, everyone steals from everyone else. Through the third virtue wickedness is suppressed, evil ones punished, the poor protected, and peace defended, so that the prince is a true rescuer or knight and justly wears the golden spur. I believe that *Ritter* comes from *retten* and that the word *Retter* has become *Ritter,* a true and splendid name for the princes and lords.[25]

An Admonishment to Pastors to Preach against Usury: How One Should Give, Lend, and Suffer[1]

Editors' Introduction: Fundamental to Luther's spirituality or way of living in faith is that God does not need our works, but our neighbor does.[2] That is, our works have nothing to do with our salvation.[3] For him, the care of the neighbor, especially the poor, is the primary vocation of the Christian in the world. Luther thus cultivated a civic piety. According to Carter Lindberg, the poor are not to be the objects of the neighbor's almsgiving for the merit of the benefactor; there should be no beggars in a Christian community. "The poor are neighbors to be served through justice and equity."[4] This is a social responsibility.

Luther was primarily a biblical theologian, not an economist, but throughout his broad experiences he observed the consequences of the development of capitalism and a growing money economy. Severe inflation was a regular factor in Wittenberg and its environs during Luther's lifetime. Not only did powerful economic forces inflate prices, but various lending institutions loaned money with interest rates as high as 40 percent. Consequently, Luther was profoundly critical of the growing tendency of the money and interest-credit economy to abuse the poor and the financially burdened with high rates. According to Luther, even if it was the rich who sometimes paid the high interest rates, the poor inevitably suffered, because the costs were passed on to them.

Luther did not have a Franciscan view of money, as if it were evil. Nor did he have a spirituality that encouraged giving alms to those in need, especially beggars. Economic resources had to be used with justice and compassion for the vulnerable precisely because money was a good. It was how it was used that could be evil. Luther favored the regulation of business and the care of the poor by the prince and the community.[5]

He was not alone in challenging high, usurious interest rates; the church had historically interpreted the Bible as condemning usury. However, Luther was a strong if unheard voice against the abuses of a nascent capitalism that many of his contemporaries tolerated.[6] He was not opposed to mortgages with reasonable rates of 5 percent. He did have an impact in Wittenberg, where a "Common Chest" was established that cared for the needy of the community and those with burdensome debts. It also offered loans at little or no interest and cultivated a sense of the commonweal.[7]

* * *

Now that the powerful worldly authorities have become Christians, how are we contemporary Christians to remain faithful to Christ's teaching about suffering? They do not allow anything in Christendom to be diminished or harmed in any way. Now, their protection and shelter should not be scorned but should be treated like other goods and creatures of God with thanksgiving, etc., because the Christians under the Turks probably do see this teaching and suffer more than we know or believe. Suffering among us now are the papists, the very holiest of Christians, martyrs beyond measure and the cross, for which they can neither sleep nor rest, if they are to persecute the gospel sufficiently. They also persecute all who believe in it, murdering them, drowning them, and filling the world with their blood, to the honor of God and to maintain the holy church. For this they anticipate countless crowns of honor in heaven.

All joking aside, however, where is such suffering among us, when we are protected by worldly authorities? No one dares seize us or insult us because we have accepted the word of God. For the others who persecute it give their subjects suffering and plagues enough, as we see before our eyes. And now, after discussing the raging of the papists, where, I ask, is our suffering? Well, just let me tell you! Run through all the estates, starting from the bottom to the very top, and you will find what you are looking for. That is, you find an upright Christian peasant or farmer, who shows Christian love and faithfulness to his or her neighbor, a poor, upright peasant or the poor pastor, by giving, lending, counseling, or helping in the person's need. On the other side you will find more than a thousand unchristian peasants or farmers, who would not give a penny to the pastor or the neighbor, even if the person were starving. Rather, like greedy thieves they scratch everything toward themselves, overcharging for their advantage, forging, embezzling, taking, stealing, and secretly robbing, whether the government, pastor, or neighbor, wherever they can. If they could suck out everyone's blood, they would do it, just to fill their greed, which, however, they can never fill. And so one could assuredly bring all the upright Christian peasants of a country together in one village, and the village would still not be very large. What does it matter? Such peasants will surely teach you that you must endure this teaching about suffering, overcoming evil with patience, because the peasants in Israel did the same thing for their priests, Levites, brothers, and friends, as we read in Malachi 2.

You can see the same thing among the city people or burghers. You may find a city hall where the mayor and the council members sincerely consider the gospel to be holy, or you may find a faithful Christian citizen who gladly gives, lends, helps, etc. Yet, on the other side, you will find a great many city halls and even more citizens who hate and scorn the gospel to the same degree. They will oppress, plague, and martyr pastors and poor peasants where they can and be just as greedy as the unchristian peasants, if not more so. In addition, they will use pure tyranny, power, and rank against whomever they can, whether a pastor or a poor person. So I suppose one could place all upright Christian councilors and citizens of a principality in one city, which would also not be especially large. These too are the masters who teach us to keep the word of Christ about suffering.

After that, take the nobility and officials, and count all of those for me who take the word of God seriously (because it is they who, before all others and out of great love for the word of God, devour it). Should you find one who takes giving, lending, and helping the neighbor seriously, then again you will find more than a hundred who play the opposite game with great violence, so that truly, it would not need to be a very large castle where the praiseworthy, upright Christian nobility of a whole principality could live and dwell together. And if you do not know what suffering means according to Christ's teaching, then be so proud as to proclaim the word of God to such an arrogant noble, when it is against him, and do not pray to God for him the way he wants and for what he wants. Then you will get what you are looking for! We will especially win praise and glory because of those whom we attack for their greed and usury, by which they have sunk deep into hell. We consider them unchristian, extend no sacrament to them or grant them the communion of the church, as we surely cannot do for our conscience's sake. And, finally, look also to the high estates of the rulers. Where one or two are Christian among rulers, they are a rare find. The others all continue to be firebrands of the devil from hell and cause suffering and misfortune for Christians.

Although the Lord proclaimed and commanded such suffering for all Christians in common, God especially commanded it for the apostles and the heirs of their office after them. Toward such as these the devil is especially hostile, because, for the sake of their office, they must publicly punish offenses, which the peasant, burgher, nobility, ruler, lord cannot tolerate. But, like their god and lord, the devil, they want to do what they please freely and without punishment, even wanting to be loved and praised for it. Therefore, the devil is not only the enemy of the upright pastor and preacher but also of the evil ones, together with all those who study or who become "writers," as he calls them; he is worried that a writer or someone educated could become a preacher and a bad pastor could one day become just. Thus, none of these is tolerated in his kingdom. And it is no wonder, because he would like to keep everyone in it a plain serf, whereby no one studies; in this way, he knows, both pastors and books would soon turn to dust. Thus he is the enemy of all the educated and the writers, even of those who do not harm him but powerfully serve him. He may well also be the enemy of all feathers and geese, since the writing quill comes from the birds.

So he now begins by saying, "One must not allow clerics[8] to become lords!" They do not say this because they are worried that the clerics might become lords. They know themselves to be lying, because they know full well it is prohibitive for clerics to become lords. First, one cannot deny that a pastor has nothing of his own in the parish; pastors are tenants as to the possessions of the pastorate and have to leave them behind when they die. While one or two through great toil may have enough to buy their widows and orphans a little cottage, the others are all pure beggars and leave pure beggars behind them, both their widows and their orphans. Even if they do scrape together something for themselves, here below they still have to remain among humble peasants or burghers, for with ten florins they cannot ride or sit very high. Such facts they know, see, hear, and grasp very well, even especially well, but they scold and mock such poor people and say, "Clerics should not be lords!" That strikes me like the rich man in the gospel saying to Lazarus, "Lazarus should not be the lord in my house," when he even begrudges him the rinds and crumbs that fell under the table for the dogs. Dear friend, how far might these mockers be away from those who crowned our Lord with thorns, spit on him, and said, "Hail, dear king!"?

Therefore, I say, they do not say such things because they are worried that clerics might become lords; they fabricate such comedies out of wanton mischief, in order to muffle the office of preaching, because they want to make themselves free and secure from having to hear the truth, by which they deserve punishment. Yet the gospel cannot bear such people; otherwise, it would soon go under. But we have to have them, in order to suffer further evil for the sake of Christ. Because, indeed, what the Lord says about suffering must also be fulfilled among our people. "No prophet is accepted in the prophet's hometown" (Luke 4:24). And Christ [says], "It is impossible for a prophet to be killed outside of Jerusalem" (Luke 13:33), and in John 1:11, "He came to what was his own, and his own people did not accept him." If our gospel is the true light, then it truly has to shine in the darkness, and the darkness must not comprehend it. If we do not want to accept that and want the world to be different, then we must take our leave of the world or create a different world that does what we want or God wills. This world does not want to and will not do it. We might want to surrender cheerfully and ponder that....

So for our gospel to proceed correctly and receive its honor, our preachers or pastors and Christians have to deal with false teaching first and after that with violence. (These two, namely, lies and murder, have been the two weapons of the devil from the beginning.) And, praise be to God, the schismatics have made an excellent start on lies. Faithfully following after them, the peasants, burghers, nobles, and lords assist with thanklessness, disdain, hatred, pride, and all kinds of deception. If the prelude has begun, then surely the real song will soon begin, if half of it has not already perhaps been sung and played. But though it means risking your neck,[9] call them unchristian or God's enemies who scorn God's word. They will tolerate it far less than Jerusalem, the holy city, would have, since they called Israel a whorehouse and a murder pit (Isa 57:3; Jer 7:11). The majority of our Christians are now the same way. They want to be evangelical, hold the word in high esteem, and be pure saints, but they are the enemy of the pastors and preachers who preach the word and speak the truth to them. Jerusalem also held the word in high esteem, but the prophets had better not preach it lest they die and be destroyed.

And why do we preachers, pastors, and writers want to complain? Take a look at the world in itself. Look at the way one country hates the other, like Italy, Spain, Hungary, and Germany; how one ruler hates the other, one lord the other, one burgher the other, one peasant the other. And all with what they call Christian love and faithfulness, meaning by that that they are jealous, hate, whack, hack, abuse, injure, and cause all sorts of misfortune or, at least, wish it. Moreover, they all want to be and have everything by themselves, so that whoever from an evangelical heart observes their nature and action will think that it is not people but pure devils who are raging here in human masks and human forms. It is a wonder that the world can remain standing for a year. Where could that power possibly come from that holds the world together amid such disunity, enmity, hatred, envy, robbery, theft, scratching, grabbing, hurting, and unspeakable arrogance, so that it does not daily collapse in a heap upon itself? It is God's wondrous, almighty power and wisdom that you must perceive and comprehend here. Otherwise, the world could not stand so long.

Therefore, do not worry about where you will find suffering. No need for that. Just be an upright Christian, preacher, pastor, burgher, peasant, noble, or lord, and carry out the duties of your office diligently and faithfully. Let the devil worry about where to find a scrap of wood from which to make you a cross, and the world, where it can find a switch to make a whip for your skin. Even if the authorities held you in their lap, no authority is so clever and mighty that it could shield and protect you from the devil, bad people, and all evil, even if it were quite righteous and diligent. Only be a genuine Christian with a simple heart who suffers for the sake of Christ, and do not give yourself cause for suffering like false fame-hungry martyrs and monks do or loose reckless fellows who, with their arrogance, bring themselves into misfortune and the gallows.

And think of the little hen in Aesop's fables that was bitten by the roosters. As she saw that the roosters bit each other too, she comforted herself and said, "I will now bear up under my suffering a measure better, since they themselves also bite each other." Should not the world bite and trample on us Christians if among themselves they so shamefully bite and trample on each other? Why do we want to have it better in the world than the world has it in itself, submitting to more suffering than it can bear? Let that be enough said about the right teaching of Christ as to how one should give, lend, and suffer, so that among Christians there can be no place for usury and greed. If it finds a place, then they are certainly not Christians, let them boast as much as they will, because Christ says in Matthew 6[:24], "You cannot serve God and wealth." And St. Paul, "No…one who is greedy (that is, an idolater) has any inheritance in the kingdom of…God" (Eph 5:5). Indeed, he calls greed idolatry, as everyone now knows, glory to God!

If the servant of wealth, however, cannot be saved, who is surely just a greedy person, and such a person's life is, indeed, called pure idolatry, where does that leave usurers? Whose servants could they be, if the merely greedy person is called the servant of the devil? For there is a big difference between a greedy person and a usurer. One who is covetous of one's own possessions might not take anything from anyone, strangle anyone, or oppress anyone by direct action or encroachment. Rather, like the rich man in the gospel, one does it covertly by not helping where one should help, watching as oppression and harm take place, when one could and should prevent them. As the common saying of Ambrose testifies: "Feed the hungry. If you do not feed them, then it is as if you had killed them."[10] A usurer, however, is an outright murderer, because not only does he not help the hungry, he rips from their mouths the scrap of bread that God and upright people gave them for their bodily necessities. He does not ask if the whole world is dying of hunger; for him, it is only about having his usury.

Indeed, perhaps you say, "I take by greed and usury nothing from the poor but only from the rich who have it. Therefore, I murder and oppress no one." Thank you, my dear scamp, for even recognizing yourself as a greedy miser and usurer, that is, the devil's servant and the enemy of God and all people. Next, you lecture us as to how you do not oppress and murder the poor, but it is the rich and those who have that you suck dry (in other words, you still confess that you are a thief and a robber). Truly fine, you are well excused, for I had not known that before, and you ought to convince me quickly, so that, being mistaken, I can take back my having scolded you as the worst murderer and robber. But listen to my answer, you highly intelligent usurer and murderer. Who is most affected when you charge usury? Does it not fall fully and completely on the poor alone—those who, because of your usury, cannot in the end hold on to a penny or a piece of bread, since through your usury all prices have increased and become inflated? Who were affected by the usury in Nehemiah 5, in which the poor people finally had to sell all they had to the usurers—their houses, vineyards, fields, and, at the end, even their children? Similarly, whom did it affect in Rome, Athens, and the other cities, where because of usury the burghers had to become serfs, as mentioned before? Was it not the poor? Yes, they had been rich, and usury devoured them up to their own bodies.

Let the devil thank you that you do not charge any usury from the poor. Why would you want to charge usury where there is nothing? One knows quite well that you do not practice your usury on an empty money pouch; rather, you start with the rich and turn them into beggars. What follows from your lovely excuse that you do not charge the poor usury amounts to sheer murder of the rich, because you make them into beggars and drive them into poverty, to say nothing about how you should be keeping them out of poverty. So by this pretty little excuse you make yourselves not only the murderers of the poor but also of the rich, yes, of the rich alone. Are you such a mighty god in the world, reducing the rich and the poor into one, and only after you have first made them both poor, will you murder them and that is your great love and friendship?

Beyond that, even if the rich could swing themselves up and bear the inflation caused by your usury, nevertheless, the poor person cannot. The poor do not have one gulden per week to spend and have many children, so that even through hard work they cannot earn their daily bread because of the way your greed and usury have increased all the prices and caused inflation. Now again, whom is your greed and usury affecting? Dear friend, to excuse yourself at this point you say you increase prices and charge usury because you wish to give the rich a reason to give more alms to the poor so that they can earn the kingdom of heaven. By that argument you suck everything out of the rich in two ways: once out of themselves and once out of them for the poor for whom they must provide, so that for all of it you get the more honor and fame afterward—that you have done a good work, have done a service to the rich by having given the rich a cause for doing good works. How could you achieve a better reputation, one that would be more agreeable to a usurer? The devil too provides endless reasons to do good works by plaguing many people, whom one, for God's sake, must help.

In a short time it has gotten to the point through usury and greed that those who could nourish themselves with a hundred gulden several years ago now cannot nourish themselves with two hundred gulden. The usurer sits in Leipzig, Augsburg, Frankfurt, and similar cities and does business with sums of money, but we feel it here in our market and in our kitchen, in that we cannot even hold onto a penny or a worthless coin here. We pastors and preachers and those who live on fixed incomes have no business and cannot increase or multiply our income. We feel how close the usurers sit to us, devouring our food with us in the kitchen, drinking the best from our cellar, sucking us dry, so that our lives and bodies hurt. Peasants, burghers, and nobles can increase their harvest and work, double or triple their income, and thereby cope with usury more easily. But those who must live from hand to mouth, as the saying goes, have to put their bodies on the line and let themselves be skinned and killed.

Now, however, preaching cannot help anymore. They have usured themselves deaf, blind, and senseless, and they hear, see, and feel nothing more. It is just that, if we preach to them, then, on their last day, when they have to ride to hell, we are excused and they have no excuse. Otherwise, they put the blame on us, their counselors, that we did not warn them, chastise and teach them, and, for the sake of a sin of omission, we have to go with them to the devil. No, they have to go to hell alone, because we did our part according to our office. We punished and taught them with diligence; their blood and sin be and remain on their own heads and not on us.

Finally, lest the usurers and the greedy think we want to crush their business completely and ruin them utterly, we want to give them good and faithful counsel, so that they can become sated and over-satisfied with greed and usury. Thus, a preacher can claim to know and proclaim a rich Lord, who gladly allows usury charged against him. The Lord searches out and calls usurers and the greedy wherever they are, that they might confidently come and be greedy and charge as much usury as they can. The Lord desires to give them as much usury as necessary, not only ten or twenty on a hundred, but a hundred on one gulden and a thousand on a hundred, for he has mountains of silver and gold galore and can afford it easily and well. This selfsame Lord is called God, the creator of heaven and earth. Through God's dear Son in the gospel we can make the offer, "Give, and it will be given to you. A good measure, pressed down, shaken together, running over" (Luke 6:38). Now bring to me your sack and pouch, jar and larder. Do you hear? So much shall be given you in return that all your sacks and containers will be completely insufficient, way too small, for they will become so full that no more will fit in them, and they will overflow. And once again, "Everyone who has left houses…or fields for my name's sake will receive a hundredfold and will inherit eternal life" (Matt 19:29).

Why not be greedy and charge usury here, where one can have one's fill of greed and usury? Why search instead to quench one's greed and usury among people who can give little in return and do not satisfy but only exacerbate greed and make one thirstier? Is it not the cantankerous devil that keeps one from being greedy and charging this rich Lord usury? This rich one offers himself to everyone as their debtor, ready to bring tribute and personal service, and will gladly pay usury; and still no one wants to or will be the beneficiary.

God too calls it usury and yearns for such usury in Proverbs, chapter 19[:17]: "Whoever is kind to the poor lends to the Lord, and will be repaid in full." Where are you, greedy, insatiable usurers? Come here, and receive the usury of your lives for yourself and enough of all good things, here now and there in eternity, without doing any harm to the next person. For by your cursed usury you become murderers, thieves, scoundrels, and the most offensive, hostile, and despised people on earth. What is more, you will lose body and soul eternally. Nor will you be able to keep the ill-gotten gain from your usury, and, as mentioned, ill-gotten gain can never be inherited into the third generation.[11] However, as was mentioned before, you can become pure, holy usurers, who are dear, beloved, and valued by God, by all the angels and by people, and, what is more, you will never be able to lose the reward of your usury.

Now just see whether the children of the earth are not irrational and possessed by all the devils, because they despise such a rich Lord and his rich, eternal offering of usury. They turn themselves over to harmful, cursed, murderous, thieving usury, which cannot last and consigns them to hell....

All right, let them go their way, but you, pastor, watch out, as I said before, that you do not make yourself an accomplice to their sin. Let them die like dogs, and let the devil devour them body and soul. Do not admit them to the sacrament, baptism, or Christian fellowship. For a plague will spread over Germany, which now cannot be long in coming. Where greed and usury become the capital deadly sin, there, for its sake, we will all have to suffer God's wrath and rod, because we have let such cursed people be among us and did not punish or prevent them but had fellowship with them. And rulers and lords in particular will have to answer severely for having carried the sword in vain, allowing such murderers and robbers (usurers and greedy misers) freely to murder and steal through usury and reckless inflation in their lands. Even if they hope to remain unpunished for their committed sins, God will punish them for such sins of omission, so that they become impoverished, oppressed, separated from their lands and people. Even their family and lineage will wither and become extinct, as has happened to many.

For God is a greater enemy to usury and greed than anyone could think, since these involve not mere murder and robbery, but

44

serial, unquenchable murder, as you have now heard above. Therefore, each and every one should see to his or her worldly or spiritual office, in which he or she is commanded to punish offenses and protect the righteous. For now let this indictment of usury be enough. A preacher can probably bring more out of the history books. At all times they have written against usury and preached about the shocking and dreadful examples of how God and the devil have openly raged against usurers and greedy misers, have scandalously killed their body and soul, and made their family line become fully extinct, their goods reduced to some evil ruins. They believed that God's wrath could hardly be so great upon them, just as the usurers feel now, until they experienced it, as experience it they must. This we daily see before our eyes, and we will continue seeing more such examples.

I have not been referring to interest that is charged on a mortgage.[12] Such a just and completely legal financial operation is not usury. And one knows well, praise God, what a mortgage with payments is, according to worldly law, namely, that there should be mortgage security and the rate should not be too high per hundred, which is not now our topic. Each person should watch out that it is a just and honest purchase [and mortgage arrangement], because one greatly misuses all business transactions quite wondrously and falsely now, which [is a subject] someone else should develop and explain, as I did some fifteen years ago. God have mercy, make us righteous that we honor God's name, increase the kingdom, and do God's will. Amen.

PREFACE TO THE REVELATION OF ST. JOHN (1522)

Editors' Introduction: This brief and critical preface appeared in the September Testament of 1522 and in other editions up to 1527. Luther declares here, "My spirit cannot abide this book, and for me it is reason enough not to hold it in high regard that Christ is neither taught nor recognized in it." He professes that books are apostolic only if they give him "Christ clearly and purely."

Here Luther's early reforming emphasis on the Christ of faith—the proclaimed Christ—is evident. One of the significant achievements in Luther's early religious breakthrough was to shift apocalyptic spirituality away from the late medieval focus on the fearful symmetry of the Last Judgment, to which all earthly pilgrimages were tending.[1] The judging Christ, seated on the tympanum of many medieval cathedrals, with the twenty-four elders seated around and the good and the damned rising or falling to either side, terrified the young Luther.[2] This late medieval apocalyptic view of a judging Christ collected around it attendant attempts at religious appeasement.[3] In this commentary on the Apocalypse, Luther points instead to the cross and resurrection as the judgment. A painting by Lucas Cranach the Elder in the parish church at Wittenberg captures Luther's insight. Luther is depicted in the pulpit pointing to the crucified Christ and centering the drama of the Last Judgment on the crucifixion/resurrection event. He follows a Johannine understanding of the crucifixion/resurrection/ascension and Last Judgment as one event. In a similar altarpiece by the elder in the town church of Sts. Peter and Paul in Weimar, the Redeemer is lifted up on the cross while the victorious Lamb of the Apocalypse lies at the foot of the cross and the resurrected Christ slays death and the old Dragon alongside. The juxtaposition of these eschatological themes is set in a medieval village context with John the Baptist pointing to the Crucified One and Luther pointing to the open scripture. Among the passages cited by the painter is John 3:14–15, "And as Moses lifted up the serpent in the wilderness, even so must the son of man be lifted up, that whoever believes in him may have eternal life."[4]

* * *

I will leave this book, the Revelation of John, to each one's opinion and will bind no one to my thoughts or estimation of it. I say what I feel, for this book leaves so much to be desired that I hold it to be neither apostolic nor prophetic. In the first place, the apostles do not use visions, but prophesy with plain, clear words, as Peter, Paul, and Christ do in the gospel. That is as it is appropriate, for the apostolic office should speak clearly of Christ and his deeds without images or visions.

Besides, there is no prophet in the Old Testament, not to mention the New, who so uses visions and images throughout. I would think it similar to the Fourth Book of Esdras, and above all I cannot tell that it is inspired by the Holy Spirit.

...Moreover, [John] rates his own book so highly (22:7)—more than other holy books do that are much more useful—and he commands and threatens anyone who detracts from it that God will do something to them (22:18, 19). On the other hand, they will be blessed who keep what is written in it, but no one knows what that is, let alone how to keep it. It is as if we did not have it at all, and there are much better books at hand.

Many of the fathers long ago rejected this book as well, although St. Jerome, to be sure, praises it with lofty words and says it is beyond praise and that there are in it as many mysteries as words.[5] Nevertheless, he cannot prove it, and at many places his praise is too generous.

Finally, let all think of this book according to their spirit, but my spirit cannot abide this book, and for me it is reason enough not to hold it in high regard that Christ is neither taught nor recognized in it. That is above all what is expected of a prophet, for [Jesus] says in Acts 1 [:8], "You shall be my witnesses." Therefore, I stick with those books that will give me Christ clearly and purely.

Preface to the Revelation of St. John (1530 and 1546)

Editors' Introduction: In 1530 two new editions of the New Testament appeared from the print shop of Hans Lufft.[1] The first of these had numerous improvements upon and revisions of earlier texts. This edition replaced the earlier brief and critical preface to the Revelation of St. John (1522) with this much longer preface, which interprets the prophecies of the Book of Revelation through past and current events of church history.[2]

By 1530 and at the time of the Diet of Augsburg, Luther's understanding of the Apocalypse had changed. The papacy's continued rejection of his reforms, the Peasants' War, and the threat of the Turkish conquest of Europe served as occasions for the development of his apocalyptic spirituality, which sharpened through much of his career.[3] As Robert Barnes comments, "Luther saw his own movement to revive the gospel as the last great act in the great conflict between God and the devil. God was allowing the light of truth to flash over the world with a final burst of clarity even as true believers were subjected to unprecedented threats and persecution."[4] The prophetic and apocalyptic writings in the Bible could now help to interpret God's actions in history and to identify the forces of opposition.

Although Luther still seemed skeptical about seeing God's revelation in history, he plunged into the method popularized by the Franciscan Nicholas of Lyra (1270–1349) and the more radical adaptation of it by Wyclif.[5] Nicholas had popularized a method that was later used because it was straightforward and based on literal/historical interpretation, which was gaining acceptance in the late Middle Ages. His careful judgments were widely ignored, however, especially by Luther and his proximate sources, with significant consequences for the history of Apocalypse interpretation.[6] Unlike Nicholas, who refused to see the Antichrist within the church, Wyclif and Luther followed a radical Franciscan Joachite tradition that identified the papacy with the Antichrist.

Nevertheless, the theme of this commentary is still the gospel, as summarized by the protagonists and antagonists of the doctrine of justification by faith through history. As Jaroslav Pelikan has shown, Luther's interest is more dogmatic than historical, more evangelical than exegetical.[7] Luther found in the Apocalypse a message of consolation for the endurance of the Holy Catholic Church. At the end of this commentary he takes it as an article of faith that the church will ever endure despite its failings and adversaries.[8]

* * *

One finds many kinds of prophecies in Christendom. One kind prophesies by interpreting the writings of the prophets, about which Paul speaks in 1 Corinthians 12 and 14 and in other places.[9] This manner of prophecy is indispensable, and one should be exposed to it daily, since it teaches the word of God, lays the foundation of Christendom, and defends the faith. In short, it regulates, upholds, establishes, and performs the office of preaching. Another kind prophesies future events that were not already in scripture, and it is of three types.[10]

The first expresses itself with words without using images and figures. So Moses, David, and other prophets prophesy about Christ, and Christ and the apostles prophesy about Antichrist and false teachers, etc. The second type employs images but includes interpretation in specific words, as Joseph interprets his dreams (Gen 40, 41) and Daniel interprets both dreams and images.[11] The third type uses only images without either words or interpretation, like this book of Revelation and like the dreams, visions, and images that many holy people have through the Holy Spirit. Peter preaches in Acts 2 [:17] from Joel (2:28),[12] "Your sons and your daughters shall prophesy, and your young men shall see visions, and your old men shall dream dreams."

As long as such a prophecy remains unclear and is not precisely interpreted, it is a hidden and inarticulate prophecy that has not yet fulfilled its usefulness and fruitfulness for Christendom. Such has been the case with this book. Many have attempted to interpret it but to this point have not come up with anything certain.[13] Some have imbued the book with many silly notions out of their own heads. Because of such uncertain interpretation and hidden understanding, we have ignored it to now, especially since some early writers thought that the author was not St. John the Apostle, as is written in *The Ecclesiastical History*, Book 3, chapter 25.[14] For our part, we still share this doubt, but no one should be prevented by this from thinking that it is by St. John the Apostle or whomever.[15]

Since we would nevertheless like to be certain of the meaning and the interpretation, we will try to give these superior spirits something to think about and shed light on our thoughts. Therefore, since it is supposed to be a revelation of future events, especially future tribulations and misfortunes for Christendom, we think that the closest and surest way to find the interpretation is to take from the histories the past events and misfortunes that have happened to Christendom up to now and hold them up to these images, comparing them word by word. If, then, the two perfectly match and coincide with one another, one could maintain that it is a certain or at least unobjectionable interpretation.[16]

Accordingly, we contend that the text itself says that the first three chapters refer to the seven congregations and their angels in Asia. They have no other purpose than to depict how these congregations were at the time, how they were encouraged to be steadfast, to increase, or to improve themselves. In addition, from these chapters we learn that the word *angel* is to be understood later on, in other images or visions, to mean bishops and teachers in Christendom. Some are good, like the holy fathers and bishops; some bad, like the heretics and false bishops. In this book there are more of the latter than of the former.

In the fourth and fifth chapters all of Christendom's future tribulations and plagues are prefigured.[17] There are the twenty-four elders before God, that is, all the bishops and the teachers in unison, crowned with faith, who praise Christ, the lamb of God, with harps (that is, they preach) and worship with censers (that is, they pray). Thus, they attempt to comfort Christians with what they need to know, namely, that [the church] will endure, despite the future plagues.[18]

In the sixth chapter the future tribulations take place. First come bodily tribulations in the form of persecutions by the temporal authorities, represented by the crowned rider with the bow on the white horse (6:2). Then war and bloodshed come, represented by the rider with the sword on the red horse (6:4). Then inflation and hunger come, represented by the rider with the pair of scales on the black horse (6:5). Then pestilence and boils come, represented by the rider in the image of death on the pale horse (6:8). For these four plagues certainly always follow the thankless and the despisers of the word of God, together with other things, like the overthrow and change of governments until the last day, as is depicted at the end of chapter six. The souls of the martyrs also proclaim this with their cries (6:9–10).

In the seventh and eighth chapters the revelation of spiritual tribulations begins, that is, a variety of heresies. Again, an image of comfort is presented first, in which the angel seals the Christians and protects them from the four evil angels. This is so that they may again be assured that, even under heretics, Christendom will have faithful angels and the pure word, as the angel with the censer demonstrates, that is, with prayer (8:3). These good angels are the holy fathers, such as Spiridion,[19] Athanasius,[20] Hilary,[21] and the Council of Nicea, and similar figures.

The first evil angel is Tatian with his Encratites,[22] who prohibited marriage and sought to be righteous through their works, like the Jews. The doctrine of works righteousness had to be the first one contrary to the gospel; it remains the last, except that it always picks up new teachers and new names, like Pelagians, etc.[23] The second is Marcion[24] with his Cataphrygians,[25] the Manichaeans,[26] the Montanists, etc.,[27] who esteem their own spirituality[28] above all the scriptures and travel like this burning mountain between heaven and earth (8:8). This is among us even now with Müntzer and the enthusiasts.[29] The third is Origen,[30] who has embittered and spoiled the scriptures through philosophy and reason, as the universities have done with us until now. The fourth is Novatian[31] with his Cathars,[32] who rejected penance and wanted to be purer than other people are. Later the Donatists were just the same,[33] and our clergy are like all four. The learned who know history will be able to figure this out, because it would take too long to narrate and prove everything.

In the ninth chapter the real misery begins. The preceding physical and spiritual tribulations were a joke compared to these future plagues, just as the angel at the end of the eighth chapter proclaims (8:13). Three woes will come, to be inflicted by the others (that is, the fifth, sixth, and seventh angels), and through this will come the end of the world. Here physical and spiritual tribulations will come together, and there are to be three—the first great, the second greater, and the third greatest.

Thus the fifth angel, the first woe, is Arius, the great heretic, and his followers. They tortured Christians so cruelly all over the world that the text says upright people would rather die than see such things but must see them and not die (9:6). Yes, he says, the angel from hell, who is called the Destroyer (9:11),[34] is their king, as if to say the devil himself rides them. For they have persecuted the true Christians not only spiritually but also with the sword. Read the history of the Arians, and you will understand this figure and these words.

The second woe is the sixth angel, namely, the shameful Mohammed with his followers, the Saracens,[35] who inflicted great plagues on Christendom by his teaching and the sword. Beside this one and with the seventh angel comes the mighty angel (10:1) with the rainbow and the bitter book (10:2) to make the woe all the greater. This is the holy papacy with its great, spiritual appearance. It measures and circumscribes the temple with its laws, shuts out the holiest of holies, and establishes a counterfeit church, a church of external holiness that merely wears a mask of the church (11:2).[36]

In the eleventh and twelfth chapters two images of consolation are placed between these evil woes and plagues: the first, the two preachers (11:3–13); and the second, the pregnant woman who gives birth to a boy, despite the dragon (12:1–17). This demonstrates that some upright teachers and Christians will nevertheless remain both during the two previous woes and during the third future woe (11:14). Now these final two woes run together and at last attack Christendom simultaneously. With this the devil lets all hell break loose.

In the thirteenth chapter comes this seventh angel's work (following the trumpet of the last of the seven angels, which blows at the beginning of chapter 12). This is the third woe, the papal empire and the imperial papacy. Here the papacy receives into its power the temporal sword to rule not only with the scroll, as in the second woe (10:8–10), but also with the sword in the third woe. For it boasts that the pope has both the spiritual and the temporal sword in his power.[37] There are now the two beasts (13:1, 11). The first is the empire. The second with the two horns is the papacy, which has now become a temporal power but in the guise of the name of Christ. The pope has reestablished the fallen Roman Empire, extending it from the Greeks to the Germans.[38] It is, however, more an image of the Roman Empire than the empire's body, the state itself, the way it actually was. Nevertheless, he puts spirit and life into this image (13:15), so that it has its estates, laws, members, and offices and actually functions to an extent. This is the image that was wounded and healed again (13:3, 12).

The abominations, woes, and injuries this imperial papacy has committed cannot be recounted here. For, in the first place, by means of this scroll (10:8–10), the world is filled with all kinds of idolatry, with monasteries, foundations, saints, pilgrimages, purgatory, indulgences, celibacy, and innumerable human doctrines and works, etc. Moreover, who can tell how much blood, murder, war, and misery the popes have instigated, both by fighting themselves and by stirring up the emperors, kings, and princes against one another?

Here now the devil's final wrath gets to work. There in the East is the second woe, Mohammed and the Saracens. Here in the West are papacy and empire with the third woe. To these are added the Turk, Gog, and Magog, who come, as will follow in chapter twenty [20:8]. Thus, Christendom is plagued most terribly and miserably throughout the world at all times by false doctrines and wars with scroll and sword. This is the rock bottom and the final plague. After this come, almost exclusively, images of comfort, telling of the end of all these woes and abominations.

In the fourteenth chapter Christ first begins to slay the Antichrist with "the breath of his mouth," as St. Paul says (2 Thess 2:8). The angel with the gospel goes against the bitter scroll of the mighty angel (10:1, 8–10). Again saints and virgins (14:4) stand around the lamb and preach the truth. The angel's voice follows with the gospel, crying that the city of Babylon will fall (14:8), and the spiritual papacy will be destroyed. The fifteenth chapter also belongs here, as the harvest is gathered and those who cling to the papacy against the gospel are thrown outside the city of Christ and into the cold of God's wrath.[39] That is, by the gospel they are separated from Christendom and condemned to the wrath of God. There are many of them, and the wine press produces much blood, or perhaps there may be some other just punishment and judgment appropriate to our sins, which are beyond all measure and are overripe.

After this in the sixteenth chapter the seven angels with the seven bowls come.[40] Here the gospel grows and hems the papacy in from every side through many learned, upright preachers. The throne of the beast, the pope's power, becomes dark and wretched and despised (16:10). Nevertheless, it grows angry and adamantly defends itself, because three frogs—three foul spirits—come out of the beast's mouth (16:13) and stir up kings and princes against the gospel. But this does not help because their battle takes place, nonetheless, at Armageddon. The frogs are the sophists, such as Faber, Eck, Emser, etc.[41] They croak much against the gospel, but accomplish nothing and remain frogs.

In the seventeenth chapter the imperial papacy and the papal empire from beginning to end are encapsulated in one image, and it is presented as in a summary to be nothing, for the ancient Roman Empire is long since gone and still exists. Some of its lands still exist, and the city of Rome is still there. This image is presented here that people might know that the beast will be condemned shortly, just as one would make a criminal stand publicly before a court to be sentenced. As St. Paul says, "annihilating him by the manifestation of his coming" (2 Thess 2:8). As he says in the text this is begun by the patrons of the papacy, those who protect him, such that the clergy will sit stark naked.

In the eighteenth chapter the destruction begins, and this glorious and great splendor falls to the ground, and the courtiers, the pilferers of foundation endowments, and thieves of the benefices will cease to be. For even Rome had to be plundered and stormed by its own protector at the beginning of the final destruction.[42] Still [these thieves] do not let up. They keep searching, consoling, arming, and defending themselves, and, as he says in the nineteenth chapter (19:19), when they are no longer able to fight with scripture and scrolls, and the frogs have croaked themselves out, they fight with earnest and by force of arms gather kings and princes to battle. Nevertheless, they falter because the one who is on the white horse, who is called the Word of God, is victorious (19:13), as both beast and prophet are captured and thrown into hell.

While this is going on, the last cup comes in chapter twenty.[43] Satan, who was taken captive for one thousand years and after one thousand years has gotten loose, now brings Gog and Magog, the Turk, and the red Jews.[44] Nevertheless, they will join him soon in the lake of fire (20:7–10). Now we think that this image, which is distinct from the former, is placed here on account of the Turks. The thousand years began about the time this book was written and the same time that the devil was bound, although the counting need not be accurate to the minute (20:2).[45] After the Turks, the Last Judgment follows quickly, at the end of this chapter (20:11–15), as Daniel 7 also shows.[46]

Finally, in the twenty-first chapter the eternal consolation is pictured. The holy city, fully prepared, shall be led as a bride for the eternal wedding (21:2). Christ shall be Lord alone; all the godless will be condemned and driven to hell with the devil. This interpretation can make this book useful, as we use it foremost for consolation, to know that no force or lies, no wisdom or holiness, no tribulation or suffering will suppress Christendom; rather, it will gain the victory and will conquer and prevail in the end. In the second place, one must be warned against the great dangerous and many-sided offense that assaults Christendom. For that such a mighty power and fraud should fight against Christendom and should lie hidden under such complete formlessness,[47] so much trouble, heresy, and other faults, makes it becomes impossible for natural reason to recognize Christendom. In opposition, natural reason falls to the ground and takes offense. It calls the Christian church that which is the enemy of the Christian church. It calls condemned heretics those who are the true Christian church, as has been the case until now under the papacy, Mohammed, and indeed with all the heretics. Thus they also lose the article, "I believe in one holy Christian church."[48]

Similarly, some clever people see heresy, dissension, and shortcomings of all sorts and many false and loose-living Christians and lightly conclude that there are no Christians at all. For they have heard that Christians should be holy, peaceful, united, friendly, virtuous people. Consequently, they think there should be no offense, heresy, or shortcomings, but only peace and virtue. They should read this book to see Christendom from a perspective other than reason. For this book [I think] shows plenty of ghastly and monstrous beasts, horrible and hostile angels, wild and terrible plagues. I will refrain from mentioning other great crimes and shortcomings that have always been in Christendom and among Christians so that under such conditions natural reason would have lost all sense of Christendom. Here we see clearly before our times what gruesome offenses and shortcomings there were when Christendom was supposed to be at its best. One might think that, compared to then, our time could be reckoned a golden year.[49] Do you not think that the heathen took offense at this and held the Christians to be stubborn, loose, and cantankerous people?

It is this piece, "I believe in one holy Christian church," that is as much an article of faith as all the others. This is why reason cannot recognize it even with spectacles on. The devil can disguise it with offenses and sects so that you have to be offended by it; God too can hide it beneath crimes and all manner of shortcomings, such that you must become a fool for it and pass false judgment on it. She will not be observed but believed. Faith, nevertheless, has to do with things that are not seen (Heb 11:1). With her Lord she also sings the song, "Blessed is the one who does not take offense at me" (Matt 11:6). As an individual Christian, one is also hidden from oneself in that one cannot see one's holiness and virtue but only vice and unholiness.[50] And, you rude, clever one, you want to observe Christendom with your blind reason and unclean eyes?

In sum, our holiness is in heaven where Christ is and not in the world before our eyes like goods in the market.[51] Therefore, let offenses, sects, heresies, and crimes be, and let them do what they will. As long as the word of the gospel remains pure among us and we love and value it, we shall not doubt that Christ is at our side and with us, even when things are at their worst. As we see here in this book, through and beyond all plagues, beasts, and evil angels Christ will nevertheless be with his saints and obtain the final victory.

PART II

Teaching the New Spirituality

Editors' Introduction to Part II: This selection of biblical commentaries, pamphlets, prefaces, and sermons introduces the reader to Luther's teachings on the New Spirituality—from his early classroom comments on evangelical hope in Psalm 5 (1515/16) and the theology of the cross in Psalm 117 (1530), to his late and magisterial comments on Galatians (1535) and Genesis (1541/42). Here we are introduced to a spirituality of the word of God that creates faith and is both critical of the late-medieval spiritualities with their external rituals that Luther inherited, and indebted to their mystical theology and monastic disciplines. Thus one should memorize the Epistle to the Romans, which Luther considered the clearest expression of the gospel, and pray and meditate on the psalms.

This is a spirituality that emphasizes the spoken and the written word of God, which renews externally and internally through the gift of the Holy Spirit, and sacramentally through baptism and the Lord's Supper. As we discover in "The Freedom of a Christian," it is a word that frees through justifying grace, and is lived out in the world with a Christian freedom that expresses itself in a spirituality that serves the neighbor. The Christian is sovereign and slave, saint and sinner, but hears from the word of Christ law and gospel, commands and promises, ascending in the rapture of faith and descending into suffering love. This teaching of a new spiritual life is lived in faith in God's justifying grace in Christ and under the cross.

As we hear in Luther's thoughts on the Magnificat, God is revealed in the depths where we least expect to find God, especially on the cross. As Luther teaches in his Genesis commentary "On Jacob's Ladder," we ascend by faith to Christ, and he descends to us in the word and sacraments. The angels ascend and descend, wondering at the union of divinity and humanity in the incarnation. As

Luther teaches in the Galatians' commentary, faith, not reason, is the power of God in us, becoming God in us in Christ. In "The Sermon at the Coburg," Luther pastorally proclaims a baptismal spirituality of dying and rising as Christians bear the cross that life plants squarely on their shoulders; the suffering of Christ does everything, ours nothing, except if it is formed in the image of Christ. One could say of these selections what Luther says of Psalm 118, which was his favorite (included in Part III of this volume on page 203), "These are living, striking, rich words that encompass everything and focus on one thing."

SCHOLIA ON PSALM 5:
ON HOPE

Editors' Introduction: This fragment, an excursus on hope from the commentary on Psalm 5,[1] was written by the young Luther sometime between the first and second psalm lectures, perhaps between 1516 and 1517 (the second lectures began in 1518). This fragment is called an *operations*, a working document that brings the work of Luther's study to the classroom. He shows his mastery of the tradition with frequent references to Scholasticism and the writers of the early church, in particular Chrysostom and Augustine. With great erudition Luther explains what evangelical hope is. It overcomes impatience, sadness, and confusion because it is the gift of faith, the way of being and acting in faith, God's power through Jesus Christ in the faith of the believer. Nevertheless, the real experience of patience is in adversity, and the real experience of hope is present in sins. Where there is no sin there is no mercy. Where there is no mercy there is no hope. Where there is no hope there is no salvation.

* * *

Let all who hope in you rejoice [Ps 5:11].[2]

[Having dealt with self-enjoyment and self-praise in two ways, Luther continues:] Like enjoying and praising oneself, hope is experienced in either of two ways: either in the "flesh" or in the "spirit,"[3] from either human or divine perspective, from the creature or from the creator. To understand the nature of hope, I must digress a little and speak of something about which the whole psalter regularly reminds us. Thereby are the first rule and conclusion established.

Impatience, sadness, and confusion are not actually caused by pressures and obstacles and loss of property but come much more from the feelings of a person who, having an aversion to these things, foolishly seeks only the good life and honor. Similarly,

59

doubt, spiritual sadness, and an uneasy conscience do not derive from numerous sins but from numerous and rich good works, that is, from a feeling of self-righteousness that, though terrified by sins, foolishly seeks its own righteousness. This is clear, as the psalm says here in the first place, "All will rejoice who hope in you and will exult in you etc."—all, namely, who, because they believe in Christ, partake in the sufferings of Christ and have many such sufferings, as the apostle says (cf. 2 Cor 1:5). Because they know how they should experience joy and praise, they are, in their wisdom, not sad, uneasy, or impatient during these sufferings, because they are not striving after good fortune, the good life, and honor. Those who do not know or want to know that they are to find their joy in God and that it is for God's sake that they should praise become sad, uneasy, and impatient. This happens for them not because obstacles and sad things occur, but because, when they come, they do not look to God but to good fortune and the good life. Therefore, they flee but cannot escape, because they do not flee to where they must flee. As Isaiah describes in verse 30:15–16: "For thus says the Lord God, the Holy One of Israel: In returning and rest you shall be saved; in quietness and confidence shall be your strength. But you refused and said, 'No, for we will flee on horses'—therefore you shall flee! And, 'We will ride on swift horses'—therefore those who pursue you shall be swift!" What is to blame in regards to this sadness is the yearning for joy and praise. If a person were not so fixated on these, one would hardly take the obstacles in life seriously.

In the second place, it is likewise clear that many great sinners have been saved. They would not have been saved if their many sins had caused them to doubt. But the rule-minded disposition that looks to its own goodness, seeking it out first in times of doubt in order to hold it up against its sins, drives itself into a corner. Failing to find this [goodness], it does not know that one must gaze on God's mercy. Therefore, of necessity it despairs. And so the unfortunate conscience of one dying and rushing to the judgment seat of God has a conversation with itself and says, "Oh, who has done any good? Who has not done evil? Who has always remained pure?" These words are so full of foolishness that they could not be worse. What else do they reveal but that this person puts hope in works and does not hope in God?

In any event, if someone were to say that he or she could confidently and assuredly hope to have had good works and righteousness, and if that person were to hope in God on the basis of the good works, he or she would, nevertheless, be putting more hope in those works than in God. What could be more outrageous and godless than this? Such people do not say, "But I, through the abundance of your great mercy will enter your house," etc. (Ps 5:7), but "through my great righteousness." For if you hope in God or would hope in God when you do good or would do good, then hope all the more in God when you sin or do evil. Then it cannot be said of you, "He confesses you, when you do good to him and yet in times of testing falls away" (cf. Ps 49:18; Luke 8:13).[4] These who present themselves as if their joy and praise are in God, but who strive after good fortune and honor, actually only trust in their own works and their honor, as the temptation proves. Thus, it is frightful and in our time especially dangerous that many who live holy and righteous lives say they hope, who knows how much, in God and do not recognize that they put their hope much more in their own righteousness. This will be the case in their hour of death, when they must appear before the judgment seat of God. They think that they can die with assurance only because they are conscious of a good life and can therefore trust in God. Such a person is like one perched on a log floating in water who tries to find a footing and is suddenly in deep water. Just so, the works of such people will be tested by God's judgment and revealed to be terrible sins, since they trusted in them and did not honor and uphold the mercy of God.

Therefore, just as the patience that relies on good fortune is nothing, so also hope that relies on merits is nothing. Just as it is easy to have patience when one has good fortune, so also it is easy to hope when one relies on merits. Nevertheless, the real experience of patience is in adversity, and the real experience of hope is present in sins. Now the law was given that the inestimable mercy of God might unite itself with us and lift up our self-assurance.[5] Through the law God has committed all to sin in order to have mercy on them (Rom 11:32). For where there is no law, there is no sin (Rom 5:13). Where there is no sin, there is no mercy. Where there is no mercy, there is no hope. Where there is no hope, there is no salvation. Thus, the power of sin is the law. The power of the law, however, is mercy; moreover, the power of mercy is hope; the power of hope is salvation; and the power of salvation is God through Jesus Christ. The law produces sin, but mercy results in, that is, fulfills, the law; hope, however, results in mercy; salvation results in hope; and God produces salvation and everything. And now the crown or excursus follows:

In temporal life God gives good things in order that we may learn to honor, love, and hope in God the more. However, in our flawed minds[6] it happens that God is pitifully and inadequately honored and trusted—yes, even to the point that God is honored, sought, and trusted more easily in temporal adversity than in good fortune. So also it happens in spiritual life: God gives spiritual gifts (1 Cor 12) and merits in order that we might learn to hope the more in God. However, to our flawed minds that become conceited, it comes about that our hope in God is pitiful and inadequate, in fact, not hope at all.

Thus, it is easier and more possible to hope in God in sinning than in merits and good work. It is dangerous for people to be left in peace while experiencing good fortune, because they do not learn to love God, except in rare circumstances and with great difficulty. So also it is dangerous for people to be left alone with many spiritual gifts for their whole lives, because they will hardly learn to hope in God, except with great difficulty—and not at all without the Holy Spirit.

Nevertheless, in order that no one take offense at these words, I submit the following: It is a serious concern when one asks, "Should one then just sin and give up doing good?" Or is it appropriate to assert that which the apostle Paul was accused of saying, "Let us do evil so that good may come" (Rom 3:8)? By this teaching we seem to be making allowance for sin and discouraging the good, as if it were harmful for salvation. In order that this may be properly understood, I answer: good works are not forbidden by this teaching but are encouraged to the highest degree. The point is that the secret and scandalous predisposition of the flesh that puts its trust in works and not in the sheer mercy of God must be torn away and discouraged as a habit, so that one knows that hope is nothing but a power poured into us.[7] Moreover, in relation to all good works and efforts, we must consider that hope is the result of

God working in us, and in this way we are made worthy of mercy. It is not that we may imagine that, as soon as we have done good works, we obtain hope as a possession, but that we know that we must always seek hope, even when we do good works.

Consequently, we do not have to sin in order to be in sin and receive hope as a possession, but we have to acknowledge that we are always in sin, no matter how much good we do, and we can only be saved by the mercy of God that we seek in a good life. Nevertheless, when a good life has not been lived, one should not despair; neither should one hope the more because such a life has been lived. If the one is difficult, the other is even more difficult. The only thing one can do is pray that despair will be conquered in both instances and that hope will not be lost either on the left or the right side, because "a thousand may fall at your side, ten thousand at your right hand" (Ps 91:7).

Therefore it follows that it is fundamentally wrong to define hope as "the expectation that proceeds from merits," insofar as one understands "proceeding from merits" as coming about "through merits and as a result of merits." Rather, it must be understood and properly maintained as "proceeding from merits," not for those who do, but for those who long (for it in prayer). This is because one can obtain hope only through the gifts we receive, pious offerings of prayer, and the good works that God works in us; it cannot be expected from oneself. This is the reason: just as the content and object of faith belong to the "things not seen" (Heb 11:1), the object of hope belongs to the same. God promised both through the word. This is addressed by the definition. There it says, "anticipation." Now the one who expects sees nothing and has nothing on which to rest, except the word of promise itself. However, the one who hopes in works sees and has something on which to rest. "Hope that is seen is not hope" (Rom 8:24). If there is hope in us that can only be proven in affliction,[8] then hope is hidden during the time of good works. This is why we pray, we trouble ourselves over the concern that, at the time of temptation,[9] hope is secure, that is, when the devil and our conscience attack us even though our merits defend us before God. Therefore, we have to prepare ourselves in peacetime for what we need in times of conflict. There are those who do not view their good works in this perspective. They do not cry for help during a time of conflict but think that they are secure because they have done good works—that is, that hope is already achieved. These fall into misfortune, since they do not trust in the longed-for mercy but in the accomplished good works. They rest on what is completed and do not yearn for that which must be sought and still done.

Now the question arises: are there then no merits? I answer that they exist, but they are known only to God and not to you, so that you will not rely on them. We do not know when we are earning merits and when we are sinning.[10] Therefore, in no way can hope grow out of merits. If merits are doubtful, then hope would necessarily become doubtful as well, and one would not know if one might hope. On the other hand, it is certain and infallible that God is the one who promises mercy, grace, and glory, which are given to us through Christ. When we understand hope rightly, it is better for us to say that merits proceed from hope, because something has to precede all merits and good works; faith, hope, and love would otherwise pour from God in vain, and similarly one's being made righteous so that one might even be able to earn merits. The one who does not believe does not do good; similarly, the one who does not hope multiplies evil, as we saw in the discussion about despair. In the same way, the one who does not love does not preserve the word of Christ (John 14:24).[11] And through this "grace upon grace," as it says in John 1:16, we have even so received love upon love; we march on "from faith to faith" (Rom 1:17),[12] from hope to hope, from "clarity to clarity," and from power to power. "The one who is righteous today will be forever made righteous" (cf. Rev 22:11).

Therefore, hope precedes merits; hope is there with merits and on the basis of merits; hope results in hope to hope. When one understands "proceeding from merits"[13] as meaning "to grow beyond oneself," then one must admit that this is the best way to understand this definition. Just so, we do not attain righteousness in this life but always reach out for it (cf. Phil 3:13), seek it, and strive for it, such that we are always made righteous and our sins are always forgiven. So, too, we pray in the Lord's Prayer that the will of the Father in heaven be done, that God's name always be made holy (Matt 6:9–10), and that, nevertheless, we may still be seen by God as righteous. As it is written in Matthew 5:6, "Blessed are those who hunger and thirst for righteousness," etc., so must we seek hope and not think that we have already obtained it just because we were experiencing hope ourselves.

Who would really yearn rightly to be given hope as a gift, if one did not hope? This is the will "of our wonderful God for the saints"—that they are righteous while striving to be justified,[14] and at the same time they are unrighteous while striving to be justified. As such and in truth they are unrighteous, but, because God accepts their faith and their pleas for mercy, they are righteous—at the same time sinner and saint. They are consciously sinners and unconsciously saints, or sinners in reality and saints in hope, so that they know that while they are confessing their sins themselves and longing for righteousness, God will not reckon their sins against them. Because the sinner strives for and yet does not obtain righteousness, God does not see the sinner as a sinner. How "wondrously God leads" (Ps 4:3)[15] in that we are both righteous and unrighteous, at the same time sinner and saint! And all of this is done to show God's great and tender mercy, so that "we taste that the Lord is good" [cf. Ps 34:8; 1 Pet 2:3]. With joy I will repeat it once again: God sees us as righteous who have not yet obtained righteousness but seek it. In this way at the same time sin and our failing righteousness remain in us; and yet sin is not sin, and unrighteousness is not unrighteousness, because the way the merciful one beholds our seeking is to accept it as righteousness. Therefore, through righteousness we are righteous on the outside, and through unrighteousness we are unrighteous on the inside, externally saints and from the inside sinners. In our lives and works we are unrighteous, but in the judgment of God alone we are righteous.

In the same way must we speak of hope, because at the same time we despair, that is, that we are without hope, and we also hope, in that we seek hope in hope. What we hope for we do not know, but over what we despair we know; for this reason we seek, yes, because we know and feel that we are despairing. Therefore, we are seen by God as ones who hope, because we long for hope. One cannot throw this before the dogs and the pigs (Matt 7:6), that is, the metaphysical theologians who in their dreaming about driving out sins and their chatter about grace seem neither to understand sin nor grace.

Thus in Psalm 32:1–2, "Happy are those whose transgression is forgiven, whose sin is covered." See, what a wonderful sentence!

The psalmist does not say that one's sins disappear but are "forgiven" and "covered"; they still exist, but are covered. How? "Happy are those to whom the Lord imputes no iniquity." Why does God impute no iniquity to them? This is the reason: "I acknowledged my sin to you, and I did not hide my iniquity. I said, 'I will confess my transgressions to the Lord,' and you forgave the guilt of my sin. Therefore let all who are faithful offer prayer to you" (Ps 32:5–6). See, every godly person who prays about being godless is therefore "holy" for praying this but "godless" because he or she longs for holiness. A person would not long for holiness if it were already a possession. And yet one has it because of the bidding that it be given and that godlessness be taken away. At the same time holy and god-less—before oneself godless and before God righteous. The person knows the godlessness, but does not recognize the righteousness, because God alone recognizes it, as God reckons it to the person.

Now, at last, to return to the psalm, when the situation is such that our righteousness is unknown and, in the same way, hope, then where will the unrighteous [so-called] holy ones stand who hope on God because they know their advantages? They hope in their works, and, in that they preempt God, they reckon these things as good for themselves and record them steadfastly as merits. Therefore, God reckons these as sins for them, because they prematurely grasp for themselves the honor of justification and a favorable judgment, not pleading and waiting for God to weigh them first. Thus they charge headlong, unworried in their confidence, and they are unknowingly unrighteous and knowingly righteous, pretentious, self-proclaimed saints, but in reality sinners, because they do not know the God who weighs them [in the scales]. They set themselves up as their own judges. In this way alone "God works wondrously," not only "in the saints"[16] but also in the sinners.

Thus, when the apostle says in Romans 5:4 that "character produces hope," does that mean that hope proceeds from merits? I answer no. How could suffering produce endurance and endurance character without hope? The one who despairs can acquire neither endurance nor character, so much the more must hope be present before affliction. Therefore, one speaks of the last and fulfilled hope that, as I have said, can only work and be recognized in affliction, whose power is always hidden until it can be seen in affliction.

[Then] one recognizes what was not known beforehand: that one's hope must rest in God and, moreover, that one continues to long for hope. Up to this point one feared that hope could not be obtained and sought to grasp it. God prefers it this way, because hope is complete when a person fully learns to seek and long for it. With all one's strength, with help from anything created excluded, one prays in despair, and, without knowing it, one has the hope that "produces character."

Nevertheless, I know how much from the holy scriptures, the words of the fathers, and the legends of the saints could be lifted up in opposition; however, if these things were rightly understood, they also would speak for us. One example is the saying of the blessed Hilary,[17] who, when he was in the throes of death, said to his soul: "Depart, soul, why are you afraid? You have served Christ for ninety-three years, and you are afraid to die?" Now, if this were understood as if he were trusting on the works of his life, then it is easier to assume that he went to hell than that he went to heaven. Why should we not also investigate the saying of Agatho[18] that is contrary to that of Hilary? He said, when gazing for three days at heaven's door, that he could not shake his fear, since he could not trust his works.

One should understand St. Hilary in this way, that his works drove him to such hope that he wished to say: "See, God has given me so much, why should God also not give me more? The one who has been so generous in this life will also not be stingy towards you; the one who has remained merciful will remain merciful in eternity; the one who has freely preserved you from many sins and who has accepted your service will also preserve you from eternal punishment."

Therefore, no one should say, "Now I will sin, and at the end I will hope." You do not know whether God might slay you because, while in dying you sought righteousness, in life you hardly asked about the righteousness of God. If you do not want to learn to hope, then you have reason to be concerned about doing good works and having confidence in them, as long as you stay in good health. I have tried to demonstrate this at great length here so that I do not have to do the same in every psalm.

Now "all who hope in you rejoice" [cf. Ps 5:11]. If they grieve about themselves—all the more because they grieve over them-selves and are displeased with themselves—they rejoice in you.

"Blessed are those who mourn, for they will be comforted" (Matt 5:4), namely, those who hope in you, you who consider them righteous, who [themselves] confess that they are mere sinners. "They sing for joy" (Ps 5:11) because they despair in themselves. Therefore, they "love your name," because they hate their own. "This is the name," says Jeremiah (23:6), by which he will be called: "The Lord is our righteousness." This is their name: strange sinful slave or strange unrighteous prisoner. But your name is worthy of love and ours worthy of hatred.

From this one should understand that, whenever one says something good about the righteous, it is only said in relation to their wickedness. The good that is attributed to their spirit and the new person in them refers to the contrary wickedness that they had in the "flesh" and in the "old Adam." They will not be able to reign with [Christ] or be glorified (Rom 8:17) if they have not first suffered and been shamed. These grand things only come about through the cross, as the water at Marah was made sweet through the piece of wood (Exod 15:22–25). Everything good is hidden in and under the cross, and therefore no one should seek or understand it anywhere else but under the cross. So with my limited insight I can find nothing in the scriptures but "Jesus Christ, and him crucified" (1 Cor 2:2). Jesus is indeed all the good that is appropriated to the righteous in the scriptures, such as joy, hope, honor, virtue, and wisdom. But he is the crucified; therefore only "they rejoice" in him who "hope in him" and "love" him and despair about themselves and hate their own names.

THE FREEDOM OF A CHRISTIAN

Editors' Introduction: Written by Luther in October 1520 in both Latin and German,[1] this pamphlet was Luther's bestseller. It is a fine example of the ability of Luther, better known for his massive, scholarly works, to summarize essential points concisely in a short tract.[2] Championing the freedom of a Christian person, the pamphlet represented a halfhearted attempt to win the pope himself over to Luther's cause of theological renewal. Luther thus kept the piece almost completely free of polemics, giving it a strong spiritual tone. However, Pope Leo X probably never read it.

Presented here is a new English translation from the German version, of which there were twenty-two editions.[3] Although the Latin version is more theologically precise and expansive, the German text is a fine example of the power of the increasing number of spiritual texts in the vernacular in the late medieval era, and it has its own spiritual vibrancy and power.[4] Luther wrote this vernacular pamphlet for the unlearned laity; the Latin version was for the educated reader. It is, according to Luther, "the whole sum of the Christian life. A Christian person is a free sovereign, above all things, subject to no one. A Christian person is a dutiful servant in all things and subject to everyone." It is this apparently contradictory set of theses that Luther explains in the tract. He draws from the Song of Solomon, Paul, and a long Christian tradition of spousal imagery to show how faith unites the soul with Christ. What he calls the *fröhliche Wechsel* (happy exchange) has a long tradition, but Luther now roots the exchange or union in terms of faith,[5] which is given to the individual through the preached word from outside us.[6] As Martin Marty summarizes in his biography of Luther, "The benefit of faith was that it united the soul with Christ as a bride is united with her bridegroom. 'They become one flesh,' as Paul puts it. What Christ has is the property of the believing soul, what the soul has becomes the property of Christ, including the soul's sins, death, and damnation. Faith negotiates the exchange."[7]

* * *

To the insightful and wise Mister Hermann Mülphordt, Mayor of Zwickau, my especially good friend and patron.

I who am called Doctor Martin Luther, an Augustinian, offer you my willing service and send my best wishes.

Your praiseworthy city preacher, the honorable Master John Egran, a learned and wise man and my good friend, praised exceedingly to me your love for and the pleasure you take in the holy scriptures, which you so diligently confess and ceaselessly extol among the people. That is why he would like for you and me to become acquainted, an event for which I am readily willing and gladly prepared. It is good and a special joy to hear about a place where godly truth is loved, for, sad to say, it is so often resisted with all manner of coercion and deceit, especially by those who presume to have the right and title to it. Of course, it is necessary that Christ be a sign and stumbling block, resisted and contradicted by those who take offense at him, who need to fall and be resurrected again.[8] Therefore, I have begun by addressing this little German tract and sermon to you for our acquaintance and friendship. In the meantime, I have written it in Latin and sent it to the pope, so that everyone has an account of my writing about the papacy and my teaching is not found to be objectionable, I hope, by anyone. I commend myself, yourself, and all of us together to God's grace. Amen. At Wittenberg, 1520.

Jesus

1. First of all, so that we might fundamentally be able to discern what a Christian person is and what freedom Christ has acquired and given this person—a freedom about which St. Paul writes a good deal—I propose two resolutions:[9]

- A Christian person is a free sovereign,[10] above all things, subject to no one.
- A Christian person is a dutiful servant in all things, subject to everyone.

These two conclusions can clearly be drawn from St. Paul in 1 Corinthians 9:19:[11] "Though I am free with respect to all, I have made myself a slave to all." Likewise, in Romans 13:8, "Owe no one

70

anything, except to love one another." Love, however, can be described as service and is subject to whatever it loves. Thus, it is also said of Christ in Galatians 4:4, "God sent his Son, born of a woman, born under the law."

2. We can understand these two contradictory sayings about freedom and servitude in that each Christian person has a twofold nature, spiritual and physical. Relative to the soul, one is a spiritual, new, inward person; relative to flesh and blood, one is a physical, old, outward person. And it is for the sake of the difference, so directly opposed to each other in what is said about them in the scripture, that I speak of freedom and servitude.

3. Let us then consider for ourselves what belongs to the inward, spiritual person, what makes one a free, upright, and Christian person. It is evident that nothing external can make one free and upright (or whatever we might call it), because this freedom and righteousness—or, conversely, this arrogance and captivity—are not bodily or external. What help is it to the soul if the body is not captive, fresh, and healthy, and eats, drinks, and lives as it wants? From the other perspective, what harm comes to the soul if the body is confined, sick, and weary, and hungers, thirsts, and suffers in the way it does not like? Not one of these things reaches all the way to the soul to set it free or bind it, to make it righteous or evil.

4. In the same way, it does not help the soul at all if the body puts on holy clothing as the priests and clergy do, nor does it help to be in churches and sacred places. It does not help if a body handles sacred objects or prays, fasts, goes on pilgrimages, or does all manner of good works that might forever take place in and through the body. Something of a completely different nature must bring and give the soul righteousness and freedom, because all these items, works, and ways just mentioned could also be assumed and done by an evil person, a phony saint, and a hypocrite. Through such measures you develop nothing but pure hypocrites. On the other hand, it does not harm the soul in the least if a body wears unholy clothes, eats and drinks in an unholy place, does not go on pilgrimages or pray, and refrains from doing all the things that the aforementioned hypocrites do.

5. Nothing else in heaven and on earth can make the soul alive, righteous, free, and Christian besides the gospel, the word of

God preached by Christ.[12] As Christ himself says in John 11:25, "I am the resurrection and the life. Those who believe in me…will live and…never die." Likewise, John 14:6, "I am the way, and the truth, and the life." Again in Matthew 4:4, "One does not live by bread alone, but by every word that comes from the mouth of God." So we can now be sure that the soul can do without all things except the word of God, and without the word of God, nothing can help it. And if it has the word of God, it needs nothing else; it has everything it needs in the word—nourishment, joy, peace, light, art, righteousness, truth, wisdom, freedom—and all these good things overflowing. Thus we read in the psalter, especially in Psalm 119, that the prophet does not cry out for anything but the word of God. And in the scripture it is considered the worst of plagues and the wrath of God when God's word is taken away from the people.[13] By the same token, there is no greater grace than when God's word is sent to a place; as it says in Psalm 107:20, "[God]sent out his word and healed them."[14] Christ came to help in no other office than to preach the word of God. Besides, all apostles, bishops, priests, and the whole spiritual estate are called and installed for the sake of the word of God alone, even if these days, sadly, things are different.

6. You may ask, however, "Which is the word that gives such abundant grace, and how shall I use it?" The answer: It is nothing but the preaching of Christ in accordance with the gospel, spoken in such a way that you hear your God speaking to you. It shows how your whole life and work are nothing before God but must eternally perish with everything that is in you. When you truly believe that you are guilty, then you must despair of yourself and confess that the verse in Hosea is true, "O Israel, in yourself you have nothing but your destruction; it is in me alone that you have your help."[15] So that you can come out of yourself and away from yourself, that is, out of your perishing, God places the dear Son, Jesus Christ, before you and allows you to be addressed by this living and comforting Word. You are to surrender yourself with steadfast faith in this Word and boldly trust God. And for the sake of this selfsame faith, all your sins will be forgiven, all your destruction will be overcome, and you will be righteous, genuine, satisfied, upright, and fulfill all the commandments and be free of all things. As St. Paul says in Romans 1:17, "The one

who is righteous will live by faith." And in Romans 10:4, "Christ is the end of the law...for everyone who believes."

7. Thus it is appropriate for all Christians to let their only work and exercise be forming the word and Christ in themselves, constantly practicing and strengthening such faith, because no other work can make a Christian. It is as Christ says to the Jews in John 6:28, when they asked him what work they should do in order to perform godly and Christlike works. He said, "This is the only work of God, that you believe in him whom [God] has sent," whom alone God the Father ordained for that purpose.

Therefore, a genuine faith in Christ is an overflowing treasure, which brings with it every blessing and takes away all ungodliness. As is written in the last chapter of Mark [16:16], "The one who believes and is baptized will be saved; but the one who does not believe will be condemned." Therefore, the prophet Isaiah beheld the treasure of this faith and said, "God will make a brief summation on earth, and this summation will flow into righteousness like a primal flood";[16] that is, faith, in which, in brief, every commandment stands fulfilled, will overwhelmingly justify all who have it, so that they need nothing else to be righteous and justified. In the same way St. Paul says in Romans 10:10, "For one believes with the heart and so is justified."

8. But how does it happen that faith alone without any works makes one righteous and provides such superabundant treasure, when there are so many laws, commands, works, statutes, and directions prescribed for us in the scriptures? Here one must pay diligent attention to and earnestly hold that faith alone without any works makes one righteous, free, and blessed (about which we will hear more later). And let it be known that the entire holy scripture is divided into two kinds of words: command, or law of God; and promises, or words of assurance. The commands teach and prescribe for us many good works. Merely prescribing them, however, does not make them happen. Laws point the way, but they do not help; they teach us what one ought to do, but they do not give us the strength to do it. They are set up only so that persons become aware of their incapacity for good and learn to despair in themselves. That is why they are called the "old" testament and why they belong in the Old Testament. For example, the command that "you shall not covet" proves that we are all of us sinners together. For no

person can pretend to be without covetous desires, do what one may. In this way one learns to give up on oneself and look for help from another place to become free of covetous desires and thereby fulfill the law, because one is not capable of doing it by oneself. In the same way all the other commandments are impossible for us.

9. Now when people have learned and become aware from the commandments of their powerlessness, they become fearful as to how they will be able to satisfy the law. For the commandment must certainly be fulfilled, or they will be damned. They become completely humbled and reduced to nothing in their own eyes. They find nothing in themselves that might make them righteous. At this point, the other word, the divine promise and assurance, comes and speaks to them: "If you would like to fulfill all the commands, become free of all your covetous desires and your sin, as the commandments compel and require. Look here: believe in Christ, in whom I promise you all grace, righteousness, peace, and freedom. Believe, and you have it; don't believe, and you won't have it.[17] For what is impossible to you through all the works of the commandments, which are so many but are of no use anyway, is quickly and easily done by faith. For I have placed all things in a compact form inside faith, so that whoever has faith has all things and is saved, and whoever does not have faith has nothing." In such a way the promises of God provide what the commandments require and accomplish what the commandments demand, so that everything belongs to God, command and fulfillment. God alone commands and alone also fulfills. Therefore, the promises of God are the word of the "new" testament and belong in the New Testament.

10. Now these and all of God's words are holy, true, righteous, peaceable, free, and completely full of good. Therefore, one who clings to God with a true faith will become so fully and completely unified with God that all the word's virtues will become the soul's very own. And thus by the word of God through faith, this soul becomes holy, righteous, true, peaceable, free, completely full of good, and an authentic child of God, as John 1:12 states, "to all…who believed in [Jesus'] name [God] gave power to become children of God."

From these words it is easy to see why faith is capable of so much and why no good works can equal it, because no good work clings to the divine word as faith does, nor can a work reside in the soul, because the word and faith alone rule there. Just as iron becomes red-hot, like fire, when combined with fire, as the word is, so will the soul be because of it.[18] Thus, we see that a Christian person with faith has enough and needs no works in order to be righteous. Therefore, one is without a doubt released from all laws and commands and, if released, is most certainly free. This is Christian freedom: faith alone,[19] which brings about not that we might become idle or do evil but that we have need of no works to attain righteousness and blessedness, about which we will say more later.

11. Furthermore, faith also brings about the following. When people believe in another, they believe the other because they regard him or her as righteous and true, which is the greatest honor one person can give another. Conversely, it is the greatest offense to regard a person as loose, deceptive, and untrustworthy. So too, when the soul believes steadfastly in the word of God, then one regards God as true, just, and righteous. One thereby accords God the highest honor that the soul can give: conceding to God that God is in the right, honoring the divine name, and allowing God to deal with one as God wills. Indeed, such a soul does not doubt that God is righteous and true in all God's words [cf. Ps 51:4]. On the other hand, one cannot dishonor God any more than not to believe in God. In doing so, the soul regards God as inept, deceptive, and untrustworthy. By its own measure the soul denies God through such unbelief, erecting one's own mind as an idol in the heart against God, as if one knew better than God. However, when God sees that the soul concedes that God is true,[20] honoring God through such faith, then God honors the soul in return, regarding it also as righteous and true. Then the soul actually is righteous and true through such faith. For the fact that a person regards God as righteous and truthful is right and truthful, which makes one right and truthful, because it is true and right to ascribe to God the truth.[21] Those who do not believe do not do this, continuing to drive themselves to exhaustion with many good works.

12. Not only does faith impart so much that the soul becomes equal to the divine word—completely full of grace, free, and blessed—but it also unifies the soul with Christ as a bride with her bridegroom. It follows from this marriage, as St. Paul says, "that Christ and the soul become one body."[22] Thus, for better or worse, all things are shared in common, so that what belongs to Christ

becomes the believing soul's very own, and what belongs to the soul becomes Christ's very own. Now to Christ belong every possession and blessedness, and they become the soul's very own. And all the vices and sin burdening the soul become Christ's very own. At this point the struggle of joyful exchange begins.

Because Christ is human and divine—who has never sinned and whose righteousness is invincible, eternal, and almighty—through the wedding ring of the bride (that is, faith), he thus takes the sins of the believing soul and makes them his own and acts just as if he had done them. In this way the soul's sins are swallowed up and drowned in Christ, because all sins combined are no match against the strength of his unassailable righteousness. Simply by means of this dowry, that is, because of faith, the soul is released and freed from all its sins and given the gift of the everlasting righteousness of Christ, the bridegroom. Is this not a joyous wedding celebration when the rich, noble, righteous bridegroom, Christ, receives the poor, despised, evil whore in marriage,[23] unburdening her of all evil and adorning her with every good thing? It is no longer possible for her sins to condemn her, because now they rest on Christ and are swallowed up in him. She now has such abundant righteousness in her bridegroom that she can resist any sin, even if sin should already rest on her. St. Paul speaks about this in 1 Corinthians 15:57: "Thanks be to God, who gives us the victory through our Lord Jesus Christ," in whom death and sin are swallowed up.

13. Here you can see again the reason it is right to ascribe so much to faith. It fulfills all the commandments, and, without any other work, it makes a person righteous, because you can see that all by itself it fulfills the first commandment, which requires, "You shall honor the one God." Now if you were made of purely good works from head to toe, then you still would not be righteous, for you would not yet be honoring God and would thus not be fulfilling the very first commandment. For God does not wish to be honored in any other way than by ascribing truth and all goodness to God, indeed, as God truly is. No good works can do such a thing, only faith of the heart alone. That is why faith alone is the righteousness of persons and the fulfillment of all the commandments. For whoever fulfills the first and main commandment surely and easily fulfills all the other commandments. Works are dead things.

They cannot praise and honor God, however they may come about and allow themselves to be done for the glory and honor of God.[24] But here we are not looking for the work that is done, but for the maker and masterworker who honors God and does the works. That one is none other than faith of the heart, which is the head and whole essence of righteousness. That is why it is a dangerous, sinister way of speaking when one teaches that God's commandments are to be fulfilled by works, because the fulfillment of the commandments must take place by faith, and works follow this fulfillment, as we shall hear.

14. Now let us see what other things we have in Christ and what a great blessing true faith is. First, it is important to know that, before and in the Old Testament, God set apart and reserved for divine purposes all firstborn males of both humans and animals [Exod 13:2]. Being the firstborn was precious and had two great advantages over all the other children, namely, the sovereignty and priesthood, or kingly and priestly reign, so that on earth the firstborn little boy was lord over all his brothers and a priest or pope before God. This is a figure signifying Jesus Christ, who is actually himself the same first male birth of God the Father by the Virgin Mary. Therefore, he is a king and a priest, but spiritually, because his kingdom is not earthly, nor does it consist in earthly possessions but in spiritual goods, including truth, wisdom, peace, joy, blessedness, etc. Temporal goods are not thereby excluded, however, because all things in heaven and on earth and in hell are subjected to him, even though we do not see him, which means that he rules spiritually and invisibly.

And so his priesthood does not consist in outward trappings and clothing, as we see among human beings, but it stands invisibly in the Spirit, in that he continuously pleads for his own before the eyes of God and offers himself and does everything a righteous priest should do. "He intercedes for us," as St. Paul says in Romans 8:34. He teaches us inwardly in our hearts. These two things are actually the true offices of a priest, for temporal priests, who are outward and human, also teach and make intercession.

15. Now as Christ has the right of the firstborn with their honor and dignity, he then shares it with all his Christians, so that by faith they all also become rulers and priests with Christ, as St. Peter says in 1 Peter 2:9, "You are a chosen race, a royal priesthood." What

then happens is that through faith a Christian person is lifted up so high over all things as to become a sovereign over all things spiritually, for nothing at all can now harm that one's salvation. Yes, now all things have to be subject and assist such a one's salvation, as St. Paul states in Romans 8:28, "We know that all things work together for good, for those who...are called according to [God's] purpose," whether it is life, death, sin, righteousness, good and evil, or whatever else we can name. Likewise in 1 Corinthians 3:21, "For all things are yours, whether...life or death or the present or the future." Not that we are bodily empowered over all things to possess them or use them the way people on earth do, for we certainly have to die bodily; no one can escape death. So too must we suffer under many other things, as we see happened to Christ and his saints. For this is a spiritual sovereignty, ruling by putting the body under subjection; that is, with respect to the soul, I can improve myself without any [earthly] thing, so that even death and suffering have to serve me and become useful for my salvation. Indeed, that is an exalted and honorable dignity and a truly almighty sovereignty, a spiritual kingdom, in which nothing is too good or too evil that it cannot serve me for the good, if I believe, for I do not need anything anyway, but my faith is sufficient for me. Look at how precious the authority and freedom of a Christian is!

16. Above and beyond that, we are priests, which is far more than being a king or queen, because the priesthood makes us worthy to stand before God and to intercede for others. For to stand before God's eyes and to intercede is the prerogative of no one except a priest. Christ has redeemed us, in order that we might spiritually represent and intercede for one another, just as a priest represents the people bodily and prays for them. But nothing works for the good of those who do not believe in Christ. They become enslaved to all things and have to get frustrated with all things. In addition, their prayer is not favored and does not ascend before the eyes of God. Who can even imagine, therefore, how high the honor and status of the Christian person is? Through one's dominion one has power over all things, and through one's priesthood one has power over God, because God does what one asks for and desires. As it is written in the psalter, "[God] fulfills the desire of all who fear him; he also hears

their cry" [Ps 145:19], to which honor the Christian person comes only through faith alone and not through any work.

From these things one can clearly see how free a Christian is from all things and over all things, needing no good works in order to become righteous and blessed. Rather, faith brings all these things to the Christian in overflowing measure. And if one were so foolish as to think that a good work could make one righteous, free, blessed, or Christian, then one would lose faith and, along with it, everything else. It is like the dog that sees a reflection of itself with a bone in its mouth and, snapping at the water to get the bone in the reflection, loses the one in its mouth and the reflection as well.[25]

17. You ask, "Then what is the difference between priests and laity in Christianity, if all are priests?" The answer: the little words *priest, cleric, spiritual,* and the like have suffered an injustice, because they were taken from the whole people and assigned to a small group, which one now calls the spiritual estate. The holy scripture makes no distinctions beyond calling the learned or consecrated ministers, servants, stewards—that is, servants, slaves, administrators[26]—who are to preach the faith of Christ and Christian freedom to others. For even though we are all equally priests, we still cannot all serve, administer, and preach. Therefore, St. Paul states in 1 Corinthians 4:1, "Think of us in this way, as servants of Christ and stewards of God's mysteries."

Out of this administration has developed such a worldly, external, sumptuous, intimidating sovereignty/authority that legitimate worldly power can in no way match it, just as if the laity were something other than Christian people. With that the whole understanding of Christian grace, freedom, faith, and everything we receive from Christ has been precluded, and Christ himself has been taken away. In its place we have received human laws and works and have completely become slaves of the most inept people on earth.

18. From all this we learn that it does not suffice merely to preach, when one speaks of the life and work of Christ superficially as mere history and chronicle, let alone preach sermons that do not speak of Christ at all but present only canon law or other human law and teaching. There are many who preach Christ in this way and permit themselves to have pity on Christ, or they vent their anger on Jews or otherwise practice more or less childish traditions

in their sermons. Yet, Christ should and must be preached so that faith is engendered and sustained in you and me. This faith is awakened and sustained when I am told why Christ came, how to benefit and have my needs fulfilled by him, and what he brought and gave me. This occurs when a person correctly explains the Christian freedom that we have from Christ and that we are rulers and priests, having power over all things, and that all we do is pleasing and acceptable in the eyes of God and is heard by God, as I have said up to this point.

When a heart hears Christ in this way, it has to rejoice to its very core, receive comfort, become sweet for Christ, and love him again. This point can never be reached with laws or works. For who can harm or frighten such a heart? When sin and death fall away, it believes the righteousness of Christ belongs to it; its sin is no longer its own but belongs to Christ, and with that, in faith, sin must vanish before the righteousness of Christ, as said above. And the soul learns with the apostle to spite death and sin, saying, "Where, O death, is your victory? Where, O death, is your sting? The sting of death is sin.[27] But thanks be to God, who gives us the victory through our Lord Jesus Christ" [1 Cor 15:55–57], and death is drowned in his victory!

19. Now enough has been said about the internal self, freedom, and the chief righteousness that requires no law or good works. Indeed, they can be harmful to this righteousness if one should presume to be justified through them.

Part II

Now we come to the second part [of our tract], which deals with the outward person. Here we will answer all those who take offense at the previous discussion and who typically speak in the following manner: "Aye, then if faith is all things and counts alone as sufficient for making one righteous, then why are good works commanded? Let us be merry, have pleasure, and do nothing."

No, my dear, not so. It would be that way, indeed, if you were a completely internal person and became wholly spiritual and internal, which will not happen until Judgment Day. What is and stays on earth is only a beginning and increase that is completed in the next world. Thus, the apostle speaks of *primitias spiritus*,[28] that is, the firstfruits of the Spirit. So it is at this point that [the proposition] stated at the beginning belongs: A Christian person is a dutiful servant and subject to everyone. That is, if one is free, one does not have to do anything; if one is a servant, one has to do all kinds of things. We will now see how this works.

20. According to the soul, one is inwardly sufficiently justified through faith and has everything that one should have—except that this faith and sufficiency should always increase until the next life. However, one still remains in this bodily life on earth and must rule one's own life and relate with people. Now works begin to play a role, and one must not be idle. The body must be compelled and exercised by fasting, waking, working, and every discipline in moderation, so that it can obey and match the form and faith of the internal person and not hinder and resist them, as it is its nature to do when not compelled. For the inner self is united with God and, cheerful and happy for the sake of Christ, who has done so much for it, puts all its pleasure in serving God freely out of love in return for nothing. In the flesh, however, the inner person discovers a recalcitrant will that wants to serve the world and seek its own pleasure. Faith cannot tolerate that and with pleasure takes the body by the throat and throttles it to subdue and restrain it. As St. Paul says in Romans 7:22, "I delight in the law of God in my inmost self, but I see in my members another law at war with the law of my mind, making me captive to the law of sin." Likewise, "I punish my body and enslave it, so that after proclaiming to others I myself should not be disqualified" [1 Cor 9:27]. And also Galatians 5:24, "Those who belong to Christ...have crucified the flesh with its passions."

21. However, these works must not be done in the belief that through them a person will become righteous before God, because faith cannot tolerate such a false belief; it alone is and must be righteousness before God. Rather, works should be done only with the idea that the body become obedient and purified of its evil passions, and the eye should only look at these evil passions in order to drive them out. For because the soul has become purified by faith and loves God, it would gladly also see all things purified, its own body first, and then everybody loving and praising God along with it. So

for the sake of one's body a person cannot be idle but must practice doing many good works in order to compel it. Works are not the true possession by which one becomes just and righteous before God, but do them freely out of love, for nothing, in order to please God, having sought nothing else in them and having regarded them in no other way than that God is pleased, for whose sake one gladly does one's very best.

Accordingly, an individual can derive the measure and insight for chastising the body, fasting, keeping vigil, working as necessary to subdue the obstinate willfulness of the body. Others, however, who think they will become righteous through works, do not consider chastisement but focus only on works and imagine that, if only they do many and great works, then they have done well and they will be righteous. In some cases they break their heads and ruin their bodies pursuing them, which is the height of foolishness and a misunderstanding of the Christian life and faith in that, without faith, they want to become righteous and blessed through works.

22. Now [to illustrate] with a few examples: One should regard the works of a Christian person who has become justified and blessed by faith and the pure grace of God, for nothing, in no other way than the way Adam and Eve related to works when they were in paradise. As it is written in Genesis 2:15, God placed the created human beings into paradise for them to work and be caretakers in it.

Now Adam was righteous and created by God without sin, so he had no need to become righteous and justified through work and caretaking. However, so that he not be idle, God put him to work planting paradise, building and conserving it. These were purely free works, done only to please God alone, and not to attain righteousness, which he already possessed and which would have already been naturally inborn in all of us as well.

It is the same with the work of the believer, who through faith is once again put in paradise and created anew. Such a person does not need work to become righteous but, simply to please God, is commanded to do such free works so as not to stand around idle but to give the body work to do that sustains it.

It is the same with a consecrated bishop who, when he consecrates churches, confirms, or performs the other works of his office, is not made a bishop by doing these various works. Indeed, if he has not already been consecrated a bishop, then none of these works would have been good enough, and they would have been the work of a pure fool. In the same way a Christian who is consecrated by faith does good works but does not become a better or more consecrated Christian through them; this can happen only by an increase in faith. If, indeed, one did not believe before and were not a Christian, then all one's works would count for nothing; rather, they would be utterly foolish, punishable, damnable sin.

23. Thus these two verses are true: Good and righteous works will never make a good and righteous person, but a good and righteous person does good and righteous works. Evil works never make an evil person, but an evil person does evil works. Therefore, the person must always be good and righteous beforehand, ahead of all good works, and good works follow and flow out of a righteous and good person.

As Christ says, "A good tree cannot bear bad fruit, nor can a bad tree bear good fruit" [Matt 7:18]. Now, obviously, the fruit does not bear the tree, nor does the tree grow on the fruit, but vice versa; the tree bears the fruit, and the fruit grows on the trees. Just as the tree has to precede the fruit and the fruit does not make the tree good or bad, but the trees make the fruit, so similarly the person must be righteous or evil beforehand in the self before doing good or evil works. One's work does not make one good or evil, but one does good or evil works.

All the trades illustrate the same thing. A good or bad house does not make a good or bad carpenter, but a good or bad carpenter makes a good or bad house. No work makes a master artisan, whatever the specific work. Rather, as the master is, so is the work as well. It is the same way with human works too; it is how a person stands in faith or unfaith that determines whether their works are good or evil, not the other way around, that the works determine whether a person is righteous or believing. Just as works do not make one have faith, they do not make one righteous either.

On the other hand, just as faith makes righteous, it also does good works. If, therefore, works make no one righteous and one must be righteous beforehand, then, obviously, faith alone out of pure grace through Christ and his word makes a person sufficiently righteous and blessed. And no work, no commandment, is necessary for a Christian's salvation; one is free of all commandments and out of pure freedom does all that one does for nothing, seeking no benefit or salvation from it, because one is already satisfied and blessed through faith and God's grace and seeks only to please God.

24. On the other side, if one is without faith, no good work will enhance one's righteousness and blessedness,[29] and then again, no evil work will make one evil and condemned. Rather, unbelief, which makes the person and the tree evil, does evil and damnable works. Thus, whether one becomes righteous or evil does not follow from works but from faith. As the author of Wisdom says, "The beginning of all sin is to depart from and not trust God."[30] Similarly, Christ also teaches that one must not begin with works saying, "Either make the tree good and its fruit good, or make the tree bad and its fruit bad" [Matt 12:33], as if he were saying, "Whoever wants to have good fruit must begin with the tree and plant it right."[31] Thus whoever wishes to do good works should not start with works but with the person who is supposed to do the works. No one makes a person good except by faith alone, and nobody makes a person evil except by unbelief alone.[32]

It is indeed the case that works make someone righteous or evil in the eyes of people; that is, [works] indicate externally who is righteous or evil. As Christ states in Matthew 7:20, "You will know them by their fruits." However, all of that is just a matter of appearance and external, and such appearances lead many people astray. They then write and teach that one should do good works and become righteous, and so, of course, they never consider faith. And off they go, the blind forever leading the blind, torturing themselves with many good works and never coming to true righteousness, as St. Paul says in 2 Timothy 3:5,7, "holding to the outward form of godliness but denying its power...[are those] who are always being instructed and can never arrive at a knowledge" of true righteousness.

Now whoever does not want to go astray with the blind needs to look beyond works, commands, or teachings about works. Such a one must look inside the person for all the things that make that one righteous. One does not become blessed and righteous through commandments and work but through God's word (that is, through God's promise of grace) and through faith. God's honor consists in the fact that God does not save us through our works but through God's gracious word, freely, out of pure compassion.

25. From all these considerations it is easy to understand in what sense good works are to be rejected and in what sense they are not to be rejected, as well as how we should understand all the teaching that instructs good works. When works include the false condition and confused notion that through them we will become righteous and saved, then they are already no good and completely damnable, because they are not free and insult the grace of God, which makes righteous and saves through faith alone. Even though [salvation] is beyond the competence of works, they still presume to be able to do it, and with that they violate the work and honor of grace. Thus, we reject good works not for their own sake, but for the sake of this evil addition and the false and confused belief that makes them good in appearance only, even though they are not good. [Such teachers] deceive themselves and everyone else, too, with them, just like ravenous wolves in sheep's clothes [Matt 7:15].

This evil addition and confused opinion concerning works is impossible to overcome where there is no faith. It remains in works-righteous people until faith comes and destroys it. Nature cannot expel it by itself. Indeed, it cannot even recognize it but regards it as a precious and blessed thing, and that is why so many are led astray by it.

On this account, even though it is good to write and preach about contrition, confession, and satisfaction,[33] if one does not continue all the way to faith, then pure devilish, misleading teachings certainly result. One should not preach in only one way but rather include both of God's words. One should preach the commandments to frighten sinners and expose their sin so that they feel contrite and become converted. It should not remain there, however. One must preach the other word, the promise of grace, as well, in order to teach faith, without which the command, contrition, and everything else happen in vain. There certainly are still preachers who preach contrition for sin and grace, but they do not emphasize the commands and promises of God in order to teach where contrition and grace come from, and how they come about. For contrition flows out of the commandments and faith out of the promises of God, and in this way the person who was previously humbled by the fear of God's commands and has come to his or her senses is justified and raised up by believing the divine word.

Part III

26. Let that in general be said about works, which a Christian person should practice in relation to his or her body. Now we will speak about more works that one does in relation to other people. For a person does not live in the body alone but also among other people on earth. For that reason one cannot be without works in relation to them. One must truly have to speak about and deal with them, even though not one of these same works is necessary for righteousness and salvation. Thus a person's position should remain free regarding all works and only be directed to being useful and serving other people. Let such a one have nothing in mind but the need of the other. In truth this is the genuine Christian life, in which faith gets to work with pleasure and love, as St. Paul teaches in Galatians 5:6.

For after he had taught the Philippians that they had every grace and sufficiency, he taught them more by saying, "I admonish you with all the consolation that you have in Christ, and all the comfort that you have in our love for you, and all the communion that you have with spiritual, righteous Christians, that you would gladden my heart perfectly by having one mind among yourselves from now on, showing one another love, serving one another, all of you not looking to yourself and your own interests, but to others and their necessities."[34] Look how clearly St. Paul depicts a Christian life to us, [showing us that] all works should be directed toward the good of the neighbor, for each and every person has enough by having faith, and all such a one's works and whole life are left over to be able to serve the neighbor freely in love. To focus on that St. Paul uses Christ as an example and states, "Have this mind among yourselves which you see in Christ, who, although he was fully in the form of God" (Phil 2:5f.) and had enough for himself, and his life, work, and suffering were not necessary in order for him to become righteous and blessed, nevertheless emptied himself of it all anyway, taking the form of a servant. He did all kinds of things and suffered, regarding nothing but what was best for us. Even though he was free, nonetheless, for our sake he became a servant.

27. Therefore, the Christian person, like Christ the head, should be fully satisfied with faith, letting it be enough and always increasing it, because it gives life, righteousness, and salvation, everything Christ and God have, as mentioned before.[35] And St. Paul states in Galatians 2:20, "What life I still live in the body, I live trusting in Christ, God's Son."[36] Thus, Christians, even if completely free, become willing servants once again in order to help the neighbor, walking alongside and dealing with each neighbor the way God through Christ dealt with them—and all for nothing, looking for nothing [in return] except God's good pleasure. They think: "Well, all right. My God, through Christ, out of sheer compassion, purely and freely, gave me, an unworthy and damned person, without my deserving it, the full riches of all righteousness and salvation, so that from this point forward I need nothing more than to believe it is so. Aye, to such a Father, who has inundated me with abundantly overflowing possessions, I shall, freely, cheerfully, and for nothing in return, do what well pleases him and in relation to my neighbor also become a Christ, the way Christ became for me, and do nothing else than what I see is necessary, useful, and a blessing to my neighbor, since through my faith I already have enough of everything I need in Christ."

Look, this is how love and pleasure for God flow out of faith, and how out of love flows a free, willing, and cheerful life, [lived] freely, serving the neighbor for nothing. For in the same way that our neighbor suffers want and needs our abundance, we suffered before God and needed God's grace. Therefore, as God helped us freely by means of Christ, we should do nothing else than help our neighbors by means of our bodies and their work. In this way we see what is involved and how high and noble a life the Christian life is. Sadly, not only has this vanished in the whole world at the present, but it is also neither known nor preached.

28. Thus we read in Luke 2:22 how the virgin Mary went to the church after six weeks to receive her purification according to the law, just as all the women did, even though she was not unclean as they were, nor did she require the same purification.

Nonetheless, she did it freely, out of love, not to disparage the other women but to remain in solidarity with the common people.

Similarly, St. Paul allowed St. Timothy to become circumcised in Acts 16:3, not because it was necessary but so that he would not give the Jews, who were weak in faith, a cause to have evil thoughts. On the other hand, he would not allow Titus to be circumcised, because of the way they pressured them, saying he had to be circumcised and that it was necessary for salvation [see Gal 2:3].

And then in Matthew 17:25–27, when they required from the disciples the payment of the tax, Christ questioned St. Peter as to whether the children of the king were not free from paying taxes. And St. Peter said, "Yes." And Jesus nevertheless sent him down to the sea, saying, "In order that we do not anger them, go down, take the first fish you catch, and in its mouth you will find a coin, and give it for you and me." That is a really fine example for this teaching, because Christ calls himself and his own the children of the king, who need do nothing. Yet he freely subjects himself, serves, and pays the tax. Now just as little as this work was necessary or served Christ for his righteousness and salvation, so little were all the other works by him and his Christians necessary for salvation. Instead, they were duties all freely assumed for the sake of and the improvement of others. All the works of priests, monasteries, and religious foundations should be done in the same way too, that all do the work of their position in life or order for nothing else than the welfare of others. They should rule their bodies to provide an example for others to do the same, who also need to compel their bodies, being careful all the time, however, not to presume and intend to become righteous and saved through them, since that belongs to the power of faith alone.

Likewise, St. Paul commands in Romans 13:1–2 and Titus 3:1 that "they should submit to the governing authorities of the world, and be prepared," not thereby to become righteous, but that they might thereby freely serve others and the authorities and do their will out of love and freedom. Now those who have this understanding could easily find their way through the countless commands and laws of the pope, bishops, monasteries, foundations, rulers, and lords, which some of the mad prelates promote as if they were necessary for salvation, calling it the command of the churches, despite

88

how wrong this is. For a free Christian speaks as follows: "I will fast, pray, do whatever is commanded, not because I need to, or that by it I could become righteous or saved. Instead, for the sake of pope, bishop, community, my fellow brother, or lord, I will provide an example, do my duty, and suffer as for my sake Christ did, suffering far greater things for me that he had far less need to do. And even now, if the tyrants wrongly require me to do things, it will still not harm me, since it is not against God."

29. On this basis each person can make a sound judgment and differentiate among all works and commands and even between the blind and mad prelates and the right-minded ones. For if a work is not oriented toward serving others or toward suffering under another's will (as long as one is not forced to act against God's will), then it is not a good, Christian work. For that reason I worry that few foundation churches, monasteries, altars, masses, and testaments are Christian and, along with that, the special fasting and prayers to some of the saints. For I fear that in all of these works each person seeks only his or her own benefits, presuming thereby to do penance for his or her sins and be saved.

This all comes from ignorance about faith and Christian freedom. Some of the blind prelates encourage the people and praise such matters, decorating them with indulgences and then never teaching faith at all. I advise you, however, if you wish to establish a foundation, pray, or fast, then do not do it in the belief that you are doing something good for yourself, but give it away freely, so that others can use and enjoy it. If you do it for their good, then you will be a true Christian. What are your possessions and good works to you, which are above what you need to keep your body in check, given that you have enough in faith, in which God has given you everything?

Look, in such a way God's possessions must flow from one person into another and be [held] in common. Each one should so accept the neighbor as if the neighbor were himself or herself. All good things flow into us from Christ, who accepted what we are into his life, as if he were what we are. These same things should flow from us into those who have need of them. In addition, I must place even my faith and righteousness before God for my neighbor, so that they cover my neighbor's sin, and then take that sin upon myself, and act no differently than if it were my very own, even as

Christ did for all of us. That, you see, is the nature of love when it is genuine. And love is genuine where faith is genuine. Hence, the holy apostle in 1 Corinthians 13:5 attributes to love that it does not seek its own interests but the interests of the neighbor.

30. Out of all these things the conclusion follows that Christians do not live in themselves but in Christ and in their neighbor—in Christ through faith and in the neighbor through love. Through faith one ascends above oneself into God. From God one descends through love again below oneself and yet always remains in God and God's love. As Christ says in John 1:51, "You will see heaven opened and the angels of God ascending and descending upon the Son of Man."[37]

Behold, that is the right, spiritual, Christian freedom which makes the heart free from all sins, laws, and commandments and which excels every other freedom as the heavens do the earth. May God give us a right understanding and observance. Amen.

THE MAGNIFICAT PUT INTO GERMAN AND EXPLAINED

Editors' Introduction: This explanation of the Magnificat was written by Luther before and after the Diet of Worms.[1] He wrote the first third in Wittenberg at the turn of 1520–21 and the last two-thirds when he was at the Wartburg in May and June 1521. The commentary is dedicated to the seventeen-year-old Prince John Frederick of Saxony (1503–54) and serves as a mirror for princes.[2] "Because they need not fear people," Luther comments, "rulers should fear God more than others, learning to know God and carefully to observe the works of God. As St. Paul says in Romans 12:8, 'Let the one who leads be diligent.'"

This early commentary is also an example of Luther's Marian piety.[3] Luther considers Mary to be the mother of God, in accordance with the tradition established by the Council of Ephesus in 431: "This holy song of the most blessed mother of God…ought indeed to be learned and kept in mind by all who would rule well and be helpful lords. The tender mother of Christ…teaches us with her words and by the example of her experience how to know, love, and praise God. With a leaping and joyful spirit she boasts and praises God for regarding her, despite her low estate and her nothingness."

George Tavard has argued that the twofold, threefold, and six-fold patterns of the commentary demonstrate the influence of Bonaventure's *Itinerarium mentis in Deum*, and its negative theology echoes the medieval German mystics.[4] For Luther, in contrast to his predecessors, the third or unitive level in the believer's progress—the level of darkness and unknowing—is simply that of faith.[5] Throughout, Luther's theology of the cross is evident. God is hidden and revealed where one would least expect to find the almighty One, in the lowliness of a poor maiden, in suffering, in the cross.

* * *

Jesus

To his Serene Highness, Prince John Frederick, Duke of Saxony,
Landgrave of Thuringia, Margrave of Meissen, my gracious Lord
and Patron
Subservient Chaplain[6]
Dr. Martin Luther

Serene and highborn prince, gracious lord! May your Grace
accept my humble prayer and service. Your Grace's kind letter has
recently come into my obedient hands, and its comforting contents
brought me much joy. Since I long ago promised and still owe this
exposition of the Magnificat to you, since the troublesome quarrels
of adversaries have so often hindered me, I decided to answer your
Grace's letter with this little book. If I put it off any longer, I shall
have to blush for shame, and it is not right for me to make any more
excuses. I do not want to impede your Grace's youthful spirit, which
inclines to the love of sacred scripture and would be stirred up and
strengthened by more attention to it. To this end I wish your Grace
God's grace and help.

This is especially needful because the welfare of so many people
depends on so great a prince, when concern for himself is removed
and he is graciously governed by God. On the other hand, when he
is left to himself and not governed graciously by God, many are
ruined. Although all human hearts are in God's almighty hand, it is
not without reason said of kings and princes, "The king's heart is…in
the hand of the Lord; he turns it wherever he will" (Prov 21:1). In this
way God wishes to drive fear into the hearts of the great princes to
teach them that they can think nothing without God's special inspiration. What other persons do brings weal or woe only to themselves
or to a few people. Rulers, however, are appointed for the special purpose of being either harmful or helpful to other people. The more
people, the wider their domain. Therefore, scripture calls upright,
god-fearing princes "angels of God" (1 Sam 29:9),[7] and even "gods"
(Ps 82:6).[8] Conversely, harmful princes are called "lions" (Zeph 3:3),[9]
"dragons" (Jer 51:34), and "wild animals" (Ezek 14:21). These God
includes among the four plagues—pestilence, famine, war, and wild
animals (Ezek 14:12–19; Rev 6–8).

Since the human heart is by nature flesh and blood, it is in itself prone to presumption. If power, riches, and honor are bestowed, it is so tempted to presumption and self-assurance that God is forgotten and subjects are neglected. Therefore, if it is at liberty to do evil without fear of punishment, it does so and becomes a beast doing whatever it wants—a prince in name but a monster in deed. Therefore, the sage Bias has well said, "The office of ruler reveals what sort of person a ruler is."[10] As for the subjects, they do not dare to let themselves go for fear of the government. Because they need not fear people, rulers should fear God more than others, learning to know God and carefully to observe the works of God. As St. Paul says in Romans 12:8, "Let the one who leads be diligent."

Now in all of scripture I know of nothing that serves as well for this purpose as this holy song of the most blessed mother of God, which ought indeed to be learned and remembered by all who would rule well and be helpful lords. Here she sings most sweetly of the fear of God and of what kind of Lord God is and, above all, how God deals with those of high and low degree. Let another listen to his love singing a worldly song. This modest virgin deserves to be heard by princes and lords, as she sings her sacred, pure, and salutary song. It is also appropriate that this canticle is sung daily in all churches at vespers and in a special and appropriate setting that sets it apart from other chants.[11]

May the tender mother of God grant me that spirit that I may profitably and thoroughly expound her song. May God grant that your Grace and all of us may take from it a salutary understanding and praiseworthy life, so that in eternal life we may praise and sing this Magnificat. So help us God. Amen.

Herewith I commend myself to your Grace, humbly beseeching your Grace in all kindness to receive my meager attempt. Wittenberg, March 10, 1521

The Magnificat

My soul magnifies the Lord,
and my spirit rejoices in God, my Savior,
for he has looked with favor on the lowliness of his
    servant.
Surely, from now on all generations will call me blessed;

for the Mighty One has done great things for me,
and holy is his name.
His mercy is for those who fear him
from generation to generation.
He has shown strength with his arm;
he has scattered the proud in the thoughts of their
    hearts.
He has brought down the powerful from their thrones,
and lifted up the lowly;
he has filled the hungry with good things,
and sent the rich away empty.
He has helped his servant Israel, in remembrance of his
    mercy,
according to the promise he made to our ancestors,
to Abraham and to his descendants forever.

In order properly to understand this song of praise, one must recognize that the Blessed Virgin Mary is speaking from her own experience, through which she was enlightened and instructed by the Holy Spirit, for no one can understand God or God's word without receiving it directly from the Holy Spirit.[12] On the other hand, no one can receive it from the Holy Spirit without experiencing, proving, and feeling it. Within this experience the Holy Spirit teaches as if in a school of the Spirit, outside of which one learns nothing but empty words and babble. Now when the Blessed Virgin herself experienced that God was working such great things in her despite her insignificance, lowliness, poverty, and despised condition, the Holy Spirit taught her this valuable insight and wisdom. God is the kind of lord who does nothing but lower what is of high degree,[13] briefly breaking what is whole and making whole what is broken.

Just as God is called the creator and the almighty because the world was created out of nothing, so God's work goes on unchanged. From now to the end of time God will make what is insignificant, despised, suffering, and dead into something valuable, honorable, blessed, and alive. On the other hand, everything that is valuable, honorable, blessed, and living, God will make to be nothing, worthless, despised, suffering, and dying. No creature can make something out of nothing.[14] Therefore, God's eyes peer only into the depths, not to the heights. As Daniel says in chapter 3:55 (Vulgate), "You...look into the depths from your throne on the cherubim";[15] in Psalm 138:6, "For though the Lord is high, he regards the lowly; but the haughty he perceives from far away." Similarly Psalm 113:5f., "Who is like the Lord our God, who is seated on high, who looks far down on the heavens and the earth?" Because God is most high with nothing above, God cannot look above or alongside, and, since nothing is God's equal, God must necessarily look within and below, and the farther you are below, the better God sees you.

The eyes of the world and of humanity, on the other hand, look only above and want to rise above themselves. As it is said in Proverbs 30:13, "There are those—how lofty are their eyes, how high their eyelids lift!" We experience daily how all strive after that which is above them: honor, power, riches, knowledge, the good life, and everything that is lofty and great. Where such people are, everyone wants to hang around, run there, serve there gladly, be at their side, and share in their glory. Therefore, it is not without reason that the scriptures describe so few princes and kings as faithful. On the other hand, no one wants to peer into the depths, where poverty, humiliation, want, lamentation, and fear are; from this all avert their eyes. Where such people are, everyone runs away, flees, shuns, and leaves them alone. No one thinks to help them, stand with them, or attempt to make something out of them. So they must remain in the depths in their low and despised condition. There is no creator among humans who can make something out of nothing, although that is what St. Paul teaches, saying, "Do not be haughty, but associate with the lowly" [Rom 12:16].

Therefore, to God alone belongs the kind of seeing that looks into the depths, to need and lamentation, and is close to all who are in the depths. As St. Peter says, "God opposes the proud, but gives grace to the humble" (1 Pet 5:5). For this reason their love and praise of God flows. People cannot praise God unless they first love God. No one can love God except by knowing God as the sweetest and best. And God can only be known in this way when we are shown, feel, and experience God's works in us. Where God is thus experienced as the kind of God who looks into the depths and helps only the poor, the despised, the suffering, the lamenting, the forgotten, and those who are nothing, God is loved so fondly that one's heart runs over with joy and leaps and dances for sheer gladness because of these gifts received. Here, then, is the Holy Spirit who can teach in just a moment such boundless knowledge and desire through experience.

Therefore, God assigns death to us all and provides for the dearest children and Christians the cross of Christ and countless sufferings and wants. In fact, God even lets them fall into sin in order to be able to see much and assist those in the depths, help many, perform many works, and be revealed as a true creator, dear and worthy of praise. Unfortunately, the world works tirelessly against this with eyes that overlook and hinder God's seeing, work, and help, and block our knowledge, love, and praise. [The world] thus deprives God of honor and its own joy, happiness, and salvation. For this reason God cast the only and beloved Son into the depths of misery. Before everyone God revealed to what end God's seeing, work, help, method, counsel, and will are directed. Thus Christ, who has most fully experienced all of this, remains eternally full of knowledge, love, and praise of God. As it is said in Psalm 21:6, "You bestow on him blessings forever; you make him glad with the joy of your presence," namely, in that he sees you and knows you. To this Psalm 44 adds that all the saints will do nothing in heaven but praise God, because God saw them in their depths and was revealed to them as worthy of love and praise.

The tender mother of Christ does the same here, teaching us with her words and by the example of her experience how to know, love, and praise God. With a leaping and joyful spirit she boasts and praises God for regarding her, despite her low estate and her nothingness. We must believe that she came of poor, despised, and lowly parents. To paint this for the eyes of the simple, there were undoubtedly daughters of chief priests and counselors in Jerusalem who were rich, young, educated, and held in high regard by all people, just as there are today daughters of kings, princes, and the rich. The same was also true of many another city. Even in Nazareth, her own town, she was not the daughter of one of the chief rulers but a poor and plain citizen's daughter, whom no one looked up to or held in high regard. To her neighbors and their daughters she was but a simple maiden, tending the cattle and doing the housework, and she was certainly no greater than any house servant who does what she is told to do around the house.

Thus Isaiah had announced (Is 11:1–2), "A shoot shall come out from the stump of Jesse, and a branch [Luther says "flower"] shall grow out of his roots. The spirit of the Lord shall rest upon him." The stump and root is the generation of Jesse or David, in particular, the Virgin Mary; the shoot and flower is Christ. Now just as it is unforeseeable, yes, unbelievable, that from a withered, rotten stump and root a lovely shoot and flower should grow, just so unlikely was it that Mary the virgin should become the mother of such a child. I think that she is not called the stump and root merely because she miraculously became a mother with her virginity intact—just as it is miraculous for a shoot to grow from a dead block of wood—but also because the royal stem and line of David was green and blossomed with great honor, power, wealth, and good fortune at the time of David and Solomon and was held in high regard by the world. Yet at the time when Jesus was to come the priests assumed this honor to themselves and ruled by themselves, and the royal line of David was as poor and despised as a dead block of wood, so that there was no longer any hope or anticipation that a king would come from it with any great glory. But when all seemed most unlikely, Christ comes, born of this despised stump, of the poor and lowly maiden. The shoot and the flower grow from a person whom Sir Annas's or Caiaphas's daughter would not have deigned to have for their humblest lady's maid. Therefore, God's work and eyes reach into the depths, while human eyes reach only into the heights. So much for the origin of her canticle, which we shall now consider word for word.

My Soul Magnifies the Lord

This word is expressed with great fervor and overwhelming joy, in which her soul and life lift themselves from within in the Spirit. Therefore, she does not say, "I magnify God," but "My soul magnifies the Lord." As if she wished to say, "My life and my whole understanding soar in the love, praise, and sheer joy of God, such that I am no longer in control of myself; I am exalted, more than I exalt myself to praise the Lord." Thus it happens to all in whom godly sweetness and God's spirit has poured, that they experience more than they can describe. It is not a human work to praise God with joy. It is a joyful suffering and God's work alone and cannot be taught with words but only by personal experience. As David says in Psalm 34:8, "Taste and see that the Lord is good; happy are those who take refuge in him." David puts tasting before seeing because this sweetness cannot be comprehended unless one has experienced it for oneself. No one attains this experience without trusting God with one's whole heart in the depths and in the distresses of life. Therefore, David adds, "Happy are those who trust the Lord." They will experience God's work and will obtain God's sensible sweetness and, through it all, understanding and knowledge.

We want to treat the words in order. The first is "my soul." Scripture divides the person into three parts.[16] St. Paul says in the last chapter of Thessalonians, "May the God of peace himself sanctify you entirely; and may your spirit and soul and body be kept sound…at the coming of our Lord Jesus Christ" [1 Thess 5:23]. Each of these three parts, as well as the whole person, is further divided into two parts, called spirit and flesh. This division is not of human nature but of human qualities. That is, according to nature, there are three parts—spirit, soul, and body—which can be altogether good or bad, that is, flesh or spirit, which is not now our topic. The first part, the spirit, is the highest, deepest, and noblest part of the person, through which one can attain untouchable, invisible, and eternal things. In short, it is the home of faith and God's word. David speaks of it in Psalm 51:10, "Create in me a clean heart…and…a new and right spirit," that is, a righteous and unwavering faith. On the other hand, concerning the unbelievers, he says in Psalm 78:37, "Their heart was not steadfast toward [God], they were not true to his covenant."

The second part, the soul, is this same spirit, according to nature, but is seen to have the separate function of making the body alive and working through it. In the Bible it is often spoken of as life, because the spirit can live without the body but not the body without the spirit. Even in sleep we see the soul living and working without interruption. It is its nature not to understand incomprehensible things but only that which reason can understand and consider. And it is reason that is the light in this house. Where the spirit in faith with its brighter light does not enlighten, the light of reason rules, and it is never without error. It is too inferior to deal with godly things. The Bible attributes many things to these two parts, including wisdom and understanding—wisdom to the spirit and understanding to the soul—and likewise hatred, love, delight, outrage, and the like.

The third part is the body with its members. Its work is to draw upon and apply what the soul understands and the spirit believes. To use an example from the Bible,[17] Moses built a tabernacle with three different courts. The first was the holy of holies; here God dwelt, and in it there was no light. The second was the holy place; here stood a lampstand with seven arms and seven lamps. The third was the outer court; it was open to the sky and to the sun's light. This is a metaphor for the Christian person, whose spirit is the holy of holies, God's dwelling in the darkness of faith without light. For the Christian believes what is neither seen, nor felt, nor comprehended. The soul is the holy place with its seven lamps, that is, every form of reason,[18] discrimination, knowledge,[19] and understanding[20] of bodily and visible things. The body is the outer court that is open to everyone, so that everyone can see what one does and how one lives.

Now Paul asks the God of peace to make us holy, not in part, but entirely—through and through—so that the spirit, soul, and body may all be holy [1 Thess 5:23]. There would be much to say concerning the reasons for such a prayer, but, in brief, when the spirit is no longer holy, then nothing is holy. The greatest battles and the gravest dangers take aim at the spirit's holiness, which stands only in the pure and simple faith, because the spirit does not concern itself with tangible things, as was said. False teachers come and draw the spirit outside. One proposes this work, the other that way of becoming righteous. When the spirit is not protected here and is not wise, it will come out and follow, and it comes upon the outer works and ways and thinks that it will be righteous in this way. Immediately faith is lost, and the spirit is dead in God's eyes.

Then the various sects and orders arise, so that one becomes a Carthusian and another a mendicant. One tries to obtain salvation with fasting, the other with prayer; one with this work, the other with that. All of these are self-chosen works and are orders never commanded by God but only imagined by people. They no longer hold true to faith but focus on works until they are so deep in them that they have a falling out among themselves. Everyone wants to be the best and despises the other, just as the monks of the stricter orders brag and puff themselves up. Against these holy workers and seemingly righteous teachers Paul prays, saying that God is a God of peace and unity. Such a God these disunited and unpeaceful saints cannot have or hold, unless they let go of their own things and come together in spirit and faith that these works create only disagreement, sin, and strife, and only faith makes one righteous and peace loving. As Psalm 68:6 says, "God grants us unity in the house,"[21] and Psalm 133:1, "How very good and pleasant it is when kindred live together in unity."[22]

This peace never comes unless one teaches that one is made righteous, just, and blessed not by a work or any external method but only by faith, that is, by a firm confidence in the unseen grace of God promised to us. This I have shown at great length in my treatise "On Good Works."[23] Where there is no faith there must be many works, and from this follows discord and disunity, and God can no longer remain there. Therefore, Paul is not content here to say simply, "your soul" or "your spirit," etc., but "your whole spirit," for all depends on this. Here he employs a fine Greek expression, *olokleron pneuma emon*, that is, "your spirit that possesses the whole inheritance." It is as if he wished to say: "Do not be led astray by false teachings about works. The believing spirit alone possesses everything." I pray that God will protect you from the false teachings that build up works as trust in God that are, nevertheless, false assurances, because they do not build on God's promises alone. When this "spirit that possesses the whole inheritance" is preserved, both soul and body are able to remain without error and evil works. Otherwise, when the spirit is faithless, it is not possible for the soul and the whole life to be righteous and without error, even if they are filled with good intentions and opinions and find within themselves their own devotion and pleasure. Therefore, because of these errors and false opinions of the soul, all the works of the body also become evil and useless, even if some fast themselves to death and do all manner of holy works. Therefore, it is important that God first protect the spirit and after that the soul and the body, so that we do not live and work in vain but become truly holy—not only free from visible sins, but even more from false and apparent good works.

Now enough has been said concerning these two words, *soul* and *spirit*, as they occur frequently in the Bible. Next is the little word *magnificat*,[24] which means to make great, to lift up, or to hold in high regard, as in reference to one who can perform, know, and will the many great things that follow in this song of praise, such that the word *magnificat* serves as the title of a book about the same topic. Thus Mary shows by using this word what her canticle is about, namely, the great acts and works of God to strengthen our faith, to comfort the lowly, and to terrify those of high degree. To this threefold use and purpose of the canticle we should focus our attention and understanding, for she sang this not for herself but for all of us, so that we would sing after her. Now, one would not normally be terrified or comforted by such great works of God, unless one believes not only that God has the ability and knowledge to do great things but also that God wills and loves to do them. Nor is it enough that you believe God will do such things for others and not for you, thus excluding yourself, as those do who, because of their power, do not fear God and those of little courage do, who, because of their tribulations, fall into despair.

Such faith is nothing and is dead, like an illusion taken from a fairy tale. Instead, without wavering or doubt you must imagine God's will for you, so that you trust firmly that God will and wills to do great things with you. This is a lively, active faith that pervades and changes the whole person. It forces you to fear when you are of high degree and to take comfort when you are of low degree. The higher you are, the more you must fear, and the more you are oppressed, the more you must take comfort, which is what those with a dead faith cannot do. What will you do in the hour of death? At that time you must not only believe that God has the ability and knowledge to help you but also wants to help you. For an unspeakably great work must occur to deliver you from everlasting death, that you may be eternally blessed and become God's heir. To this faith all things are possible, as Christ says (Mark 9:23). This faith alone abides. It also experiences God's works and thereby God's love, leading to godly praise and song, so that this righteous person holds God in the highest regard and truly magnifies God.

God is unchangeable. God is not made great by us in essence, but in our understanding and experience, that is, when we both lift up and esteem the grace and goodness of God. Therefore, the holy Mother does not say, "My voice or my mouth, my hand or my thoughts," or "My reason or my will magnifies the Lord." There are many who praise God with great voice, who preach with well-chosen words, who speak much of God, who dispute, write, and paint; there are many who reason and speculate about God; moreover, there are many who lift God up with false devotion and will. By contrast she says, "My soul magnifies the Lord," that is, my whole life and being, mind and strength esteem God highly. She is enraptured by God and feels herself lifted up into God's grace and good will, as the following verse shows.[25] In the same way, when someone does something especially good for us, our lives turn toward that person and we say, "I hold that person in high regard"; in other words, "my soul magnifies that one." How much more will such a lively emotion be excited in us when we experience the goodness that is so rapturously great in God's works that all our words and thoughts fall short. Our whole life should be excited, as if everything in us wants to sing praises.

But now there are two false spirits that cannot rightly sing the Magnificat. The first are those who will not praise God unless things go well with them. As David says, "They praise you when you do good to them."[26] These persons seem to praise God, but, because they do not want to suffer oppression and be in the depths, they never experience the proper work of God and therefore never properly love and praise God. Thus, the world is filled with worship and praise, singing and preaching, organ and pipes. The Magnificat is sung gloriously, but it is a pity that this exquisite song should be sung by us without strength and savor, except when it goes well with us; and we do not sing it at all when things do not go well. God sinks in our estimation, and we think that God cannot or does not want to work for us, and, therefore, the Magnificat must also be left out.

The others are even more dangerous. They err on the other side. They exalt themselves because of the gifts God has given them and do not attribute them to God alone. They want credit for them. They want to be honored for them and to be considered more worthy than others. They consider all the good things that God has done for them and cling to them, claiming them as their own doing and regarding themselves as better than those who have no such things. This is certainly a slippery stance. God's good gifts naturally produce proud and complacent hearts. Therefore, we must heed Mary's last word, "God." Mary does not say, "My soul makes itself great," or "holds me in high regard." She thought nothing of herself. God alone makes her great. She credits God with everything and gives all the glory to God, from whom she has received it. Although she experienced such a great work of God within herself, she did not consider herself greater than even the lowliest person on earth. Had she done this, she would have fallen with Lucifer into the depths of hell.

PREFACE TO THE EPISTLE TO THE ROMANS

Editors' Introduction: This very early preface from the September Testament (1522) presents the core of Luther's Reformation understanding of spirituality. In it Luther claims that the Epistle to the Romans, the clearest expression of the gospel, should be known by heart. It contains the whole of Christian and evangelical teaching, including an introduction to the entire Old Testament. From this epistle Luther defines for the reader what a Christian needs to know, namely, the meaning of law, gospel, sin, punishment, grace, faith, righteousness, Christ, God, good works, freedom, love, hope, and cross.

According to Luther, the epistle shows us how we should relate to everyone, whether righteous or sinner, strong or weak, friend or foe, and even how we should consider ourselves. The preface contains perhaps Luther's clearest statements on faith as a lively, creative, active thing and its relationship to the way a Christian lives. Faith is unflappable trust in God's grace through Jesus Christ; sin is unbelief.[1] The law, as proclaimed in the scriptures, must always be recognized for its proper functions and limits and be distinguished from the good news of the gospel.

Paul's distinctions between flesh and spirit, maintains Luther, address the whole person, consisting of body and soul with reason and all the senses, and thus one can be spiritual in one's daily vocation as well as in one's inner life; one can be worldly both internally and externally. Furthermore, we are always righteous and sinful at the same time. Even as faith alone justifies and gives the spirit and the desire to do good outward works, so also unbelief alone sins and gives the flesh the desire to do evil. The gifts and the spirit grow in us daily but are not perfect, since evil desires and sin remain at war against the spirit. Faith is a godly work in us that changes us, makes us to be born anew of God (John 1:13), puts to death the old Adam, and turns us into completely new persons in heart, in soul, in mind, and in all our powers.

Luther argues that one may be called spiritual when one does the simplest of external works, as Jesus did in washing the feet of the disciples (John 13:4–10) and as Peter did as he steered the boat and fished (Luke 5:4–5. and John 21:3–7). Hence, the term *flesh* is the whole person oriented away from God and neighbor, while *spirit* is the whole person oriented toward God and neighbor.

Therefore, the true freedom from sin and the law about which Luther writes in concluding this chapter is a freedom to do good with delight and to live rightly without coercion from the law. He also shows how the spirit comes from Christ, who has given us his Holy Spirit, who has made us spiritual and subdued the flesh and assures us that we are still God's children, no matter how hard sin rages in us, as long as we follow the spirit and fight against sin in order to kill it.

* * *

This epistle is truly the main text in the New Testament and the gospel in its clearest expression. Thus, it is worthy and valuable for a Christian not only to know it word for word by heart but also to indulge in it daily as the soul's daily bread. It can never be read or pondered too often. The more one indulges in it, the more valuable it becomes, and the better it tastes. Therefore, I would like to offer my services and, with this preface, provide an introduction by God's help, so that it can better be understood by every person. Up to now it has been clouded with glosses and all sorts of empty comments.[2] By itself it is a brilliant light and is sufficient to illumine the whole of the scriptures.

First, we must make the terminology clear and know what Paul means by words like *law, sin, grace, faith, righteousness, flesh, spirit*, and similar words. Otherwise, it is of no use. You must not understand the little word *law* here in human terms, as if it were a teaching about work that needs to be done or not, as is the case with human laws, even if the heart is not in it. God looks to the depths of the heart, and therefore God's law requires a response from the depths of the heart; it is not content with works.[3] God punishes all the more works that are not done from the depths of the heart; they are hypocrisy and lies, as everyone is called a liar in Psalm [116:11].

This is because no one can keep the law from the depths of the heart, because everyone discovers an internal resistance to the good and a longing for evil. If now there is no willing desire to do the good, since the depths of the heart are not set on the law of God, then certainly sin and God's wrath are deserved, even if many good works and an honorable life appear on the outside.

In chapter 2, therefore, St. Paul asserts that the Jews are all sinners and says that only the doers of the law are righteous before God [Rom 2:13]. He intends by this not that the one who does works keeps the law, but he asserts all the more to them, "You that forbid adultery, do you commit adultery?" (Rom 2:22); similarly, "when you judge others…you condemn yourself, because you, the judge, are doing the very same things" (Rom 2:1). As if he were saying: "You live a fine outward life in the works of the law, and you judge those who do not live accordingly. You know how to teach everyone, as you see the splinter in the other's eye, but you do not notice the log in your own eye" (Matt 7:3). Although you keep the law outwardly by works out of fear of punishment or love of reward, you nevertheless do all this without a willing desire for and love of the law but rather with resistance and force. You would prefer to do something else, if the law were not there. Therefore, one can conclude that from the depths of your heart you are the enemy of the law. You, then, that teach others "Do not steal!" are all the while a thief in your heart (Rom 2:21), and you would gladly be one outwardly if you dared. To be sure, the outward work does not lag far behind for such hypocrites. Thus, you teach others but not yourself (Rom 2:21), and you do not know what you teach, and you do not really understand the law. In this way the law multiplies sin, as he says in chapter 5[:20]. The more the law demands what one cannot do, the more one becomes an enemy of the law.

Therefore, he says in chapter 7, "The law is spiritual" (Rom 7:12).[4] What is this? Were the law corporeal, it could be satisfied by works. Since it is spiritual, no one can fulfill it unless it comes from the depths of the heart. But only the Holy Spirit provides this heart and makes a person into the likeness of the law with a heart whose delight is in the law (Ps 1:2). Consequently, one does everything not out of fear or compulsion but with a willing heart. The law is thus spiritual in that it wants to be loved and fulfilled with such a spiritual heart and demands such a spirit. Whenever this spirit is not in the heart, there is sin, resistance, and enmity toward the law even though the law is good, just, and holy (Rom 7:12).

Accustom yourself to the language that it is one thing to do the works of the law and another to fulfill the law. The works of the law are all that a person does and can do in relation to the law by free will and one's own powers.[5] Nevertheless, since along with these works there remains in the heart resistance and a sense of being under compulsion to the law, such works are lost and remain useless. This is what St. Paul means in chapter 3, where he says that through the works of the law no one is justified in God's sight (Rom 3:20). Thus, you can see that the school wranglers and the sophists mislead when they teach that one can prepare oneself for grace with works.[6] How can one prepare oneself for grace by works if one does them only with resistance and unwillingness in one's heart? How can a work please God that proceeds from a resisting and unwilling heart?

But to fulfill the law is to do one's works with delight and love, free of the constraint of the law, to live a godly and good life as if there were no law or punishment. The Holy Spirit gives this delight or love for the law to the heart, as he says in chapter 5[:5]. But the Holy Spirit is not given except in, with, and by faith in Jesus Christ, as St. Paul says in the preface. Faith comes only through God's word or the gospel that preaches that Christ is God's son and human, who died and rose for us, as he says in chapters 3, 4, and again in chapter 10.[7]

Therefore, faith alone justifies and fulfills the law, and this is because faith brings us the Spirit gained by the merits of Christ. The Spirit creates a glad and free heart, as the law demands. Thus, good works proceed from faith itself, as he says in chapter 3, after he rejects the works of the law and sounds as if he wished to overthrow the law through faith. "By no means!" he says. "On the contrary, we uphold the law" (Rom 3:31). That is, we fulfill the law through faith.

Sin in the scriptures is not only defined as outward works done by the body but as all the activities that are excited and set in motion with the outward actions, namely, the depths of the heart with all its powers. Also, the little word *doing* refers to the case when a person gives in completely and falls into sin. No outward act of sin occurs without a person falling into it with both body and soul. In particular, the scriptures look into the heart and onto the root and the main source of all sin, which is unbelief at the depths of the heart. Even as faith alone justifies and gives the spirit and the desire to do good outward works, so also unbelief alone sins and gives the flesh the desire to do evil outward works, as happened to Adam and Eve in Genesis, chapter 3.

Therefore, Christ calls unbelief alone sin when he says in John 16 that the Spirit will punish the world because of sin, "because they do not believe in me" (John 16:9). Before good or evil works occur, just like good or evil fruit (Matt 7:17), first there must also be either faith or unbelief in the heart. Unbelief is the root, sap, and chief power of all sin, which in the scriptures is called the serpent's head. It is also called the head of the old dragon that the seed of the woman, Christ, must tread underfoot, as was promised to Adam (Gen 3:15).

The words *grace* and *gift* differ in that *grace* actually means the faithfulness or favor that God bears toward us by God's own choice, by which God is disposed to give us Christ and to pour the Holy Spirit with the gifts of the Spirit into us, as is clear in chapter 5[:15]. There he speaks of "the grace and gift in Christ," etc. The gifts and the Spirit grow in us daily but are not perfect, since evil desires and sin remain at war against the Spirit, as he says in Rom 7[:21–23], Gal 5[:17], and as is promised in Gen 3[:15]. That is the conflict between the seed of the woman and seed of the snake. Nevertheless, grace does so much that before God we are reckoned completely and fully justified, because God's grace cannot be divided and distributed, as is true of the gifts. On the contrary, it takes us fully and completely into the faithfulness of God for the sake of Christ our advocate and mediator and to initiate the gifts in us.

Now you understand chapter 7, where Paul calls himself yet a sinner,[8] and in chapter 8 he says that there is no condemnation for those who are in Christ (8:1) because of the incompleteness of the gifts and of the Spirit. Insofar as the flesh is not yet killed, we are still sinners. But because we believe in Christ and have a beginning of the Spirit (Rom 8:1), God is so favorable and gracious to us that our sins are not regarded and not judged. Rather, God relates to us according to our faith in Christ until sin is killed.

Faith is not the human illusion and dream that some hold faith to be. When they do not see the improvement of life and good works following, although they hear and speak much of faith, they fall into the error of saying that faith is not sufficient, but one must do works to be righteous and be saved. The reason is that, when they hear the gospel, they miss the point and create an idea in their hearts by their own powers, saying, "I believe." That is what they consider to be the right faith. Nevertheless, since it is a human construction and idea that does not reach the depths of the heart, it does nothing, and no improvement of life follows.

Faith is a godly work in us that changes us and makes us to be born anew of God (John 1[:13]) and puts to death the old Adam, turning us into completely new persons in heart, in soul, in mind, and in all our powers. It brings the Holy Spirit along with it. Oh, it is a living, creating, acting, and mighty thing, this faith. It is impossible for it not to do good works continuously. It also does not ask if good works have to be done; rather, before one even asks, it has done them already and is always about doing them. An individual who does not do these works is a faithless person, who gropes and looks around for faith and good works and knows neither what faith is nor what good works are, despite talking nonsense about faith and good works.

Faith is an unflappable confidence in God's grace, so certain that one would die a thousand deaths for it. This confidence and knowledge of God's grace that the Holy Spirit accomplishes though faith makes one happy, courageous, and joyful before God and all creatures. Therefore, without constraint a person is willing and desires to do good to everyone and to serve everyone, to suffer all manner of things out of love and praise for God, who has revealed this grace. Therefore, it is impossible to separate works from faith, just as it is impossible to separate burning and light from fire. Beware, therefore, of your own false ideas and the useless talk of fools. Pray to God that God will work faith in you; otherwise, you will always be without faith, no matter how you try to deceive yourself or whatever you wish or can do.

"Righteousness," then, is such faith and is called God's righteousness, the righteousness that God holds good because God gives it and shapes a person, such that everyone gives what is due. For through faith a person becomes free from sin and gains the desire to fulfill God's commandments. In this way a person gives God the honor, and what is owed is paid. Likewise, a person serves others willingly in every possible way and thus also pays what is owed. Nature, free will, and our own powers cannot bring this righteousness into being. Even as one cannot give oneself faith, so also one cannot rid oneself of unbelief. How should one then attempt to remove even one little sin? Consequently, every act that is not done from faith or is done in unbelief is false and hypocritical (Rom 14:23), no matter how much it glistens.

Flesh and *spirit* must not be understood as if flesh had only to do with chastity and spirit only with the inward state of our hearts. Rather, like Christ in John (3[:6]), Paul calls flesh everything that is "born of the flesh," namely, the whole person consisting of body and soul with reason and all the senses,[9] because everything in a person strives toward the flesh. Additionally, you can call one "of the flesh" who, without grace, spins, teaches,[10] and chatters about highly spiritual things. You can learn this from the "works of the flesh" that he teaches in Gal 5[:19–21], where he calls factions and enmity works of the flesh. And Rom 8[:3] says that the law is weakened by the flesh, which refers not to unchastity but to all sins, especially in reference to unbelief, which is the most spiritual of vices.

Again, one is called spiritual when one does the simplest of external works, as Jesus did in washing the feet of the disciples (John 13:5–11) and as Peter did as he steered the boat and fished (Luke 5:4–5 and John 21:3–7). Hence, the term *flesh* applies to a person who lives and works internally and externally for the purpose of the flesh and to serve this temporal life. The term *spirit* applies to a person who lives and works internally and externally to serve the purposes of the Spirit and the future life. Without such an understanding of these words, you will never understand this epistle of Paul or any book of the holy scriptures. Therefore, beware of all teachers who use these words in other ways, whoever they may be, even Jerome, Augustine, Ambrose, Origen, their equals, or persons more important than they. Now, let us take up the epistle.

The first duty of the evangelical preacher is, through revelation of the law and of sin, to rebuke and declare as sin everything that is not lived out of the Spirit and out of faith in Christ, so that people are brought to recognize themselves and their misery and will be humbled and long for help. This St. Paul does as well, beginning in the first chapter to rebuke the gross sins and unbelief that are plain as day. Such were and still are the sins of the heathen who live without God's grace. Paul says that through the gospel the wrath of God from heaven is revealed over all humankind because of humans' godless ways and wickedness (Rom 1:18). For although they know and daily recognize that there is a God, nevertheless nature itself, without grace, is so evil that it neither thanks nor honors God. Instead, it blinds itself and falls continuously into wickedness, until after idolatry it commits the most abominable sins and every vice shamelessly. If unpunished, it commits other sins.

In the second chapter he extends this rebuke to those who outwardly appear righteous or those who secretly sin, as [is] true of [some people] and of all hypocrites now who live well without joy and love. In their hearts they are enemies of the law, but they love to judge other people. As is the way with all hypocrites, they consider themselves spotless, yet they are filled with envy, hate, pride, and all kinds of iniquity (Matt 23:25). These are precisely those who scorn God's goodness, and, because of their hardheartedness, they store up wrath for themselves (Rom 2:5). As a true revealer of the law, St. Paul therefore lets no one be without sin, declaring the wrath of God upon all who wish to live decent lives by nature out of their free will. He makes them out to be no better than overt sinners, calling them hardhearted and impenitent (Rom 2:5).

In chapter 3 he throws both into one heap, saying that one is just like the other; they are all sinners before God. The Jews, moreover, have had the word of God, but many did not have faith in it. Nevertheless, God's faithfulness and truthfulness are still effective. He adds a citation from Psalm 51[:4] that God is still justified in God's words. Afterward, he returns to the point and proves from the scriptures that they are all sinners, that through the works of the law no one is justified, but that the law was given that sin may be recognized. Then he begins and teaches the right way to become righteous and to be saved [Rom 3:23–27]. He says that all are sinners and fall short of the glory of God and must be justified without merit through faith in Christ, who merited this for us though his blood. For our sakes Christ has become God's mercy seat,[11] and so God forgives all of the sins that we have committed in the past to demonstrate that we are helped only by God's righteousness, which is given in faith. Now this is revealed by the gospel; earlier it was attested to by the law and the prophets. Thus, the law is supported by faith, though the works of the law are abrogated, despite the praise given them.

Having revealed sins and taught the way of faith for righteousness in the first three chapters, St. Paul begins in chapter 4 to address certain protests and objections. He first takes up the common case for all those who, hearing that faith justifies without works, ask, "Should one then not do good works?" He himself then considers the case of Abraham (Rom 4:1–5), asking, "What did Abraham accomplish with his good works? Was everything in vain? Were his works of no use?" He concludes that Abraham was justified through faith alone without works. The scriptures even praise Abraham as justified through faith alone before the "work" of his circumcision (Gen 15:6). If the work of circumcision, which God had commanded (Gen 17:10) and which was a good work of obedience, did nothing for his righteousness, then certainly no other good work could contribute to righteousness. For just as Abraham's circumcision was an outward sign that attested to his righteousness through faith, so also good works are only outward signs that follow faith and prove, just as do good fruits (Matt 7:16), that a person is already internally righteous before God.

With this powerful example from the scriptures St. Paul proves his earlier teaching about faith in the third chapter and adds another witness in David from Psalm 32[:1–2].[12] David too says that a person is justified without works, even though one does not remain without works when one has been justified. After this, he expands the example against all other works of the law (Rom 4:9–12) and concludes that the Jews cannot be Abraham's heirs merely because of their blood and far less because of the works of the law; rather, they must inherit Abraham's faith if they want to be his true heirs. This is because Abraham was justified before both Moses and circumcision and is called the father of all believers. Besides, the law creates much more wrath than grace, because no one does it with love and joy; thus, more disfavor than grace comes from the law's works. It follows that only faith can obtain the grace promised to Abraham. Such examples are written for us so that we should believe.

In the fifth chapter he treats the fruits and works of faith. These are peace, joy, love of God and everyone, and also assurance, certainty, courage, spirit, and hope in trouble and suffering. All of this follows true faith because of the overwhelming goodness that God shows us in Christ; before we could ask, while we were yet enemies, God let Christ die for us (Rom 5:8). Thus we have it that faith justifies without any works, and yet it does not follow that one should not do good works but that the true works should not be lacking, about which the self-righteous know nothing. They dream up works of their own, and therefore they do not have peace, joy, assurance, love, hope, certainty, assurance,[13] or true Christian works or the way of faith.

Then Paul makes a pleasant digression and excursus (Rom 5:12–21) and relates whence both sin and righteousness, death and life come, juxtaposing Adam and Christ. He wishes to say that Christ had to come as a second Adam, who would bequeath his righteousness to us by means of a new spiritual birth in faith, just as the first Adam bequeathed sin to us through old birth in the flesh. Here he makes clear and establishes that one cannot help oneself from sins to righteousness with works, even as one cannot prevent oneself from being born in the flesh. This also proves that the divine law—which by right should help, if anything could help in obtaining righteousness—not only provided no help when it came but even increased sin. The more the law forbids, the more our evil nature grows in animosity toward it, and the more it pursues its own desires. Thus, the law makes Christ all the more necessary and requires more grace to help our nature.

In chapter 6 he takes up the particular work of faith, the battle of the spirit with the flesh, finally killing the remaining sins and desires that are left after justification. He teaches us that we are not freed from sins through faith so that we can be lazy and secure, as if there were no longer any sin in us. There is sin in us, but it is not reckoned for our condemnation for the sake of faith that battles with sin. Therefore, we have enough to do throughout our lives to discipline our bodies, to kill its desires and control its members to obey the spirit and not its desires. This self-discipline is needed in order that we might conform to the death and resurrection of Christ and fulfill our baptism. Baptism also signifies the death of sin and the new life of grace (Rom 6:3, 4) until we are free from sins and rise bodily with Christ and live forever.

This we can do, he says, because we are in grace and not in the law (Rom 6:14).[14] He explains what this means. To be without the law is not the same thing as to have no laws and to be able to do whatever one desires. Rather, "under the law" means that we live without grace and in the works of the law. For here sin rules through the law, since no one takes a delight in the law by nature, and this is great sin. Grace moves us to love the law, and sin is no longer there, and the law is not against us but one with us.

Therefore, the true freedom from sin and the law about which he writes at the end of this chapter is a freedom only to do good with delight and to live rightly without coercion from the law. This is a spiritual freedom that does not abrogate the law but provides that which the law demands, namely, the desire and love to satisfy the law, such that it has nothing more to drive or demand. It is as if you were in debt to a lender and could not pay. There would be two ways of settling the matter and setting you free. The first is that he would take nothing from you and would tear up the bill; the second is that a righteous person would pay for you and give you enough to pay your debt. It is in this manner that Christ set us free from the law, and therefore it is not a wild, fleshly freedom that is not supposed to do anything. Rather, it is a freedom that does many and various works and is free of the demands and obligations of the law.

In the seventh chapter he shows such things by an analogy to married life (Rom 7:2). When a husband dies, the wife is free, entirely released from the other. The point is not that the wife can or should take another man, but much the more, that she is now really free to take another man, which she could not do formerly, before she was free from her husband. Similarly, our conscience is bound to the law under the old sinful person. When it is killed by the Spirit, the conscience is free, and thus one is entirely released from the other. This does not mean that the conscience should do nothing, but that for the first time it should really hang on Christ, the second husband, and bear the fruit of life.

Then (Rom 7:5–6) he expands on the mode of sins and the law, how by means of the law sin is properly stirred up and made strong. For the old self becomes even more the enemy of the law, because one cannot pay what the law demands. For sin is its nature, so by oneself one can do nothing else.[15] Therefore, to [that old self] the law is death and torment. The law is not evil, but the evil nature cannot bear the good—namely, that it demands good from one—in the same way that a sick person cannot bear to be told to run and jump and other things that one would ask of a healthy person.

Thus, St. Paul concludes here that, when the law is properly understood and construed in the best way, it does nothing but remind us of our sins, kills us through them, and makes us guilty of eternal wrath. All this our conscience learns perfectly by experience when it meets the law face to face. Consequently, one needs more than the law to make persons righteous and to attain salvation. Those who do not understand the law properly are blind. They go about blindly in their presumption, thinking to satisfy the law by means of their works. They do not understand how much the law demands, namely, a free, willing, and joyful heart. Therefore, they do not see Moses clearly; the veil is put between them and him and covers him (Exod 34:29–35; 2 Cor 3:12–15).

Thereupon he shows how the spirit and the flesh fight with one another in a person, and he uses himself as an example (Rom 7:14–25) so that we properly understand the work of killing sin in ourselves. He calls both the spirit and the flesh laws because, just as it is the mode of the divine law to drive us and make demands, so also the flesh drives, strives, and rages against the spirit and wants its own way. On the other hand, the spirit drives and strives against the flesh and wants its own way. This fight rages in us as long as we live, in one more than another, depending on whether the spirit or the flesh is stronger. Nevertheless, the whole person is both spirit and flesh, and the fight within goes on until one becomes wholly spiritual.[16]

In the eighth chapter he comforts those struggling, saying that this flesh does not condemn them. He shows, further, what the modes of the flesh and the spirit are. He also shows how the Spirit comes from Christ, who has given us his Holy Spirit, who has made us spiritual and subdued the flesh, and assures us that we are still God's children, no matter how hard sin rages in us, as long as we follow the Spirit and fight against sin in order to kill it. But because nothing else is so effective in disciplining the flesh as are our cross and suffering, God comforts us in our suffering with the presence and support of the Spirit, of love, and of the whole creation. That is, the Spirit sighs within us, and the creation longs with us that we may be rid of the flesh and of sin. So we see that these three chapters [Rom 6—8] focus on the one work of faith, that is, to kill the old Adam and to discipline the flesh.

In the ninth, tenth, and eleventh chapters he teaches about the everlasting predestination of God, from which initially proceeds who shall believe or not, who should rid themselves of sin and who should not be able to do so. This is so that our righteousness is truly taken out of our hands and put into God's hands alone. And this is most needful, since we are so weak and uncertain that, if it depended on us, surely not a single person would be saved, for the devil would overwhelm everyone. But since God is dependable, and since God is certain that God's predestination cannot fail and that no one can resist it, we still have hope against sin. Here must be stopped, once and for all, the impious and arrogant spirits who apply reason at first and begin to probe God's predestination from the top to the bottom, worrying in vain as to whether they are predestined. They are bound to plunge to their own destruction, either through despair or by throwing caution to the winds.

You, however, must follow the order of this epistle and concern yourself first with Christ and the gospel, so that you may recognize your sin and God's grace. Then fight your sin, as the first eight chapters teach. Afterward, when you arrive at the eighth chapter, and you are under the cross and suffering, chapters nine, ten, and eleven will teach you how predestination is comforting. For without suffering, cross, and the perils of death, you cannot deal with predestination without harm and without secret anger against God. Therefore, Adam must first be put to death before you can bear this thing and drink the strong wine. Beware of drinking wine when you are still nursing infants.[17] Every doctrine requires us to be of the appropriate ability, age, and maturity.

In the twelfth chapter Paul teaches the true way to serve God and renders all Christians as priests, who should not offer money or cattle, as the law requires, but their own bodies by killing their lusts. After this (Rom 12:3–21) he describes the outward conduct of Christians under the discipline of the Spirit, saying how they are to teach, preach, govern, serve, give, suffer, love, live, and act in relation to friend and foe and everyone. These are the works of a Christian, as I said above; faith takes no holidays.

In the thirteenth chapter he teaches that we are to honor and be obedient to the temporal government. Although temporal government does not make people righteous before God, nevertheless it is instituted in order to accomplish at least this much, that the good may have outward peace and quietness without fear and the wicked ones cannot do their evil freely in peace and quiet without fear. Therefore, the righteous should also honor the government, even if they do not need it. Finally, he sums everything up in love and concludes with the example of Christ. That is, as he has done for us, so we should do for others and follow him.[18]

In the fourteenth chapter he teaches how to deal gently with and spare those who have weak consciences, who are weak in faith, so that one does not use Christian freedom to damage but to assist the weak. When one does not act this way, discord and contempt for the gospel follow, and this is the most important thing [to prevent]. It is therefore better to yield a little to the weak in faith until they become stronger than to lose the most important thing, the teaching of the gospel. Only love can do this work, and it is especially important now, while we are eating meat and rudely and roughly taking other liberties, thus needlessly shaking weak consciences before they know the truth.

In the fifteenth chapter he sets Christ as an example, so that we will bear with other weak persons, even including overt sinners and those who have unrefined habits. These one must not reject but carry until they become better. For thus Christ has done and does with us daily. He bears with our many shortcomings, bad habits, and all sorts of other imperfections, and helps us constantly.

Then in conclusion he prays for them, praises them, and commends them to God. He speaks of his own office and of his preaching and begs them earnestly to give gifts for the poor in Jerusalem. All that he speaks of or does is from pure love. Therefore, we find in this epistle in the richest form what a Christian needs to know, namely, what law, gospel, sin, punishment, grace, faith, righteousness, Christ, God, good works, love, hope, and cross are. We find how we should relate to everyone, whether righteous or sinner, strong or weak, friend or foe, and even how we should consider ourselves. In addition, everything is poignantly proven with scripture and witnessed by examples of himself and the prophets. Thus one cannot wish for anything more. It seems, then, that St. Paul wished in this epistle to gather concisely at once the whole Christian and evangelical teaching with an introduction to the whole Old Testament. Without a doubt the one who knows this epistle from the heart has the light and the power of the Old Testament as well. Therefore, every Christian ought to study Romans regularly and continuously. May God grant the grace for this. Amen.

The last chapter consists of greetings, but among the greetings he mixes a noble warning about human-made doctrines that intrude alongside the gospel and cause aggravation (Rom 16:17–19). It is as if he had foreseen that from Rome and from the Romanists would come the misleading and aggravating canons and decretals and the whole crawling mass of human laws and regulations. These have now drowned the whole world and swallowed up this epistle and all the holy scriptures, as well as the Spirit and faith. Nothing else remains than their god, the belly, whose servants St. Paul rebukes here. God deliver us from them. Amen.

PREFACE TO THE GERMAN WRITINGS

Editors' Introduction: Over his objections a group of Luther's friends in Strasbourg began to organize his collected works, which would eventually become the Wittenberg edition, published by Caspar Cruciger and Georg Rörer. The German collection for which this is the preface appeared in 1539. The collected works in Latin appeared in 1545. The complete German and Latin works were finally published in 1559.[1]

In this preface Luther begins by commending the Bible to his readers and insisting that he translated the Bible into the vernacular German so that it and not his books would be accessible to all. He had labored hard to put the word of God into the everyday language of the German people so that hearing and reading the scriptures would inform their biblical spirituality. He considered the gospel more as an oral message *(mundhaus)* than as a literary text *(federhaus)*.

In this preface Luther also provides three rules for the practice of theology that he learned from Psalm 119: prayer, meditation, and overcoming the assaults of the devil.[2] First, one must distrust one's own ability to reason and submit oneself to prayer from the heart, so that one will understand the scriptures through Christ by the Holy Spirit. Second, one must meditate by using all one's senses, especially that of repetitive hearing, to experience the external word for understanding. Third, one does not fully experience the sweetness of the word and become a theologian unless one suffers the assaults of the devil. Only when one suffers the assaults of the devil through temptation can one truly become a theologian.

Finally, Luther mocks himself and all those who take pride in their written accomplishments by depicting himself and other scholars as braying donkeys, compared to those who humble themselves.

* * *

I would have been glad to see my books remain altogether in obscurity and sink into oblivion, because, among other reasons, I shudder at the example I am setting. I can well see what use it has been for the church to collect numerous books and large libraries in addition to and besides the holy scripture and indiscriminately store all sorts of writings, especially of the church fathers, councils, and teachers. Through that practice not only is precious time for studying scripture wasted, but the pure knowledge of God's word is forever lost as well, until (as happened in the Book of Deuteronomy in the time of the kings of Judah) the Bible is left forgotten in the dust under a bench (2 Kgs 22:8).

Although it is useful that some of the writings of the fathers and councils have survived as witnesses and histories, I still think that "there is a reason why things happen" *(Est modus in rebus)*, and thus it is not so bad that many of the books of the fathers and councils, by God's grace, have been lost. For if they had all survived, there would be no space left to move for all the books, but they still could not have improved on what one can find in the holy scripture.

What we also had in mind, when we began translating the Bible itself into German, was the hope that writing would decrease and the studying and reading of the scripture would increase. For all other writing should lead into and point toward the scripture, just as John [the Baptist] pointed to Christ, saying, "I must decrease, Christ must increase" (John 3:30), so that each one might drink for himself or herself from the fresh source, as all the fathers had to do if they wanted their work to be done well.

For the councils, church fathers, or we, even with our highest and best achievement, cannot match what God has done in the holy scripture. Even if we ourselves possess the Holy Spirit, faith, godly speech, and works in order to be saved, we must still let the prophets and the apostles stand at the lectern, while we take our places here below at their feet to hear what they have to say. It is not they who must hear what we say.

Now I really cannot prevent my books from being collected (with little honor to me) against my will for publication, and I shall have to let them risk the expense and labor involved. I comfort myself with the thought that in time my books will also end up lying somewhere forgotten in the dust, especially if (by God's grace) I have written anything good. "I will not be better than my fathers" *(Non ero melior Patribus meis)*; what comes later is best forgotten first. For if one could let the Bible itself lie under a bench, and if the writings of the fathers and councils become better when more quickly forgotten, then there is good hope that, once the overly curious zeal of this time has been sated, my books shall not long remain. Especially now, it has started snowing and raining books and teachers that already lie there decaying and forgotten so that one no longer even remembers their names. These, you can be sure, certainly hoped they would always have many of their books dominating the market and the churches.

Very well, let it happen in God's name, except that I make this friendly request: if you want to have my books at this time, do not, on pain of death, let them hinder you from studying the scriptures themselves. Rather, place them at your disposal, the way I do the pope's decretals and excretals and the books of the Sophists. That is, I occasionally look at what they have done, or I read about and ponder the history of the time. I do not study them or feel that I have to follow precisely what they thought, and I do not treat the writings of the fathers and councils much differently.

In this matter I follow the example of St. Augustine, who, among other things, was the first and about the only one who, refusing to be absorbed by all the books of the fathers and saints, wanted to be subject to the holy scriptures alone. This brought him into sharp conflict with St. Jerome, who reproached him with the books of his ancestors, but he did not at all care to follow them. And if one had followed St. Augustine's example, the pope would not have become the Antichrist, and the innumerable noxious books, like squirming and worming insects, would not have found their way into the church, and the Bible would probably have remained on the pulpit.

Beyond that, I want to point you toward a correct way to study theology that I have myself practiced. If you keep to it as well, you would also become so learned that you yourself could write books (if it became necessary) as good as those of the fathers and the councils. Just so, I myself (in God) presumptuously and without arrogance and lying am permitted to boast that, when it concerns the writing of books, I do not stand very far behind some of the fathers.

When it comes to my life, however, I cannot boast to be equal at all. This is the prescription[3] that the saintly King David teaches in Psalm 119 (and was practiced without a doubt by all the patriarchs and prophets). In it you will find three rules, richly presented throughout the whole psalm. They are prayer, meditation, and trial (*oratio, meditatio, tentatio*).

First of all, you need to know that the holy scripture is the kind of book that makes the wisdom of all other books into foolishness, since none of them teaches about eternal life except this alone. Therefore, you should immediately take no hope from your own reason and understanding. With them you will not reach eternal life. On the contrary, by such presumption you and others with you will plunge from heaven into the abyss of hell, as happened to Lucifer. Instead, kneel down in your little room and pray to God with true humility and sincerity that God through the dear Son might give you the Holy Spirit, who will enlighten and direct you and give you understanding.

As you see, David in the above-mentioned psalm always prays, "Teach me, Lord, instruct me, lead me, show me," and uses many other words like these. Even though he knew the text of Moses and many other books well and daily heard and read them, he still wanted to have God, the true master of scripture, there, in order to be certain not to fall into the trap of reason and become his own teacher. For that is what creates schismatics, who allow themselves to believe that the scriptures have been subjugated under them and are easily grasped by reason, as if they were Markolf[4] or Aesop's fables, which need neither Holy Spirit nor prayer to understand.

Next you should meditate, not only in your heart but externally, aloud, so that, in constantly repeating the words, you can compare your oral words with the ones written literally, contrasting them, as it were, reading and rereading them, with diligent attention and reflection in order to understand what the Holy Spirit means by them. And be on guard that you do not become satisfied and start to think that, after reading it once or twice, you have read, heard, and spoken it enough and have now gotten to the bottom of it and understood it. For you will never be a very good theologian that way, but you will be like untimely fruit, which falls from the stem before it has become half ripe.

Therefore, in the same psalm you see how David, day and night and forever, continually boasts that he wishes to speak, compose, say, sing, hear, and read nothing but the word of God alone and the commandments. For God does not want to give you the Holy Spirit without the external word. Orient yourself according to it, because God did not command you in vain to write, preach, read, listen, sing, and say, etc., externally.

Third, there is trial, that is, assault. It is the acid test that does not merely teach you to know and understand but also consciously to experience how right, how authentic, how sweet, how lovely, how powerful, how comforting God's word is, wisdom above all wisdom.

That is why you see David in the mentioned psalm lamenting about all kinds of enemies, godless rulers and tyrants, false spirits, and schismatics, whom he must suffer because he meditates, that is, because he is dealing with God's word (as said) in a variety of ways in this rule. For as soon as the word of God rises up within you, the devil will track you down and afflict you. [This will] make a real doctor of you and, by making you suffer such devilish assaults, will teach you to look for and love God's word. For I myself (if I, mouse dirt that I am, might mingle myself with pepper) have a great deal to thank my papists for, because they beat, belted, pressed, and frightened me so through the rampaging of the devil that they made a rather good theologian out of me, which I otherwise would not have become. And for what they have thus won against me, I gladly, indeed, from the heart, grant them the honor, victory and triumph, because that is what they so much wanted.

Look, there you have David's rules. If, according to his example, you study well, then in the same psalm you will also sing and boast with him, "The law of your mouth is better to me than thousands of gold and silver pieces" (Ps 119:72). Also: "Your commandment makes me wiser than my enemies, for it is always with me. I have more understanding than all my teachers, for your decrees are my meditation. I understand more than the aged, for I keep your precepts, etc." (Ps 119:98–100). And then you will experience how stale and rotten the books of the fathers taste in comparison. You will not only despise the books of your opponents but yours as well; the longer you both write and teach, the less will you please yourself. When you have arrived at this point, then hope with confidence that you have started to become a true theologian, who can teach not only the younger, more immature Christians, but also the maturing and perfect ones. For the church of Christ has all sorts of Christians in it, young, old, weak, sick, healthy, strong, fresh, rotten, gullible, wise, etc.

However, you may sense and let yourself believe that you have arrived, and you may flatter yourself because of your own little books, teaching and writing as if what you have done is very precious and your preaching excellent. It may please you very much to be praised before others; perhaps you even yearn to be praised, or else you would grieve and quit. If you fit that description, my friend, then reach up and grab your ears, and, if you grab them just right, you will find a beautiful pair of big, long, hairy donkey ears. Then do not spare any expense, but decorate them with golden bells, so that, wherever you go, they can hear you and point their fingers at you and say, "Look, look, there goes that fine animal, who can write such precious books and preach so excellently well." Then you will be blessed and more than blessed in the kingdom of heaven—yes, in that heaven where the devil and all his angels have prepared hellfire for you. To summarize, let us seek honor and be arrogant as much as we like; in this book the glory belongs to God alone. And that means: God opposes the proud but gives grace to the humble *(Deus superbis resistit, humilibus autem dat gratiam).* To whom be the glory forever and ever *(Cui est gloria in secula seculorum).* Amen.

PSALM 117:
THE ART THAT CANNOT
BE MASTERED

Editors' Introduction: This commentary on Psalm 117,[1] printed by George Rhaw in the middle of October 1530, is a revision of an earlier version that Luther had published at the Coburg (his desert). It is dedicated to Hans von Sternberg, who had taken a pilgrimage to the Holy Land and had told Luther about it. This commentary represents Luther's critique of medieval spirituality, including an account of his own pilgrimage to Rome. He recommends instead a pilgrimage through the gospels, psalms, and other parts of the holy scriptures—a spirituality of the word—and he commends his own practice of daily devotions, proclaiming himself a student of the catechism.

Luther also affirms the goodness of temporal government and its laws and the spirituality of everyday work. The monastic life is not superior to all the crafts, ways of life, and trades that exist.[2] Monasteries should be preserved as schools, as they were founded, he argues, to raise young Christian persons, teaching the faith and discipline in order to prepare excellent candidates for Christian offices. The life of the baptized is like being under a heaven or kingdom of grace that the devil and sin can sometimes cloud. In this commentary, written in German, the late-medieval development toward a democratization and secularization of spirituality is complete.[3]

Luther is not unaware of the irony that he has written such a long commentary on the shortest psalm in the psalter. We have included a significant portion of the commentary in this volume because tucked away in it are devotional and spiritual insights that are typical of Luther. In this psalm one finds the spirituality that derives from his theology of the cross. God is often found in the

125

lowest and most difficult places for us, that is, places of suffering where one is least likely to expect the Almighty One to be.[4]

* * *

Praise the Lord, all you nations!
Extol him, all you peoples!
For great is his steadfast love toward us,
and the faithfulness of the Lord endures forever.
Praise the Lord!

To the worshipful and honorable Hans von Sternberg, Knight, my gracious lord and friend.[5]

Grace and peace to you from Christ our Lord. Your Worship and Honor, gracious lord and friend:

Recently I published a booklet on Psalm 117, but, from haste and poor planning, it became unwieldy and went out bald and naked. I put it back through the forge again and improved it (although not much) so that it might be better dressed, more pleasing, and more useful. For it is worthy of holy scripture that, whenever one can, one must richly honor and adorn it so that it might attract lovers, because it has enough enemies and persecutors as it is.

I wanted to publish this booklet under your name, not only to gain the respect of those who disdain knowledge and teaching, but also as testimony that there are still some fine people among the nobility. For most of the nobility these days behave in such a sacrilegious and scandalous fashion that they create bad blood among the common people and arouse suspicion that the nobility as a whole is useless. Such suspicion among the people is dangerous, for it is not good that so little thought and respect should be accorded those who are supposed to rule in the world. The devil could well find time and opportunity from such, as happened with Müntzer and his revolt.[6]

We still recall the clergy who sat tight and lived so scandalously that the whole world despised them. They never thought it possible that they could be so despised and brought low, but, nevertheless, it did happen, and they will never regain the honor they once had. The nobility are following this pattern, and I am concerned that things will turn out the same for them, and they will inherit the fate of the clergy if things continue as they are. God does not lie when declaring,

"Those who despise me shall be treated with contempt" [1 Sam 2:30]. The nobles think that, because they are getting away with it, there is no emergency. They are defiant and insolent with both God and the people; they despise God's word, teachings, and honor. But just as God surprised the clergy, God will also catch up with the nobility. God is big enough and will give them such a beating and pounding that they will fade away like ashes in the wind.

If they wish to be held in honor and feared, they must similarly honor and fear God so as to have a good and virtuous reputation among the people. Otherwise, if they want to bluff their way with vanity, defiance, and pride, despising virtue and honor, the nobility will soon become peasants. In truth they are peasants, who only strut about as long as they can in the feathers and under the name of the nobility. God is a master who humbles the proud and causes the despisers to be despised, having no patience with them.

Now, lest this vile impression have too strong an impact, it is important to praise those nobles who are worthy of praise. God always provides that each estate God has founded has some who are upright and just, few though they may be, to ensure that creation and good order are not in vain, even if there is only one Lot in Sodom. What estate on earth is so good that the majority is not wicked? When one considers people individually, one gets the impression that the whole estate is useless. If one comes up with a few upright ones, it is nonetheless annoying to have to suffer so many evil and destructive ones in order to find these few.

Therefore, since God our Heavenly Father has endowed you with due earnestness and love for God's holy word and every virtue, I did not want to neglect to praise and laud this grace of God in you (for it is by God's grace and not your merit). I did this in order that some of the misbehaving and unruly nobles would be moved by your example to strive to act like nobles and not like peasants or pigs. As long as they want to be regarded as highest in the world, they are obligated to be examples of honor and virtue for their subjects. God demands it of them and will repay them for the evil that is produced by their offensive and scandalous lives. Even if I fail to accomplish all this, I nevertheless want to help correct the damaging impression that the nobility—or any other estate, for that matter—is useless; rather, God has a share in each and will get interest.

I wish that this and similar booklets will please you and that your heart will find in it a better and holier pilgrimage than the one you made to Jerusalem. Not that I want to disparage that, for I should like to take such a trip myself, but I cannot do that anymore. Still, I gladly hear and read about such pilgrimages, just as I recently listened eagerly to your account with such pleasure and attention. Nevertheless, we have not made such pilgrimages in the proper spirit. For instance, when I was in Rome, I was such a holy one that I ran through all the churches and crypts and believed all the stinking lies. I even performed one pilgrimage, doing about ten masses in Rome, when I was almost sorry that my father and mother were still living, for I would have loved to have freed them from the fires of purgatory with my masses and other excellent works and prayers. There is a saying in Rome that goes like this: Blessed is the mother whose son performs a mass on Saturday at St. John's. How I would have loved to redeem my mother, but the crowds pressed on too hard, and I could not get in, so I ate a smoked herring instead.[7]

Well, that is what we used to do; we did not know any better, and the Holy See did not punish such gross lies. Now, however, thanks be to God, we have the gospels, psalms, and other parts of the holy scriptures, to which we can make pilgrimages with profit and salvation. We want to see and visit the proper blessed land, the true Jerusalem—yes, the true paradise and heaven—not via the physical locations of the saints, their graves, but by gazing through their hearts, thoughts, and spirits. With this I commend you and yours to God. Forgive me my chatter, but it is a joy to see and to listen to upright nobility, since the noise of the others is so great. God help us all.

Out of the wilderness on the Saturday after St Bartholomew's Day, 1530.

Psalm 117[8]

This is a brief and delicate psalm, and it is without a doubt written in this fashion so that everyone can attend to it and retain what it says. No one can complain about its length or mass, much less about the sharpness, loftiness, or depth of the message. The words are short, fine, bright, and plain and can be understood by everyone who pays attention and wants to reflect on them. The word of God demands that we do not race over it and think that, by doing so, we have completely grounded ourselves in understanding it, as superficial, overstuffed, and bored souls do. When they hear the word of God once, they think it an old thing and long for something new, as if they understood everything they have heard. This is truly a dangerous plague and an evil and malicious trick of the devil. Through it the devil makes people self-assured, inflexible, and presumptuous, opening them to all manner of error and raising turmoil among them. This is the vice described as *acedia*, sloth in service to God, against which St. Paul exhorts in Rom 12[:11], namely, that we be "ardent in spirit." In Revelation 3[:15–16] the spirit speaks about it in this way: "I wish that you were either cold or hot. So, because you are lukewarm, and neither cold nor hot, I am about to spit you out of my mouth." Truly, these half-educated people are the most useless people on earth, and it would be better if they knew nothing at all. They do not listen to anyone, and they know everything better than anyone else in the world and think they can make judgments about all art and literature. They cannot teach anyone anything properly and will not learn from anyone. They have devoured the whole schoolbag that no one can master, and yet there is not one book in it that they could properly teach others. The devil now has such wicked people particularly among the rabble. The most common bungler who hears a sermon or who can read a chapter in German makes himself into a doctor and, crowning himself an ass, convinces himself that now he can do everything better than his teachers. He is called Master Smart Aleck, who bridles a horse's rear end. All of this is as a result, I say, of reading or hearing God's word in a superficial way and not paying attention with fear, humility, and diligence.

I myself have often experienced just such a demonic attack, and even today I cannot protect myself enough with the sign of the cross. I confess this freely as an example for whomever it pleases, as now I am an old doctor of theology and preacher and certainly can or should do as much in the study of the scriptures as all these wise ones. However, I have to become as a child and early every morning recite by mouth the Lord's Prayer, the Ten Commandments, the creed, and my favorite psalms and scripture verses, just as one teaches and trains children to do. Daily I need to struggle with the scriptures and fight with the devil. I dare not say in my heart, "The Lord's Prayer is old-fashioned, you already know the commandments, you know the creed by heart," etc. No, rather I learn from it daily and remain a pupil of the catechism.⁹ I feel too that this really helps me, and I know from experience that God's word can never be completely mastered but that what Psalm 147 says about it is true, namely, "his understanding is beyond measure" [Ps 147:5], or Ecclesiasticus, "Those who drink of me will thirst for more" [Sir 24:21]. Now if it goes like this for me, what will happen to those self-assured, overstuffed, self-satisfied charlatans who neither fight nor labor?

Therefore, I maintain there is no one who can know everything that the Holy Spirit says in this short psalm. If they had to proclaim or teach something from this psalm, they would not know where to begin. In order to shame these evil people and to honor the word of God, I have decided to interpret this psalm myself. I would like people to see both how clear and common it is and how it is nonetheless unfathomable. Even if it seems obvious (which it is not), nonetheless in virtue and power it is unfathomable, and it always renews and creates a clean heart and refreshes, washes, comforts, and strengthens us without end. I see and learn daily how the beloved prophets studied the Ten Commandments from where their sermons and prophecies had their sources and springs. Let us now divide this psalm into four parts—prophecy, revelation, instruction, and admonition.

*Prophecy*¹⁰

With a few short words the psalmist prophesies and announces the mighty work and wonder of God, namely, the gospel and the reign of Christ, which are at the same time promised but not revealed. The psalmist writes, "Praise the Lord, all you nations!" This is to say that God is the God not only of the Jews but of nations and not of just a few but of all nations over the whole world. For when the psalmist mentions all nations, none is excluded. In this way those of us from the nations are confident and sure that we also belong to God in heaven.

TEACHING THE NEW SPIRITUALITY

On the Revelation

This psalm also reveals a great and peculiar mystery that few discovered at the time of the apostles and that now under the papacy has nearly disappeared, namely, that the reign of Christ is not a temporal, transitory, earthly reign governed with laws and regulations. On the contrary, it is a spiritual, heavenly, and eternal reign that must be governed above all without laws, regulations, and outward means. Here the nations are told to remain the nations, as I pointed out above. They are not expected to leave their lands and go up to Jerusalem, or to put away their temporal regulations, customs, and manners to become Jews. By the same token, God does not expect the Jews to give up their laws. God expects something higher and entirely different from outward, temporal rules, laws, or ceremonies. Every land and city can keep and alter its own rules. God does ask that law keeping not hinder God's reign. God's word says here, "Praise God, all nations." The nations include those who live in lands and cities, as I said above. Lands and cities cannot exist or survive without regulations, customs, and local rules, so that they can govern, judge, punish, protect, and maintain the peace. They may change these things on occasion, but they cannot get along without them.

When we hear about nations and kings in the scriptures, we cannot think only of the person with the crown, but we must consider the whole government with its laws, offices, ordinances, customs, usages, and habits by which their reigns are maintained and managed. Otherwise, what would become of kings and lords? They would be false kings, or painted lords, as we find in Psalm 72 (10): "The kings from the sea coast and the islands will bring gifts." Yes, with these words the Holy Spirit legitimizes the worldly ordinances and government of all lands and calls them kings. By this we are to understand that they are to retain their authority and that everyone should be subject and obedient to one's king and lord [cf. Rom 13:1–7]. God does not punish them for being kings or nations or peoples. God created them, established them, and divided the world among them to be governed, as St. Paul attests in Acts 17[:26]. If God wanted to rebuke or punish them, they would not have been addressed as kings, nations, or peoples, but by other words. Since God names and establishes them as kings and nations, we should all the more let them be kings and nations, that is, nations or worldly authorities, and honor them as such.

At the same time, in such temporal governments, according to their own laws, God establishes all the crafts, ways of life (estates), and trades that exist—call them what you wish, as long as they are honest and praiseworthy. People may be citizens, farmers, shoemakers, tailors, clerks, knights, masters, servants, etc.; for without such, as Ecclesiasticus says, no city or land could exist [Sir 38:32]. We are to understand that these ways of life are not inherently against the will of God, and one should not abandon them to serve God by crawling into a monastery or establishing a sect.[11] Rather, these are all ways of life set up by God for God's service, according to Genesis 3[:19], "By the sweat of your face you shall eat bread." God wants these words upheld.

What God in the psalm expects from nations and peoples is very different. The psalm does not say, "Do your crafts, all nations," because this is what is demanded in Genesis 3, as was said above. It does not satisfy God that you become a Carthusian,[12] a monk, a nun, or pope. This pleases God even less than the lowliest manual labor on earth. God rejects and condemns these self-chosen ways of life because they flee, avoid, and despise what is demanded of all people in Genesis 3, namely, the sweat of one's face. They act as if they can devise a better service to God than what God established by the sweat of our faces—just as clever and rascally reason always wants to master and get the advantage of God.

What is it that God expects? It is to praise the Lord. Oh, this is a huge expectation, and, as the world understands and interprets these things, it is an unbearable and insufferable levy and tax. As such, this psalm becomes the most heretical and poisonous sermon ever to descend upon the earth....[13]

Thus in our day it should also happen to the monasteries and convents that they be torn apart and torn down, as has already begun, despite their seeming to be a fine and beautiful good.[14] [The monasteries and convents] also blaspheme the Lord of the nations, whom they should praise and whom they cannot bear. Yet they have to lift up and praise their own works and habits as if they want not merely to be Christians and be saved but want to be higher and better than the ordinary Christian. Moreover, they sell and share with them the works and merits of other Christians and understand themselves to be helping them to gain heaven. All of this is an unspeakable abomination, and they do nothing but say with their deeds, "An ordinary, common Christian person is nothing compared to us. The Christian way is much lower than our way. No one can rise to the level we achieve with our tonsures and cowls. A Christian would never be saved if our way of life did not help them."

What is being said other than that baptism means nothing, the blood of Christ counts for nothing, Christ's death and life are nothing, God's word is nothing, even God is nothing? They are better than and above baptism, Christ, and God. For if they considered themselves less than God, they would truly consider themselves less than Christ and his blood. If they considered themselves less than Christ's blood, they would also consider themselves less than baptism, which is blessed with Christ's blood—yes, we baptize in Christ's blood. If they considered themselves less than baptism, they would consider themselves less than average Christians and their way of life. But if they were to hold their way of life lower than that of the ordinary Christian, where would that put them? If they are to stay in their splendid garb and fame, they need to make themselves out to be higher, better, and holier than the average Christian, that is, above all of holy Christianity or the Christian church, above baptism, above Christ's blood, above the Holy Spirit, and even God. Consequently, they praise themselves and thereby blaspheme the Lord of the nations. No one can contradict that they have done this and exalted their way of life over the average Christian way of life. There are letters and books and acts enough to prove it.

If they would preserve their monasteries and convents but use them to raise young Christian persons, teaching the faith and discipline in order to prepare excellent persons for Christian offices, if they were simply Christian schools as they were originally founded, and if they called the prelates provost, deacon, scholar, cantor, and the like, then they would be fine foundations. However, to consider theirs a way of life better than the ordinary Christian way of life is wrong and denies and curses Christ. They should serve and enhance the Christian way of life, as do schools, upbringing at home, the temporal government, and the rest of creation, but they should not be better or above the Christian way of life. The Christian way of life should hover over everything like heaven over the earth, for it is Christ's own way of life and God's own work. Now, because they do not want to do this, like the stiff-necked Jerusalem they have to be torn apart and torn down. There is nothing else that can be done. One must praise the Lord of all nations and let God be God, or everything will go to wrack and ruin....

Let this be said about the revelation from this psalm. For even today it is a lofty and great insight to know that the Christian way of life is above and beyond all temporal and spiritual regulations, laws, external holiness, government, and whatever else these may be called, whether among the Jews or the nations. St. Paul himself affirms that it came as a revelation even to the apostles that the nations could be God's people without Moses' law and beyond the law. As we read in Acts 10 and 11, St. Peter himself did not know about this until he had a vision from heaven that he needed to visit Cornelius, the pagan; and, as far as I understand, the whole Book of Acts was written—and this psalm and similar passages were written—to witness that the nations could become God's people without the law of Moses.

Acts 15 describes a special council that was held in Jerusalem, where Peter, Paul, and Barnabas stood for this point against the whole collection of the faithful. It is difficult for our reason and nature to understand that temporal and ecclesiastical ways of life are nothing when compared to that of the Christian. Reason always wants to mix the two—to turn the Christian way of life into a temporal or ecclesiastical government and to frame and rule it with laws and works. It forgets that it does not know what the Christian way of life is, as we discovered all too well under the papacy.

It is called a revelation and remains such, as you will not find anything about this in the whole canon law or the laws of all the popes, whether they are called decretals, sextes, clementines, extravagantes, or any other name.[15] In all the summas, in all the writings of the sentences, in all the monks' sermons, in all the canons of the synods, in all the orders of monasteries and convents, in all the rules of all kinds of monks and nuns, in all the postils on the scriptures, in all the articles of the councils, in all of St. Jerome or St. Gregory, in all the questions of the theologians, in the lectures at the universities, in all the masses and vigils, and all the ceremonies of all the churches, in all the foundations for souls, in all the brotherhoods of all the sects, in all the pilgrimages to all places, in all the worship of Mary and all the saints, in all the indulgences and all the bulls, in the chancellery of the pope, in the whole court of the pope, in all the courts of the bishops, nowhere in all of this, I say, will you find a trace of this truth but rather impediments to and perversion of this revelation.

What have the pope and bishops done with the gospel and the Christian church but turn it into an unvarnished ecclesiastical and temporal government? What else are the rebellious spirits, the fanatics, and the foolish saints now looking for but to turn the gospel into an external holiness or a new monasticism in gray coats and a long face?[16] The psalm says, "Praise the Lord, all you nations." Be the nations, remain the nations, become the nations! Found ecclesiastical orders, make rules and codes, make laws and temporal government, be chaste, get married, and whatever you can imagine for the external life, as you wish. But do not imagine that you can become Christians in this way or be saved. Do not think that this can be called Christianity or define the essence of the Christian life, because all of these examples can be accomplished and established by human reason apart from Christ.[17] There is one thing that is higher than all that you can imagine and do, namely, that you praise the Lord. However, the things mentioned above praise yourselves and not the Lord, for these things arise from yourselves and from your reason and are planted and created in your human nature.

The Instruction

With that [the psalmist] teaches the highest wisdom on earth—faith, which is godly, not human, secret, not revealed. It is a heavenly, not an earthly wisdom, which no human being knows, as Paul says, and the rulers of this world do not recognize (1 Cor 2[:8]). Therefore, it must be called the most insidious heresy by the world, the devil's damned instruction. It is an utterly intolerable thing that this psalm sings, "God's goodness thunders over us!" It is supposed to be why the nations should praise God, namely, that they have all their grace and mercy, all goodness from God, purely for free, without any deserving, effort or law. Against that the Jews shout that they have God's law and their own work. St. Paul witnesses to the Romans [2:23], and Psalm 147[:19–20] also says, "[God] declares his word to Jacob, his statutes and ordinances to

Israel. He has not dealt thus with any other nation; they do not know his ordinances." And, it is true, they alone have had the law and the prophets until the time of Christ, as St. Paul says in Romans 3[:2], but after and with Christ all the nations have the gospel, that is, the preaching about grace that this psalm conveys.

There are extraordinarily fine words in this verse, which one should not rush through in a cold and superficial way. First, God speaks "goodness," that is, not our work, holiness, or wisdom, but God's grace and mercy. But what is God's grace? It is that which, out of pure mercy and for the sake of Christ, our dear bishop and mediator, forgives all our sin; assuages all wrath; leads us from idolatry and error to truth; purifies, illumines, hallows, and justifies our hearts with faith and the Holy Spirit; and chooses us to be children and heirs. God embellishes and garlands us with gifts, delivers and protects us from the power of the devil, and, in addition, gives us eternal life and blessedness as a present. Nevertheless, God provides, gives, and still preserves this temporal life with all its necessities through the service and cooperation of all the creatures of heaven and earth. Not a piece of it, not the most insignificant one, could the whole world ever earn, let alone the sum total of them all together. Nor could the great ones earn some of them; indeed, they have deserved pure wrath, death, and hell because of their idolatry, ingratitude, contempt, and all manner of incessant sins.

Where this, however, is true (as it undoubtedly must be), then it surely follows that our work, wisdom, and holiness before God are nothing. For if it is God's goodness, then it is not our deserving. If it is our deserving, then it is not God's goodness (Rom [11:6]). Therefore, the Jews cannot endure with their law and works, and far less can the nations with their idolatry, as far less as the Sophists[18] with the offense of their masses, foundations, monasteries, pilgrimages, and the like, their innumerable human inventions and works. Why do they all persecute this teaching about the grace of God and call it a heresy? They do this because they do not want to have their teaching and work scorned and rejected. For that God's grace gives us so much, as is said, they might perhaps still tolerate; but that their thing should be so utterly nothing and that only pure grace alone counts before God, that has to be heresy. They still want to have a part in the decision and through free will do enough to earn and buy grace from God—as well as all the already mentioned goods—so that it is not God's grace but our merit that first achieves grace. By that [way of thinking], we are the ones who lay the first cornerstone, upon which God later builds God's grace and goodness, so that God must thank, praise, and worship us. Thus it is that they think goodness first began entirely through us, and the foundation for God's grace is built by our merit and deserving.

These people prattle the psalms with their lips, but in their hearts they read and interpret them thus: "The whole world glorifies us, and all the people praise us, because our works reign over you and our teaching shall remain forever." That they read the psalms in this way in their hearts they cannot deny. They witness to it with all the charters and documents of their brotherhood. In these they seal, document, promise, and sell, legally and by right, an unassailable, perpetual sale of their vigils, masses for souls, and all their good works. They share the same with their benefactors, with both their ancestors and their descendants, in order thereby to deliver them from sins and purgatory for eternal bliss as if they had never been baptized or had never been Christian. What has here become of God's prevenient grace, which does such things without works? Ah, it must therefore first be bought by means of strange work.[19] Cannot that be called a blasphemous and offensive substitution and emphasis of our works for and over God's grace? Can that not be called rejecting God's divinity and denying Christ? And they do not wish to repent of this practice and improve their ways, but with hardened hearts they would rather preserve and promote it. But their seals and letters, their indulgences and books are too many and, open to the day, are too mighty a witness against them and will not permit a cover and disguise.

Now choose what you will. This verse can be understood in a threefold way. The first sounds like this: our own works reign over us and have precedence over the grace of God. Another: our work is efficacious without Christ, but nonetheless beside the grace of God above us. The third: God's grace through Christ reigns over us without and for all works. The first two are invented by Jews, Turks, Sophists, and all false Christians out of their own heads. The third interpretation is that of the Holy Spirit and of all true Christians. That the first two are also those of the Sophists...is proven not only by their legal letters, seals, indulgences, and books, but also by action, for they defend their same work and on its account murder, burn, and persecute people in the most heinous way. For if they held the third interpretation to be true, then they would not only have to abstain from persecution, but also have to change and improve all their foundations, monasteries, and their whole nature, because they have been accustomed to doing nothing in the past but selling their works to the people in order to deliver them from sins and bring them to heaven. That cannot be denied, because I myself and we all have been stuck in this scandal and have helped teach and do it. But praise be to God who helped us get out of it.

Moreover, it says "endures"; that is, it reigns over us. Grace commands and rules *(Imperat et regnat gratia)*. It is a kingdom of grace that is more powerful in and over us than all wrath, sin, and evil. This word has never yet been understood by the Sophist or the works righteous. They are as incapable of understanding it as a Jew or Turk, because, as they want to come beforehand with works and achieve grace, it is impossible for them to know what is called the kingdom of grace, the kingdom of heaven, or the kingdom of Christ. For their hearts must stand as mine stood for me, when I was a Sophist: when they do good, they have grace. When they sin or fall or feel sin, then grace falls as well and is lost. Then by their own works they must look for it and find it again, and they cannot think differently about it. But that is not a kingdom of grace that reigns over works, but a kingdom of works that reigns over grace. But "to endure," *Gabar* in Hebrew, here means "to prevail" and "to have the upper hand" and "to be powerful." Thus, you have to conceive of the kingdom of grace in a more childlike way. That is, through the gospel, God has built a great new heaven over those of us who believe, and it is called the heaven of grace; and it is much bigger and more beautiful than this visible heaven, and, beyond that, it is eternal, certain, and everlasting.

Now whoever is under this heaven cannot sin or be in sin, because it is a heaven of grace, without end and eternal. Someone who sins or falls would not thereby fall out from underneath this heaven, unless that person did not want to remain under it, preferring to travel to hell with the devil, the way the ungodly do. Sin may make itself felt and death flash its teeth and the devil give fright, but here there is far more grace, which wields power over all sin. And there is far more life, which has power over death, and far more of God, who overpowers all the devils. Therefore, sin, death, and devil are nothing more in this kingdom than a dark cloud under the lovely sky; the cloud may well cover the heavens for a while, but it cannot rule over it. The cloud must remain below the heavens and allow the heavens to remain above it and have power and govern it; and, finally, it has to pass away. Thus, the bite of sin, the threat of death, and the devil's attacks of temptation are still mere clouds over which the heaven of grace rules and prevails. They must submit to that grace and finally retreat. Such things cannot happen through works but through faith alone, which brings certainty that this heaven of grace is above one without works, and one can gaze upon it as often as one sins or feels sin and comfort oneself that way, without either merit or work.

Those who would like to render sins and death harmless through works will necessarily find the following happen to them. That is, because it is impossible to recognize all sins [Ps 19:12]—indeed it is the lesser part that they can recognize—the devil and God's judgment will reveal those sins that they cannot know or recognize. Then inevitably the conscience will take fright and say, "Oh, Lord God, about this sin I have never done anything." For it had intended to make satisfaction for sins through works, and now here it is suddenly overcome by so many and such great sins that it never even knew about, let alone made satisfaction for.

So the conscience must despair. Then the devil adds more fuel to the fire by changing all the good works into sins. Where now can the conscience go? It does not know about God's kingdom of grace, that God's goodness reigns over us, and it is not accustomed to trust in God's grace. Then both works and the teaching of works are crushed and vanish like smoke. Yes, it is fine to speak of works and satisfaction as a way of profiting, so long and until the moment comes when the devil and God's judgment touch the conscience. Then one discovers how dangerous, poisonous, harmful, and condemning such teaching is, but at that point one has tarried too long, unless God performs special signs and wonders.

But whoever is in the kingdom of grace has a heart set in the following way. Whether it feels real sin or not; whether the devil invented the sin or not, takes one's good works and reduces them to nothing or leaves them alone; whether God's judgment threatens or frightens, it speaks in this way: "Those may well be dark and bitter clouds, but God's grace endures and reigns over us. The heaven of grace is mightier than the cloud cover of sin. The heaven of grace remains eternally, while the clouds of sin pass away." For this verse does not deny, indeed it confesses, that believers feel God's judgment, sin, death, and the devil and are also frightened by them. But to counter that, it says that they have a comfort, and grace prevailed and kept the upper hand and remained in authority, so that they can sing, "Praise to the Lord that God's grace reigns over us and is mightier than our sin, etc." Behold, that happens without works and has to happen without works; otherwise, both grace and heaven would be lost in the twinkling of an eye. As David was often tempted and laments in Psalm 119[:92], "If your law had not been my delight, I would have perished in my misery." But whoever has not experienced temptation does not know anything about it and will probably be compelled to attack sins with works in order to make satisfaction for them and to suppress them. That is nothing more than trying to put out a fire with straw or measure the wind with bushel baskets or do other such wasted and self-destructive work.

Third, the psalm says "toward us." Who are they, the ones from whom the psalmist separates himself by using this word, "us," from all others who are not with us? That is, as said above, over poor sinners who know and feel themselves to be stuck in sin, death, and all manner of misfortune? They are the works righteous, because they do not stand in need of grace; they do not see in themselves sin, death, or the devil, but pure holiness, life, and the kingdom of heaven. They are the innocent child! The other children can't "tell on them"; they are as pure as the driven snow. Because of that, this verse can be taken in two false, lying ways. First, that to our enemies, our part— that is, our teaching and faith, such as it is—is not God's grace, but purely the teaching of the devil and must be God's wrath. The other, that our outward nature cannot be viewed in any other way than that God is our enemy and has given us over to the devil, that both life and teaching cannot be looked upon in any other way than that it is the devil that reigns over us and not God's grace.

Then again, over there by our enemies, it seems to them as if God is their friend and reigns over both their teaching and their life.

Therefore, both of these words have to be understood spiritually, with faith in the spirit alone, and should not be judged according to outward appearances; otherwise, this psalm turns into pure temptation and lies. Because the eyes find it to be different in reality, very different from the way these words sound. They could be changed to read thus: "Howl and blaspheme, all you nations, for God's wrath and rage reign over us eternally, without ceasing, forever...."

Fourth, the psalmist says, "And God's faithfulness," that is God's truth, which pledges and binds the divine self to us through the dear word that God wants to be our God and not deflect such divine grace from us. Thus, we can rely securely on the promise that, as God began it, so it shall always remain and reign. This is in order that we should not doubt God's promise, even though it seems to be so different outwardly to the eyes, as mentioned, which see pure wrath and no grace. For God wishes to be faithful and to maintain a tight grip over God's promise, if we on our side also hold tight, cling firmly with our faith, and do not fall away because of faithlessness and impatience. It is only about a little patient waiting while we carry the cross and not getting tired and weary. "And hope will not disgrace us,"[20] as St. Paul says in Romans 5[:5]. And God cannot lie (Rom 3[:4] and Titus 1[:2]). Therefore, we have to learn that the above-mentioned goodness and grace are not visible. The cross and the contradiction are what is visible.[21] That is what we feel. Our adversaries have outward goodness and grace, even though they do not know it. And they pay much less attention to the secret wrath by which God threatens them through the divine word.

Thus this kingdom of grace remains a secret, hidden kingdom to the world, contained in the word and in faith until the time of its revelation. Therefore the ungodly do not want it or like it but say in Psalm 2[:3], "Let us burst their bonds asunder and cast their cords from us." We will not tolerate such a kingdom to reign over us, they say. Luke 19[:14], "We do not want this man to rule over us." Why not? Such a kingdom, as mentioned above, condemns and rejects the whole of their own external doing and nature, upon which they trust, and challenges them to trust in God's grace alone, which, hidden and in secret, can be grasped only through God's word of promise and with faith. Therefore, instead of praise and thanks, they practice pure blasphemy, cursing, and persecution against the lovely kingdom of grace, like people without sense who fight and rage wildly against their own welfare and salvation until they are ruined, having attained what they were fighting for. As Psalm 109[:17] says: "He loved to curse; let curses come on him. He did not like blessing; may it be far from him." *Volenti non fit iniuria.* (An injury is not an injury when someone accepts it voluntarily.) One cannot force someone to be grateful.[22]

Now the same thing that happens with grace also happens with faithfulness and the truth of God. Grace appears outwardly as if it were pure wrath, so deeply does it lie hidden under two thick hides or fur covers, namely, that our opponents and the world damn and avoid this grace as if it were a plague and the wrath of God, and we in ourselves do not feel any different, which is probably why St. Peter says, "the word alone shines upon us as in a dark place" (2 Pet 1[:19]).[23] Yes, certainly in a dark place![24]

Therefore, God's faithfulness and truth must always forever first become a big lie before it is changed into truth. To the world it is called heresy. So we also perpetually think to ourselves that God will forsake us and not keep God's word to us, and God begins to seem a liar in our hearts. Ultimately, God cannot be God unless God becomes the devil beforehand; and we cannot come into heaven unless we have first gone to hell; and we cannot become children of God unless we have first become the children of the devil. For whatever God says and does, the devil has to have said and done. Our very flesh perceives it that way, but the spirit in the word illuminates and sustains us and teaches us to believe differently. Then again, on the other hand, the lies of the world cannot become lies unless they have first become the truth; the godless do not go to hell unless they have first gone to heaven, and they do not become children of the devil unless they were first God's children.

In summary,[25] the devil is not and does not become the devil without first being God. The devil does not become an angel of darkness without first being an angel of light. What the devil says and does must have been said and done by God; that is what the world believes, and it motivates us ourselves on the whole as well. That is why this is spoken highly, and a higher understanding must be here for God's grace and truth, or goodness and faithfulness, to reign over us and prevail. It is comforting to whoever can grasp it to be certain that it is God's grace and faithfulness, even though it allows itself to be seen differently. And then that person can say with spiritual assurance, "All right, I surely know that first God's word must become a big lie even in myself before it becomes truth."

Then again I know that the devil's word must first become the tender truth of God before it becomes a lie. I must allow the devil his pleasure for a moment of godliness and allow devilishness to be ascribed to our God. But with that all days have not yet drawn into evening. Finally, it is still written, "God's goodness and faithfulness endure forever."

Fifth, the psalm says "eternally" or "forever," "without ceasing and without end," because this kingdom of grace will reign and endure, not only here on earth for this lifetime, but also eternally after this life there in heaven. Moreover, it will be so strong in this life that it can never be moved or fall. For even if we are uncertain and might stumble and fall at times because of sin and error, grace does not fall and sway the same way, and you should not seek a new grace or another kingdom. For up there heaven still remains open, and the same kingdom of grace waits for me when I return. It does not turn out, as some lie and deceive, that Christ made satisfaction only for prior sins, the sins that happened before baptism, while, for future sins following that, we ourselves have to make satisfaction. Nor is it as St. Jerome says, doubtfully and badly, that penance is the other plank to which one must cling when the ship of innocence after baptism has broken up. Do not mention the other plank to me; the ship does not break up, baptism does not stop, the kingdom of grace does not fall, but, as the psalm here says, "It reigns or endures eternally over us." If I fall out of the ship, all right, I'll climb back in; if I turn away from baptism, all right, then I'll turn back to it; if I stray from the kingdom of grace, all right, I'll come back into it. Baptism, ship, and grace endure forever and do not fall or shake by my falling or shaking. Otherwise, God's divine self would also have to fall, and God has promised to sustain such grace forever.

Concerning Admonition

There in the psalm it admonishes us—yes, also teaches us— how we should serve God, and it calls upon us to give glory and praise. For when we consider that we have nothing from ourselves, but everything from God, it is good to recognize that we can give God nothing; nor can we pay or return anything for divine grace. Nor does God require anything from us. Therefore, the only part that remains is that we give God glory and praise. First, in our heart, we have to acknowledge and believe this, that we have everything from God, and God is our God. After that, we have to go out and with our mouths freely confess it before the world, preach, praise, and give glory and thanks. That is the true and only service to God [or worship], the true priestly office, and the loving, pleasing sacrifice, as St. Peter says in 1 Peter 2[:9], "You are a royal priesthood that you may proclaim the mighty acts of him who called you out of darkness into his marvelous light."

The world tries to shut our mouths when we give such glory. The world does not want to and cannot hear it. But one has to risk that, if one wants to bring God this sacrifice, because it is written, "Praise the Lord, all you nations." It does not say, "Praise the people or the world," but "the Lord and God's work or grace"—not human works, which it rather more condemns.

With this sacrifice of praise and offering of thanks, all the service of God and the sacrifice of the Old Testament are fulfilled, so that they are required no more. For this psalm imposes on the nations no other service to God than praise and thanksgiving, confessing and preaching God's grace and faithfulness....

Yes, they say, but both godly and worldly laws teach that what one vows one should also keep. Answer: There are two kinds of vows, one pledged to God and the other pledged to humans. We cannot pledge anything to God except that we will hold God to be God, thanking and glorifying God for all God's good deeds and grace. As the holy patriarch Jacob speaks and pledges in Genesis 28[:21], "The Lord shall be my God," which is the pledge that the first commandment also requires. For we can give God nothing; nor does God need what is ours, and that is certain because God gave it to us first. But God would like to be our God. That is why the Sophists do not understand the verses in the psalter and in the scripture about vows made before God. They interpret them as self-chosen vows, even though pure thank-you vows and obedience to the first commandment are meant. As the psalm [116:12–14] says, "What shall I return to the Lord for all his bounty to me? I will lift up the cup of salvation and call on the name of the Lord. I will pay my vows in the presence of all his people."

There you see that the psalmist knows nothing about returning something to the Lord other than that he calls on and thanks God before all the people and thus wishes to keep the pledge according to the first commandment. The psalmist calls it "the cup of salvation"; that is, it saves, as Psalm 50[:23] also says, "Thank offerings praise me, and that is the way I show you my salvation."[26] And Romans 10[:9], "If you confess with your lips, you will be saved." The word *cup* in the scripture means each one's part and wishes to say, "Some want to buy God with works, and I let them have their part and their way, which is a cup of destruction. My cup, my portion, shall be to praise God, which is wholeness and salvation."

Now, where pledges conflict with these thanksgiving pledges, as now all the monasteries and the other above-mentioned pledges [or vows] do, they should be condemned and cease. For they all take place out of the godless and damned impression that one will win God and earn grace with them, and they do not want to have pure and unearned grace. For the pope himself says, "*In malis promissis non expedit servare fidem*," that is, "One should not keep evil pledges." So too, when one pledges anything to people, the reservation should and must at all times be implicitly understood, even if it is not made explicit, namely, "insofar as it is not against God." For one can pledge nothing against God. When, for example, the emperor at his coronation swears this or that to the pope and later finds one or several articles that are against God, he needs no absolution from his oath, because it was never ever an oath in the first place. It could not have meaning or be sworn with the power of an oath, because he had earlier sworn in his baptism to God that he would do nothing against God, but help praise and glorify God's gospel and name. Against such an oath the pope cannot require anything of him, by whatever name it may be called.

What I say about the emperor's oath, however, I say about the oaths of all people. For it is surely undeniable that not all oaths are good; one can err in oaths as easily as one errs in all other matters. Therefore, one should certainly not bluster and shout, "Yes, yes, you have vowed and sworn it, you must keep it." Yes, dear friend, it is not enough that I pledged it. I might have vowed to become a Turk or a Jew, but I pledged more to God in my baptism, and I am more duty bound to keep the latter than all other vows. And where the other vows are by a hair's breadth at odds with the first vow, there I will tread them underfoot, lest I deny my God or reject God's grace. It is most important to draw a great and painstaking distinction between vows, since the very sensitive and dangerous thing about them is that they appear to be so much like the service of God, such that even very spiritual people can easily fail and err in this regard. And not everyone is competent to judge in these matters, as wild and impudent heads suppose.

Such are the four parts to which, in this little psalm, I wished this time to lead you. Notice, it is the right and useful way to treat the holy scripture, the way St. Paul did in 1 Corinthians 14[:6]. Likewise boasting of these four parts that he wanted to treat in scripture, he says, "Dear brothers and sisters, if I came to you speaking in tongues, what use would I be to you if I did not speak to you through revelation or insight or prophecy or teaching?" Here, of course, he talks of speaking in tongues, which is nothing but reading the scriptures aloud at people, even though he still wishes to treat such tongues or the simple scripture in a manifold way. Not that he should make the several [fourfold] senses out of it, as Origen and Jerome, together with others of their like, do with their allegories, but he wishes in the one simple sense to give much, as I hope that I have just now done. For here in this place he calls "prophecy" interpreting the writings of the prophets concerning Christ. "Teaching" he calls preaching faith (Titus 2[:1–2]), "how it makes us righteous, without our deserving it." He calls "knowledge" instruction and the distinction of outward behavior and customs (1 Cor 8[:1ff.]), which I have here called "admonition," but in which instructions I have also touched upon offering [or sacrifice] and vows. "Revelation" is certainly something more than allegory; that is, [it means] to strike something special in the scripture that not each and everyone can find who may well have some of the first three parts or even all of them.[27]

Such I do especially because through it I can give cause and instruction to all those who need it in their search to grasp the main point of our Christian teaching everywhere in the scripture. That is, we must become righteous, alive, and saved without any of our deserving through God's pure grace in Christ, which is given us as a gift. Beyond that, there is no other walk or way, no other wise or work that might help us.[28] For I see and experience daily all too well how the obstinate devil sets various snares for this main point in order to root it out. And when these easily tired saints notice something trivial, they thoroughly and persistently pursue it, because they let themselves think that they know it fully well and have learned everything there is to know.

I know well how their vain thinking fails the mark, and they know absolutely nothing about how much depends upon this point. For when this single point remains clear in the plan, then Christianity also remains pure and fine, harmonious, and without heretics. Most important, this single article and nothing else makes and sustains Christianity. All other points may well shine among false Christians and hypocrites, but where this one does not remain, it is not possible that one can prevent errors or the spirit of heresy. I know that for the truth, and, although I have tried many times, I could challenge the faith of neither Turks nor Jews if I should try to work without this article.

And wherever heresies arise or begin, you may have no doubt that they have fallen away from this main point, even if they chatter on and on about Christ with their lips and use fully polished and fancy phrases for themselves. For this point permits no heresy, especially since it is impossible for the Holy Spirit to be there, who does not allow heresies to begin but gives and sustains harmony. In particular, should you hear of untimely and immature saints who boast that they know full well that we must be saved without our works through God's grace, but who act as if for them it is a simple matter, then have no doubt about it, such persons do not know what they are saying. They may well never experience or taste it either. For it is not an art that one can fully learn or boast of as an ability. It is an art that wishes to keep us as students forever and remains our master.

All who truly have the ability for it and understand it do not boast that they can do everything, but they indeed sense something like a pleasant taste and smell, after which they follow and run. They are dumbfounded that they cannot in the end completely take hold and grasp it as they would and should like, so forever they hunger and strive increasingly for it, and they do not become filled by hearing or dealing with it. St. Paul himself confesses in Philippians 3[:12] that he himself had not yet grasped it. And Christ himself in Matthew 5[:6] pronounces blessed those who hunger and thirst after righteousness.

And whoever it pleases can think about me with this example, which I here would like to confess. The devil caught me several times when I did not consider this main point and plagued me with verses from the scripture in such a way that heaven and earth narrowed and began to crush me. Suddenly human works and laws seemed all right, and there was no error in all of the papacy. Presently, no one had ever erred but Luther alone. All of my best works, teaching, sermons, and books had to be condemned....

Thus, dear brothers and sisters, do not become proud or all too sure and certain that you know Christ well. You hear now how I confess and witness to you what the devil was capable of against Luther, who should actually even be a doctor in this art, because he has certainly preached, thought, written, spoken, sung, and read so much about it. Yet he must still remain a student in the matter and at times may not even be a student or a master of it. Thus, let me advise you, do not shout, "Hurray!" You are standing? Watch out that you do not fall. You can do everything? Watch out that your skill does not desert you. Have fear, be humble, and pray that your skill in this art will grow and be protected from the treacherous devil, who is called the clever one or know-it-all, who can do everything and who also learns everything in an instant.

If you need or want to deal with matters that concern the law and works or verses and examples of the fathers, then for all these take this main point with you. And do not let yourself be found without this piece, so that the dear Sun, Christ, will then shine in your heart that you will be able to speak and judge freely and surely about all laws, examples, verses, and works. Well and good, if there is anything good and right in them, then I know right well that they are not good and right beyond this life. Because for grace and that life only Christ is good and right. And if you should not take this to heart, then you will certainly find that the laws, verses, examples, and works with their pretty appearance and their great respect for persons will make you so confused that you will not know where you really stand. I have also seen in St. Bernard that, when he begins to speak of Christ, you can follow him with pleasure. When, however, he departs from this article and speaks of rules and works, then it is no longer St. Bernard. And the same goes for St. Augustine, Gregory, and all the others too, when Christ is not with them; then they are just worldly teachers, like philosophers and jurists.

Therefore, in the scriptures Christ is called a cornerstone, upon whom everything must be grounded and built if it is to stand before God. What is not grounded on him or is built without him must come to nothing and cannot stand. What are the heretics and mad saints now lacking, except that they have left this cornerstone and fallen into works again? And they cannot get back out of them but have to continue on and make of baptism and the sacrament (which are, of course, God's word and command) pure human works of their own. As the Anabaptists say, "Baptism is nothing if the person is not righteous beforehand." They do not want to become righteous from and through baptism, but through their righteousness they want to make baptism good and holy. That, in my opinion, is fundamentally losing the cornerstone, not being saved through the grace of Christ that baptism provides. They, rather, wish to become holy first through themselves. Then baptism gives nothing, creates nothing, and brings nothing; we bring and give everything to baptism beforehand, so that it is nothing but an unnecessary sign through which one is supposed to recognize these holy people. For baptism cannot be a permanent sign or mark, by which one might be able to recognize people, since it takes place only once and, after that, no one can see it by looking any more.

The enthusiasts[29] do the same thing with their sacrament. It must not make righteous or give grace but witnesses and shows how righteous and holy they are without such a sacrament. In the papacy, what did such separation of innumerable sects, heresies, and idolatries, all manner of mad saints, reverends, monks, and nuns do, but that they fell away from Christ and wanted to become righteous beforehand through works? Thus St. Paul diligently teaches the Ephesians and Colossians that Christ is our head and that we ourselves should hold to our head earnestly and remain with one another as members of one body and increase, because the devil does not celebrate or sleep. He would gladly tear us away from this head. He knows right well that this article breaks his neck and treads on his serpent head, as is promised in Genesis 3[:15].

But God, our dear eternal Father, who has so richly enlightened us through God's dear Son and our Lord and Savior, Jesus Christ, might, through the Holy Spirit, also strengthen us with complete faith and give us the power to follow such a light faithfully and diligently, and praise and glorify God together with all the nations, with both [our] life and teaching. To God be thanks and honor for all God's ineffable grace and gifts eternally. Amen.

SERMON AT COBURG ON CROSS AND SUFFERING

Editors' Introduction: This sermon,[1] based upon a harmony of Matthew 27, Luke 25, and John 19, was preached on the day after Luther arrived at the Coburg Castle, where he stayed during the Diet of Augsburg. The congregation included such personages as the Elector John, Count Albrecht of Mansfeld, Philip Melanchthon, Justus Jonas, Veit Dietrich, and John Agricola. Notes on the sermon were recorded by Veit Dietrich, who prepared the printed version of 1530.[2]

According to the sermon, Christians must suffer; however, the cross they carry cannot be self-selected but is given to them by the devil and the world. They recognize the unsurpassed gift that Christ has become theirs in his suffering and serving. Thus Christ's suffering is so powerful that "it fills heaven and earth and tears apart the power and might of the devil, hell, death, and sin." When one's suffering and affliction are at their worst, if one can think on Christ, God, who is faithful, comes to help, as God has helped God's own from the beginning of the world. To explain this, Luther invokes the legend of St. Christopher, a story by which simple people can have an example of the Christian life and how it should be lived. When one puts Christ, the dear child, on one's back, one must either carry him all the way through the water or drown. Christopher sinks, but he has a tree on which to cling, which is the promise that Christ will do something special with our suffering. In the world are trials and tribulations, but in Christ one has freedom. "In our drowning," says Luther, "we have the tree to which we can cling against the waves, namely, the word, and the fine, strong promises that we shall not be overwhelmed by the waves."

* * *

151

April 16, 1530

Sermon on Cross and Suffering, Preached at Coburg the Saturday before Easter, Based on the Passion History, April 16, 1530.

Dear friends, you are aware that the passion is a time for preaching. Thus, I do not doubt that you have heard the nature of this passion and suffering many times and the purpose for which God the Father ordained it. It is that God wanted not the passion of Christ, but to help, because it was not Christ but we and the whole human race who deserved this suffering. Furthermore, it is intended as a gift, given out of grace and mercy. This aspect we will not treat now, since I have spoken much about it already. We have many wayward fanatics about who dishonor the gospel and do us ill by asserting that we know nothing of teaching and preaching except about faith, as if we leave out the teachings about good works and suffering. They also say that they have the right spirit to proclaim such things. Therefore, we now want to speak about the example of the passion—what kind of cross we carry and suffer, and how we should carry and suffer it.

First, we must note that Christ's suffering did not just deliver us from the devil, death, and sins; his suffering is also an example for us that we should follow in our own suffering. Even though our suffering should not be overblown, such that through it we should be saved or earn the tiniest merit, we should nevertheless imitate Christ so that we may be conformed to him. For God decided not only that we should believe in the crucified Christ, but that we should also be crucified with him and suffer with him, as he clearly shows in many places in the gospels. "Whoever does not take up the cross and follow me," says the Lord, "is not worthy of me" [Matt 10:38]. And again, "If they have called the master of the house Beelzebub, how much more will they malign those of his household" (Matt 10:25)! Therefore, each one must carry a piece of the holy cross, and it cannot be otherwise. St. Paul says as well, "In my flesh I am completing what is lacking in Christ's afflictions" [Col 1:24]. It is as if he were saying that his whole Christianity is not yet completely prepared, and we also must follow so that nothing is lost or lacking from the cross of Christ, but all brought together into one heap. Everyone must ponder that the cross cannot remain external.

Moreover, it has to be such a cross and suffering that it has a name and honestly grips and hurts, such as some great danger to property and honor, or body and life. This is the kind of suffering that one really feels, and it hurts, because it would not be suffering if it did not hurt very much.

However, it should be the kind of suffering that we ourselves do not choose, as the fanatics choose their own suffering. It should be the kind of suffering that, if it were possible, we would gladly be rid of, that the devil or the world gives us. Then it is important, as I said before, that we hold fast and stick to the knowledge that we must suffer to be conformed to Christ,[3] so that it cannot be otherwise that each one must experience a cross and suffering. When one knows this, it is easier and more bearable, and one can comfort oneself by saying, "Well, if I want to be a Christian, I must wear the colors of the court. The dear Christ issues no others in his court; there must be suffering."

The fanatics who pick their own crosses cannot do this; rather, they become stubborn about it and resist. What a pretty and praiseworthy suffering this is, and still they blame us, as if we do not teach correctly about suffering, for they alone know it. We teach, however, that no one should pick up or choose a cross or suffering, but, when it comes, it should be carried and endured with patience.

Nevertheless, they do not err only in that they have a self-selected cross, but also in that they exalt their suffering so highly and award themselves great merit, thereby blaspheming God because it is not a true but a stinking, self-selected suffering. We, however, say that we earn nothing from our suffering, and we do not display it in beautiful monstrances as they do. It is enough for us to know that it pleases God that we suffer, so that we are conformed to Christ, as I have said. Thus we see that those who boast and teach the most about suffering and the cross know the least about either the cross or Christ, because they make their own suffering meritorious. This is not what it is about, nor is one pressured or forced to suffer. If you do not want to do it for nothing and without any merit, then you can let it lie and so deny Christ. The way is at the door. If you do not wish to suffer, you simply need to know that you are not worthy of the court. So you can chose between the two, either to suffer or to deny Christ.

If you wish to suffer, so be it. The treasure and comfort that is promised and given you is so great that you ought indeed to suffer gladly and with joy, because Christ together with all his suffering is given to you and becomes your own. If you can believe this, you can freely say in the greatest fear and crisis, "Even if I suffer for a long time, how can it compare to the treasure that my God has given as my possession, namely, that I will live with my God eternally?" Thus, suffering becomes sweet and light, not eternal suffering but a snippet that lasts a moment and passes away. It is as St. Paul [2 Cor 4:17] and St. Peter [1 Pet 1:6] and Christ himself say in the gospels [John 16:16–22]; they recognize the unsurpassed gift that Christ has become ours in his suffering and serving. Thus Christ's suffering is so powerful that it fills heaven and earth and tears apart the power and might of the devil, hell, death, and sin. When you hold up your treasure in the face of your affliction and suffering, it seems to be such a small loss over against such a great good to lose a little property, honor, health, spouse, child, your own body and life. If you refuse to regard this treasure and to suffer for it, so be it, go on and let it lie; the one who does not believe will not partake of these unspeakable goods and gifts.

Second, every Christian should attend to the fact and certainly understand that this suffering will turn out for the best, because on account of his word, Christ will not only help to bear such suffering but also turn and transform it for the best. By this means, again, such a cross should become so much sweeter and more bearable, because our loving God wants to pour so many spices and saltwater into our hearts so that we can carry all our afflictions and burdens. As St. Paul says (1 Cor 10:13), "God is faithful, and he will not let you be tested beyond your strength, but with the testing he will also provide the way out so that you may be able to endure it." This is true when suffering and affliction are at their worst and stress and strain one to such a point that one thinks one can stand no more but must drown. If, however, at this point you can think on Christ, God, who is faithful, comes to help, just as God has helped God's own from the very beginning of the world. For God has remained the same through all the ages, and the cause of our suffering and that of all the saints from the beginning has been the same.

Of course, the whole world must bear witness that we are not suffering because of public scandal or vice, such as adultery, fornication, murder, etc. We suffer because we remain true to God's word and preach, hear, learn, and practice it. Now since this is the cause of our suffering, so let it always be; we have the same promise and the same cause for suffering that all the saints then and now have had. Thus we might also comfort ourselves with the same promise and cling to the same in our suffering and trouble, as is most necessary.

Therefore, we should always pay attention to the promises in relation to our suffering, namely, that our cross and affliction will turn out for the best in a way that we could not wish or imagine. This is exactly what is different between Christian suffering and all other human suffering and afflictions. Other people also have their crosses and tragedies, just as they also can sit in their rose gardens and employ their good fortune and their goods as they please. Nevertheless, when they experience suffering and affliction, they cannot comfort themselves, because they do not have the mighty promises and the trust in God that Christians have; therefore, they cannot console themselves that God will help them carry their afflictions. They can see far less that their afflictions and suffering will turn out for the very best.

Thus, we can see that they cannot overcome even the small afflictions, and when they experience great and powerful afflictions, they despair altogether, commit suicide, or want to die because the world becomes claustrophobic for them. Likewise, they cannot keep a balance, whether in fortune or misfortune....

So that you will understand this better, I will give you an example by which to see how Christian suffering is painted and depicted. You know well how St. Christopher is regularly painted. You should not think that he existed as a man called by that name or who physically did what has been said of him. Nevertheless, the one who created the legend or fable was without doubt a good and reasonable person, who wanted to paint this picture for the simple people so that they would have an example and picture of the Christian life and how it should be lived. He met the mark in painting it. A Christian is like a great giant with great, strong arms and legs, as St. Christopher is painted, because the Christian also bears a burden that the whole world, emperor, king, or prince could not carry. Therefore, each Christian is called Christopher or Christbearer in that he or she takes up the faith.[4]

How does it work then? When a person takes up the faith, he or she does not think it to be a heavy burden but a small child that is cute and well formed and easy to carry, as happened for Christopher. At first, the gospel appears to be a dear, friendly, and childlike teaching, as we said at the beginning, and it happened that everyone wanted to be an evangelical.[5] There was such a hunger and thirst that there could be no oven as heated as the people were then. But how did it go? It turned out just as it did with Christopher; he did not discover how heavy the child was until he was in the deepest part of the water.

So it also went with the gospel as it broke in—the waves came, and the pope, bishop, princes, and the rabble set themselves in opposition. Then the child began to feel heavy to carry. [The water] rose so high for the good Christopher that he came close to drowning. As you see, it is happening in the same way now on the other side that is against the word; there are so many tricks and stratagems, so much deceit and cunning, all aimed to drown us in the water. There is such threat and terror that we might be frightened to death, were it not for the comfort that we have against it.

Consequently, when one puts Christ, the dear child, on one's back, one either has to carry him all the way through the water or drown. There is nothing in between. It is not good to drown; therefore, we want to get through the water with Christ, even if it might seem that we will get stuck in there. We have the promise that one who has Christ can say with David in the words of Psalm 27:[3], "Though an army encamp against me, my heart shall not fear; though war rise up against me, yet I will be confident." Let them paw and stamp their feet, threaten and frighten as they wish; no matter how deep the water may be, we will go through it with Christ.

So it is with everything else; when it gets going, it becomes too heavy, whether it is sin, the devil, death, or hell, or even our own conscience. Well, then, how should one do it? Where should one run for protection? We cannot see it any other way than that the whole thing will collapse. But on their side they are confident and proud, thinking that they have already won. I also see that the dear Christopher sinks; nevertheless, he comes through it, because he has a tree to which to cling. This tree is the promise that Christ will do something special with our suffering. "In the world," he says, "you will have trials and tribulations, but in me you will have freedom." Similarly,

St. Paul writes, "God is faithful and helps us out of affliction, so that we may be able to endure it" [cf. 1 Cor 10:13]. These sayings are branches, even trees, to which one can cling and let the water rush and roar as it will.

Thus, we have an example in Christopher and a picture that can strengthen us in our suffering and teach us that the fear and trembling are not as great as the comfort and the promise. We should know that in this life we will have no rest when we carry Christ, but that in our afflictions we should turn our eyes from the present suffering and toward the comfort and promise. Then we will learn what Christ says is true; "in me you...have peace" [John 16:33].

This is the manner of the Christian that we all must learn, namely, that we set our eyes on the word and turn them away from all the attendant and weighty misery and suffering. The flesh cannot attain this manner; it can focus only on the present sufferings. This is the manner of the devil, who shoves the word far from sight so that one can see nothing but the current misery, just as is true now. What the devil wants is that we should deny and forget the word altogether and gaze only at the danger around our neck. If he succeeds in this game, he drowns us in misery, so that we see nothing but the rush and roar. But this should not be, for it follows that if one wants to be a Christian and acts according to feelings, one soon loses Christ. Beat the suffering and the cross from your heart and mind as quickly as you can; otherwise, if you brood over them for a long time, the evil grows worse. If you find yourself in trouble and suffering, then say, "I did not choose and set up this cross for myself; it is the fault of the dear word of God and because I have and teach Christ that I suffer in this way. So let it go in God's name. I will let God take care of it and fight it out, who said long ago that I would suffer these things and promised me God's gracious help."

If, however, you plunge yourself into the scriptures, you will feel comfort, and your situation will improve, through which you would otherwise not be able to steer by any act or means on your own. A merchant will, for the sake of money and property, bring himself to leave house and home, wife and child, and risk his life for evil profit without a specific promise or pledge that he will return home healthy to his wife and child; still, he is foolhardy and bold enough to venture into such danger without any promise whatsoever. Now, if a merchant can do that for money and riches, for shame that we should spurn bearing a little cross and still want to be Christians. Moreover, in our drowning we have the tree to which we can cling against the waves, namely, the word, and the fine, strong promises that we shall not be overwhelmed by the waves.

The knight does the same thing. He plunges into battle, where innumerable spears, halberds, and firearms are aimed at him. He has no promise by which to console himself except his irrational spirit; nevertheless, he goes forward, even though his whole life is hard and filled with suffering....

...Although God does not want to attack and plague us, the devil wants to do exactly that and cannot endure the word. The devil is by nature so wicked and poisonous, unable to bear anything good, and aggrieved that an apple grows on a tree. It hurts and vexes the devil that you have a healthy finger, and, if he could, he would throw everything down and tear it apart. Nothing, however, is more hateful to the devil than the dear word, and that is because, while the devil can hide under all creatures, the word uncovers him, such that he cannot hide, and everyone knows how evil he is. Then the devil fights back and resists and draws the bishops and princes together and thinks that he has again concealed himself. Nevertheless, it does not help; the word drags him out into the light. Therefore, the devil does not rest, and, because the gospel will not suffer him, he will not suffer the gospel. If our dear God did not protect us through the angels and we were able to see the devil's cunning blows and deceit, we should die from the sight alone, as many are the cannons and guns he has ranged against us. But God protects us so that they do not hit us.

Thus, the two champions clash, and, as each does as much as possible, the devil brews one calamity after another, because he is a mighty, wicked, and restless spirit. Now it is time for our dear God to be concerned about God's honor. The word with which we fight is a weak and miserable word, and we who have it and proclaim it are also weak and miserable people and carry this treasure in clay jars [2 Cor 4:7], as Paul says, that can be easily shattered and broken. Therefore, the evil spirit spares no effort and confidently lashes out to break the little vessel; for there it is under his nose, and he cannot stand it. Thus, the struggle begins with water and fire to dampen and drown the little spark.

For a while our dear God looks on and lets us lie between a rock and a hard place, and from our experience we learn that the weak, suffering word is stronger than the devil and hell's gates. The devil and his followers can storm the fortress all they want. They will find something there that will make them break into a sweat and still not win the day; it is a rock, as Christ calls it, that cannot be overcome. Thus, let us suffer what we will; we will experience that God will stand by us to guard and protect us against the enemy and all his followers.

Third, it is important to note that we do not suffer only to demonstrate God's honor, might, and strength over against the devil, but also because this treasure that we have, when it is not accompanied by danger and suffering, causes us to become sleepy and secure. We see all too commonly that they so misuse the holy gospel that it becomes sin and shame, as if they are so liberated by the gospel that they do not need to do anything, give anything, or suffer anything.

God can only stem this wickedness through the cross. Therefore, God must discipline and drive us, so that our faith grows and becomes stronger and we bring the Savior deeper into our hearts. Just as we cannot live without eating and drinking, so we also cannot live without affliction and suffering. Therefore, we must experience peril from the devil through persecution or a secret thorn piercing our hearts, as St. Paul laments (cf. 2 Cor 12:7). Since it is better to have a cross than not to have one, no one should be upset or terrified over it. You have a good, strong promise on which and by which you can comfort yourself. Besides, the gospel cannot come out in the open except through suffering and the cross.

Lastly, Christian suffering is more noble and more exquisite than any other human suffering, because, since Christ himself suffered, he made all Christian suffering holy. Are we not poor and mad people? We run to Rome, Trier, and other such places to visit the shrines; why do we not also cherish the cross and suffering to which Christ was much closer? These touched him more than some piece of clothing touched his body, touching not only his body but also his heart. Through the suffering of Christ, the suffering of all his saints has become completely holy, for it has been touched by Christ's suffering. Therefore, we should accept all suffering as a holy thing, for it is true holiness.

Since we know that it is God's good pleasure that we suffer, and God's honor is revealed and seen in our suffering better than in any other way, and since we are the kind of people who would not remain in the word without some suffering, and since we have, nevertheless, the precious and true promise that the cross that God sends us is not an evil thing but a completely exquisite and noble holy thing, why then should we avoid suffering? Let the one who does not want to suffer go and be a knight; we will preach only to those who want to be Christians. The others would not carry this out anyway. We have ample comfort and promise that God will not leave us stuck in suffering but will help us out, even if all manner of people would doubt this.

Thus, even though it hurts, you must suffer somewhat; things cannot always be on an even plane. It is as good—in fact, a thousand times better—to suffer for Christ, who gives us comfort and help in our suffering, than to suffer for the devil and despair and perish.

See, in this way, we learn from the cross, and we need to learn to distinguish carefully the passion of Christ from all other suffering. The former is heavenly; the latter is worldly. His suffering accomplishes everything; ours nothing, except as we are formed in the image of Christ. The suffering of Christ is noble suffering; ours is that of a slave. Those who teach something else know nothing of Christ's suffering, nor ours. Reason knows nothing else; it wants to obtain merits through its suffering and all its other works. Therefore, we must make distinctions. Now we have spoken enough about the example of the passion and our suffering. May God grant that we learn and comprehend it properly. Amen.

Lectures on Galatians 3:6— "Thus Abraham Believed God"

Editors' Introduction: The Letter to the Galatians is sometimes called St. Paul's Magna Carta of Christian freedom. In Luther's characteristic way, he called Paul's Galatians "the epistle to which he was betrothed, his Katie von Bora" (LW 26:ix). He lectured on its six chapters at least twice, first in 1516–17, published in 1519 (LW 27:153–410; WA 2:436–618), and then for a second time from July 3 to November 14, 1531, published in 1535 (LW 26 and 27:1–149; WA 40/1 and 40/2). The lectures of 1519 include some fiery exegetical sections that match those of Luther's later work.

This selection comes from the 1535 lectures on Galatians 3:6,[1] and it is quite controversial in its modern reception. Luther argues that faith as the power of God creates God in us—God not per se but *in nobis*—and in that place where reason tries to seduce us away from faith in God, it has to be slain. With that, some will critique Luther as a fideist (faith without reason) and others for saying God is a human creation.[2] Luther, however, stressed that faith was the power of God in us, becoming God in us fully in Christ. Reason is queen in its own earthly house but cannot be allowed to reject and displace faith.

* * *

Abraham believed God, and it was reckoned to him as righteousness [Gal 3:6].

Up to now Paul has argued from experience, vigorously pursuing this argument based on experience. "You have believed," he says, "and in this way you have done miracles and performed many outstanding and mighty deeds. You have also suffered evil. All of these are the effect and operation not of the law but of the Holy Spirit." The Galatians were forced to confess this because they were

161

unable to deny what they could see and what was available to their senses. Thus, the argument from experience, based on its effects on the Galatians themselves, is most powerful and clear.

Now he adds the example of Abraham and recites the testimonies of scripture. The first is from the fifteenth chapter of Genesis: "Abraham believed, etc." He commends this passage strongly here, just as he does especially in Romans 4:[2]. "If Abraham," he says, "was justified by works of the law, he has righteousness and has something to boast about, but not before God," only before humans. Before God, Abraham has sin and wrath. Before God, moreover, he was not justified because he worked but because he believed. For scripture says, "Abraham believed God, and it was reckoned to him as righteousness *(iusticia)*" [Rom 4:3]. Here Paul magnificently explains and amplifies this passage as it deserves. Abraham, he says, "did not weaken in faith when he considered his own body, which was as good as dead (for he was about a hundred years old), or when he considered the barrenness of Sarah's womb. No distrust made him waver concerning the promise of God, but he grew strong in his faith as he gave glory to God, being fully convinced that God was able to do what he had promised. Therefore it was reckoned to him as righteousness. Now the words, 'it was reckoned to him,' were written not for his sake alone, but for ours also" [Rom 4:19–24].

With these words Paul makes faith in God the supreme worship, the supreme allegiance and sacrifice. Let the orator expound on this topic, and one will see that faith is something omnipotent and that its power is inexpressible and infinite. It attributes glory to God, for whom nothing greater can be done. Moreover, to attribute glory to God is to consider God truthful, wise, righteous, merciful, and almighty. In sum, it is to know God as the author and giver of all good. Faith does this, not reason. Faith fulfills the deity and, I might say, is the creator of divinity, not in the substance of God, but in us.[3] For without faith God is for us diminished in glory, wisdom, righteousness, truthfulness, mercy, etc. That is, God has no majesty and divinity where there is no faith. Nor does God ask anything more from us than to attribute glory and divinity to God, that is, not to have God as an idol, but as one who has regard for us, listens, has mercy, helps, etc. When God has obtained this, God retains the whole and unimpaired divinity; that is, God has whatever a believing heart attributes to God. To be able to attribute such glory to God is wisdom beyond wisdom, righteousness beyond righteousness, religion beyond religion, and sacrifice beyond sacrifice. And from these things one can understand what righteousness faith is, and, by antithesis, what a great sin unbelief is.[4]

Therefore, faith justifies, because it pays God back what is owed, and the one who does this is righteous. (The laws also define what it is to be righteous, to give to each what is one's due.)[5] For faith speaks as follows: "I believe you, God, when you speak." What does God say? If you consult reason, God says things that are impossible, lies, things that are foolish, weak, absurd, abominable, heretical, and diabolical. For what is more ridiculous, foolish, and impossible than when God says to Abraham that he is to receive a son from Sarah's infertile and as-good-as-dead body?

Thus, when God proposes articles of faith, God always proposes things that are simply impossible and absurd—if, that is, you wish to follow the judgment of reason. To reason it seems ridiculous and absurd that in the Lord's Supper the body and blood of Christ are presented to us; baptism is "the washing of rebirth and renewal by the Holy Spirit" (Titus 3:5); the dead will be raised on the last day; Christ, the son of God, was conceived and carried in the womb of a virgin; he was born, suffered the most ignominious of deaths on the cross, and was raised again; he is now sitting at the right hand of the Father and has "authority in heaven and on earth" (Matt 28:18). Paul calls the gospel concerning Christ crucified "the message about the cross" (1 Cor 1:18) and "the foolishness of our proclamation" (1 Cor 1:21), which Jews regard as scandalous and Greeks as foolish teaching. Thus reason judges all the articles of faith. For it does not understand that the best worship is to hear the voice of God and to believe, but it supposes that what it chooses on its own and what it does with a so-called good intention and from its own devotion is pleasing to God.[6] Therefore, when God speaks, reason determines God's word to be heresy and the word of the devil; [God's word] seems so absurd to it. Such is the theology of all the Sophists and the sectarians and all who measure the word of God by reason.

But faith slaughters reason and kills that beast that the whole world and all creatures are not able to kill. Thus Abraham killed it by faith in the word of God, by which an heir was promised to him from

Sarah, who was sterile and past childbearing. Abraham's reason did not immediately assent to the word but assuredly struggled in him against faith, calling it ridiculous, absurd, and impossible that Sarah, who was not only already ninety years old but also sterile by nature, should give birth to a son. But faith conquered in him and slaughtered and sacrificed that bitterest and most pestilential enemy of God.

So by faith all the righteous entering with Abraham into the darkness of faith slay reason,[7] saying, "Reason, you are foolish. You do not know divine things (Matt 16:23). Do not be troublesome to me; be quiet, do not judge, but hear and believe the word of God."

Thus by faith do the righteous slaughter the beast greater than the world and exhibit the most pleasing sacrifice and worship of God. Compared to the sacrifice and worship of the righteous, the worship of all the nations, all the monks and all the just are absolutely nothing. In the first place, by this sacrifice, [the righteous] slay reason, the greatest and most invincible enemy of God because it despises God and denies God's wisdom, justice, power, truthfulness, mercy, majesty, and divinity.

In the second place, through this sacrifice they attribute glory to God; that is, they believe that God is just, good, faithful, truthful, etc., and they believe that God can do all things and that all God's words are holy, true, living, efficacious, etc. This is the most acceptable allegiance to God. Therefore, there is no greater, better, or more pleasing religion and worship to be found in the world than faith.

On the other hand, the workers who lack faith do many things. They fast, pray, and lay a cross on themselves, and they think by doing these things they are placating the wrath of God and meriting grace. These persons do not attribute glory to God; that is, they do not consider God to be merciful, truthful, one who keeps promises, etc., but rather, they consider God to be an angry judge who needs to be mollified by their works. In this way they despise God, making accusations that all God's promises are lies, and they deny Christ and all his benefits. In short, they dethrone God and put themselves there instead. Having neglected and despised the word of God, they choose the worship and works that please themselves. They suppose that God is pleased with these, and by them they hope to receive a reward. Therefore, they do not put God's bitterest enemy, reason, to death; they give it life. They take away God's majesty and divinity and attribute it to their own works.

Therefore, faith alone attributes glory to God, as Paul attests in Romans 4:20, when he says, "[Abraham] grew strong in his faith as he gave glory to God." He adds from Genesis 15:6 that this was imputed to him as righteousness. Nor was this in vain. Christian righteousness consists of two things, namely, faith in the heart and the imputation of God. Faith is indeed a formal righteousness, but it is, nonetheless, not enough. After faith remnants of sin still cling to the flesh. The sacrifice of faith began in Abraham, but it was finally consummated only in death.

Therefore, the second part of righteousness must be added to make it perfect, namely, divine imputation [reputatio]. Faith does not give enough to God formally, because it is imperfect. Indeed, it is merely a spark of faith that begins to attribute divinity to God, because "the firstfruits of the Spirit" (Rom 8:23) are present not yet the tenth part.[8] Nor is reason completely killed in this life. Thus concupiscence is still left in us, as well as wrath, impatience, and the other fruits of the flesh and infidelity. Not even the more perfect saints have a full and constant joy in God. As scripture testifies concerning the prophets and the apostles, their feelings change; sometimes they are sad, sometimes joyful. But such faults are not imputed to the saints because of their faith in Christ, for otherwise no one could be saved. We conclude, therefore, from these words, "It was imputed to him as righteousness," that righteousness indeed begins with faith, through which we have the firstfruits of the spirit. Nevertheless, because faith is weak, it is not perfected without the imputation of God. Therefore, faith begins righteousness, but imputation perfects it until the day of Christ.

The Sophists also contemplate imputation relative to the acceptance of a work.[9] However, they speak apart from and contrary to scripture, for they apply it only to works. They do not consider the uncleanness and internal diseases of the heart, such as unbelief, doubt, and contempt and hatred for God, which deadly beasts are the source and cause of all evil. They consider only outward and crass unrighteousness, which are little streams that proceed from those fountains. Therefore, they attribute acceptance to good works; that is, God accepts works not because it is owed to them but by "congruity."[10] But we exclude all works and come to grips with the head of the beast called reason,[11] which is the fountainhead of all evils. It neither fears nor loves nor trusts in God but smugly despises God. It is moved neither by God's threats nor by God's promises. It does not delight in God's words or deeds but murmurs against and is angry with God. It judges and hates God. In sum, "it is the enemy of God" (Rom 8:7)[12] and does not give glory to God. Were this disease, namely, reason, to be killed, external and crass sins would be nothing.

Therefore, the first thing that must be done is through faith to kill unbelief, contempt and hatred for God, and murmuring against God's wrath, judgment, and all God's words and deeds, for then we kill reason. It can be killed by nothing other than faith, which believes God and gives glory to God and does not object when God speaks those things that seem foolish, absurd, and impossible to reason. Nor does it object when God describes God's self in a way that reason can neither judge nor grasp, as in this way: "If you wish to please me, do not offer me your works and merits, but believe in Jesus Christ, my only son, who was born, who suffered, who was crucified, and who died for your sins. Then I will accept you and proclaim you righteous, and whatever sin remains in you I will not impute to you." Thus, if reason is not slaughtered, and if all the religions and forms of worship under heaven that have been created by humanity to obtain righteousness before God are not condemned, then the righteousness of faith cannot stand.

Hearing this, reason is immediately offended, rages, and shows its hostility toward God, saying, "Are good works nothing then? Have I borne the burden of the day and the scorching heat for nothing?" (Matt 20:12). This is that raging of the nations, of the peoples, of the kings, and of the rulers against the Lord and his anointed (Ps 2:1, 2). The pope with his monks does not want to be seen as having erred; much less will he let himself be condemned. So it is with the Turk, etc.

I have said this in interpretation of the sentence, "And it was reckoned to him as righteousness," in order that students of the sacred scriptures might understand how Christian righteousness is to be defined properly and accurately, that is, as trust in the Son of God or the trust of the heart in God through Christ. Here this clause must be added for distinction: "which faith is imputed as righteousness for the sake of Christ."

As I have said, two things complete Christian righteousness. The first is faith in the heart, which is a divinely granted gift that formally believes in Christ. The second is that God reckons this imperfect faith as perfect righteousness for the sake of Christ, God's Son, who suffered for the sins of the world and in whom I begin to believe. Because of this faith in Christ, God does not see the sin that still remains in me. For as long as I live in the flesh, sin is certainly in me; nevertheless, Christ protects me in the meantime under the shadow of his wings and spreads the wide heaven over me, namely, the forgiveness of sins, under which I am safe. This keeps God from seeing the sins that still cling to my flesh. My flesh distrusts, is angry with, and does not rejoice in God. Yet, God overlooks these sins, and before God it is as if they were not sins. This is accomplished by imputation, because of the faith by which I begin to take hold of Christ; and on his account God reckons imperfect righteousness as perfect righteousness and sin as not sin, even though it really is sin.

Thus, we live under the curtain of the flesh of Christ (Heb 10:20). He is our "pillar of cloud by day and pillar of fire by night" (Exod 13:21) to keep God from seeing our sin. Although we see it and feel remorseful in our consciences, nevertheless, running to Christ our mediator and propitiator, through whom we reach completion, we are saved. For in him are all things,[13] and we have everything in him who supplies all things in us. On his account God overlooks all our sins and wants them covered as if they were not sins. God says, "Because you believe in my Son, even though you have sins, they shall be forgiven, until you are completely absolved from them by death."

Let Christians strive to learn fully and perfectly this doctrine of Christian righteousness, which Sophists neither understand nor are able to understand. Let them not, however, think that they can learn this all at once. Therefore, let them make the effort to read Paul often and with the greatest diligence. Let them compare the first with the last; in fact, let them compare Paul as a whole with himself. Then they will find that this is the situation, that Christian righteousness consists in two things: first, in faith, which attributes glory to God; second, in God's imputation. For because faith is weak, as I have said, therefore God's imputation must be added. That is, God does not want to impute the remnant of sin and does

167

not want to punish it or damn us for it. He wants to cover it and to forgive it, as though it were nothing, not for our sakes or for the sake of our worthiness or works but for the sake of Christ himself, in whom we believe.

Thus the Christian person is righteous and a sinner at the same time, holy and profane, an enemy of God and a child of God.[14] None of the Sophists will admit this paradox, because they do not understand the true meaning of justification. This is why they forced many to go on doing good works until they would not feel any sin at all. By this means they drove to the point of insanity many who tried with all their might to become completely righteous in a formal sense but could not accomplish it. Innumerable persons, even among the authors of this wicked dogma, were driven into despair at the hour of death, which is what would have happened to me if Christ had not looked at me in mercy and liberated me from this error.[15]

We, on the other hand, teach and comfort an afflicted sinner this way, and we console the afflicted sinner: "Friend, it is impossible for you to become so righteous in this life that your body is as clear and spotless as the sun. You still have spots and wrinkles (Eph 5:27); nevertheless, you are holy." You, however, say, "How can I be holy, when I have sin and I perceive it?" "It is good that you perceive and recognize sin. Give thanks to God, and do not despair. It is one step toward health when a sick person recognizes and admits the disease." "But how will I be liberated from sin?" "Run to Christ, the Doctor, who heals the contrite of heart and saves sinners. Believe in him. If you believe, you are righteous, because you give glory to God that God is omnipotent, merciful, truthful, etc. You justify and praise God. In sum, you attribute divinity and all things to God. The sin that still remains in you is not imputed to you but pardoned for the sake of Christ, in whom you believe and who is perfectly righteous in a formal sense. His righteousness is yours; your sin is his."[16]

As I have said, therefore, any Christian is the highest pontiff, because the Christian first offers and slaughters reason and the mind of the flesh, then attributes the glory to God, that is, being righteous, true, patient, kind, and merciful. This is the continual morning and evening sacrifice in the New Testament.[17] The evening sacrifice is to kill reason, and the morning sacrifice is to glorify God. Thus, a Christian is involved, daily and perpetually, in this double sacrifice and in its practice. No one can adequately proclaim the value and the dignity of Christian sacrifice.

Therefore, this is a marvelous definition of Christian righteousness, that is, the imputation or reckoning[18] of righteousness or to righteousness on account of faith in Christ or on account of Christ. When the Sophists hear this definition, they laugh, because they suppose that righteousness is a particular quality that is infused into the soul and then distributed through all the members. They are not able to strip off the thoughts of reason, which says that righteousness is right judgment and a right will. Therefore, this indescribable gift excels all reason, namely, that God imputes and reckons one righteous without any works who alone by faith holds onto the son of God, who was sent into the world, who was born, who suffered, who was crucified, etc., for us.

Insofar as it pertains to the words, it is simple; that is, righteousness is not in us formally, as Aristotle argues,[19] but outside us in divine grace alone and by reckoning. In us there is nothing of the form of righteousness, except for that weak faith or firstfruits of faith by which we have begun to take hold of Christ. In the meantime, however, sin truly remains in us. Nevertheless, this is not to be taken lightly. It is serious and most important, because Christ is given to us and we apprehend him by faith. As Paul said above, "He loved us and gave himself for us" (Gal 2:20), and "He became a curse for us, etc." (Gal 3:13). It is not idle speculation that Christ was handed over for my sins and became a curse for me so that I might be snatched from eternal death. Thus, to take hold of that Son and to believe in him from the heart, which is the gift of God, causes God to reckon that faith, although imperfect, as perfect righteousness. Here we are in an altogether different world outside reason, where we do not debate what we must do or by what kind of work we merit grace and the remission of sins. Here we are in divine theology, where we hear this gospel that Christ died for us and that, believing this, we are reckoned righteous, regardless even of the grievous sins remaining in us.

Christ also defines the righteousness of faith in this way in the Gospel of John. "The Father himself," he says, "loves you" (John

16:27). Why does he love you? Not because you were Pharisees beyond reproach in the righteousness of the law, circumcised, doing good, fasting, etc., but because "I have chosen you out of the world" (John 15:19). You did nothing except that "you have loved me and have believed that I came from God." This object pleased you, namely, this "I" sent from the Father into the world. Because you have taken hold of this object, therefore, "the Father loves you, and you please him." Nevertheless, in another passage he calls them evil and commands them to ask for the forgiveness of sins. These two things are diametrically opposed: that a Christian is righteous and loved by God and nevertheless at the same time is a sinner. God cannot deny God's own nature; that is, God is of necessity unable not to hate sin and sinners, for otherwise God would be unjust and would love sin. Then how can these two contradictory things be true at the same time? I am a sinner and am most deserving of the wrath of God, and God loves me? Here nothing intercedes in any way except Christ the Mediator. "The Father," he says, "does not love you because you are worthy of love, but because you have loved me and believed that I came from God."

Therefore, the Christian remains in pure humility, feeling sinful in a real and true fashion, worthy of wrath, the judgment of God, and eternal death. Thereby the Christian remains humble in this life. Yet, at the same time, the Christian maintains a pure, holy pride by turning to Christ. Through him the Christian rises against that feeling of divine wrath and judgment and believes in the love of the Father, not for one's own sake but for the sake of Christ the beloved.

Thus, it is certain how faith justifies without works and how the imputation of righteousness is necessary. Sins remain in us, which God particularly hates. Because of them, it is necessary that we have the imputation of righteousness, which occurs for us on account of Christ, who was given to us and is grasped by us in faith. Meanwhile, as long as we are alive, we are supported and nourished at the bosom of divine mercy and forbearance, until the body of sin (Rom 6:6) is abolished and we are raised up as new beings on that day. Then there will be new heavens and a new earth (Rev 21:1), in which righteousness will dwell. Meanwhile, under this heaven sinners and the wicked dwell, and the righteous are sinners. This is the sin that Paul complains about in Romans 7:23 that still remains in the saints.

Nevertheless, in Chapter 8[:1] he says that "there is no condemnation for those who are in Christ Jesus." Who will reconcile these utterly conflicting statements that the sin in us is not sin, that the one who is damnable will not be damned, that the one who is rejected will not be rejected, and the one who is worthy of wrath and eternal death will not receive these punishments? Only the mediator between God and humanity, Jesus Christ (1 Tim 2:5). As Paul says, "there is no condemnation for those who are in Christ Jesus."

ON JACOB'S LADDER

Editors' Introduction: This text is one of the few in this volume written when Luther was older—about sixty.[1] This portion of a lecture on Genesis (28:10–22) seems to have been written sometime between the end of 1541 and the summer or early autumn of 1542.[2] The text has been strongly edited by those who recorded the lecture, but it represents Luther's spirituality of the word that proclaims the union of God and humanity in the divinity and humanity of Christ. According to Luther, Jacob's vision of the angels ascending and descending on the ladder represents the incarnation of Christ. As Luther notes, according to the historical, simple, and literal sense, the ladder is the union of the divinity with human flesh, on which the angels ascend and descend in ceaseless wonder.

According to Luther, there is another union—a union between humans and Christ. This is the allegorical meaning of the ladder. However, the allegory is meant to nourish faith and not teach about our affairs or our works. Thus, we are carried along by faith and become one flesh with Christ, "that they may all be one. As you, Father, are in me and I am in you, may they also be in us" (John 17:21). In this way we ascend to Christ, carried along through the word and the Holy Spirit. Through faith we cling to him, since we become one body with him and he with us. He is the head; we are the members. On the other hand, he descends to us through the word and the sacraments, teaching us about himself. The first union, then, is that of the Father and the Son in the divinity. The second is that of the divinity and the humanity in Christ. The third is that of the church and Christ.

* * *

And he [Jacob] dreamed that there was a ladder set up on the earth, the top of it reaching to heaven; and the angels of God were ascending and descending on it. And the Lord stood above it and said, "I am the Lord, the God of Abraham your Father and the God of Isaac; the land on which you lie I will give to you and to your offspring; and your offspring shall be like the dust of the earth."

This is the most beautiful sermon and most remarkable gem in this whole narrative, and it must be considered accurately and diligently. As we often say, we must observe particularly when God speaks with the fathers and the saints in their legends or narratives. This is why they are holy and are called saints.

There are two kinds of holiness: the first by which we are made holy through the word; the other by which we are holy through work and life. We must distinguish these two modes of holiness most precisely. That prior and purest holiness is the word, in which there is no vice, no blemish, no sin. Thus it is so holy that it does not require any remission of sins, because it is the truth of God, according to John 17[:17]: "Sanctify them in the truth; your word is truth." We who are called through the word are glorified in that holiness and it is outside us *(extra nos)*; it is not our work. It is not formal righteousness *(formalis iustitia)*,[3] but heavenly holiness communicated through the word, and indeed orally. We preach this righteousness and oppose all the righteousness and holiness of the pope and of all the hypocrites, because ours is a perfect holiness. Insofar as I have the word, I am holy, I am just and pure, and without any guilt and accusation. Christ himself said, "You are clean on account of the word that I have spoken to you" (John 15:3)....

...Let us remember that there are two kinds of holiness. One is the word, which is holiness itself. Moreover, this holiness is imputed to those who have the word. A person is simply reputed as holy, not for our own sakes or on account of our works, but on account of the word. Thus, the whole person becomes righteous, which is why the church is called holy and we are called holy, because we have an unspotted holiness not of our accord but heaven's. This holiness must not be condemned, nor is it shameful that we are called holy. Unless we are glorified in this holiness, we injure God, who sanctifies us by the word. You say, "I am a sinner." God, however, says, "I know that you are a sinner; if you were not, I would not wish to sanctify you, nor would you need the word. Therefore, because you are a sinner, I sanctify you."

The other holiness is of works. It is the love that makes one acceptable to God. Here, it is not just that God speaks, but I strive to follow what God says. Because weakness clings to us, however, this is not pure righteousness. Here the Lord's Prayer reigns and must be prayed: "Holy be your name." This pertains to our holiness and works, which are formal and pertain to the holiness of the Ten Commandments and the Lord's Prayer. But the first holiness must be referred to the symbol, to the creed, because I do not obtain the promise of the word through the Ten Commandments. Nor do I do so through the Lord's Prayer. Through them I grasp my love and my works. Through faith, however, I take hold of the word, which is purity itself.

These things cannot be said and repeated internally enough. Yet the distinction between the law and the promise is easy. On the one hand, there is the word, which justifies the believer apart from my love and righteousness; on the other, I take hold of the law of God, so that I do not steal, commit adultery, etc. The papists are overcome and absorbed in their shadows, so that, while hearing this teaching, they do not hear, nor do we ourselves retain it sufficiently. Therefore, learn from the reading of these stories what we have always been accustomed to do in our reading, namely, to linger at the passage when God speaks with the patriarchs, because here the best and most precious things are read.

Now let us look at the sermon itself. Here one can see to what extent Jacob's spirit was trapped in sadness and anguish. He is in outer darkness, I would say, exiled from home, from country, abandoned and alone, and uncertain where to hide safely. The devil comes upon him, who is accustomed to assail spirits in a thousand strange ways. Thus the common saying is true that no disaster is isolated, because "like a roaring lion your adversary the devil prowls around" (1 Pet 5:8), seeking where the fence is lowest to cross and where the wagon is leaning to push it over. Thus, to adversities and to trials the devil piles on temptation to lead them into despair, blasphemy, or impatience.

These are the works of the devil, his customary and constant snares. Therefore, besides the physical cross and exile, Jacob was undoubtedly assailed by the fiery darts of the devil [cf. Eph 6:16]. Perhaps he thought about how he had stolen the birthright and how he had deceived his father. For in this way the devil is accustomed to make a great and enormous sin out of an excellent work. The fact that God speaks with Jacob is a sign of this very grievous trial. God is not accustomed to issue words in vain and does not speak unless an important and necessary cause impels speech. Nor is God accustomed to address or console those who laugh, who exult and rage at God in the pleasures or in the wisdom of the flesh, who lie smugly, without fear of and reverence for God. "Wisdom is not found in the land of those who live comfortably," says Job [cf. Job 28:12–13]; it is found under the cross of those who are oppressed and are in conflict with spiritual trials. Then there is both a reason and a place for consolation; then God is present and consoles the afflicted, "so that the righteous might not stretch out their hands to do wrong," as Psalm 125:3 says. And "God will speak peace to God's servants" [cf. Ps 122:8]. For if God were absent too long, no one could endure and persevere in those trials and ragings. This, then, is a great consolation in his great and exceedingly sad disturbance, and it appears that this, rather than bodily exhaustion, lulled Jacob to sleep. For the devil came to terrify him within his heart while he was in flight and in exile.

This then is Jacob's dream. A ladder has been placed on the earth, the top of which touches heaven, and on it angels ascend and descend. And the Lord is leaning on it and speaks that promise to this third patriarch. This is God speaking directly, not through a human person. It is what we have said must be carefully attended to in the stories of the fathers.

Moreover, the ladder is a picture or a certain image, by necessity signifying something. According to Psalm 104:4, the angels are spirits and fire: "You make your angels spirits and your ministers a flaming fire."[4] Thus, they did not need a ladder to ascend or descend. Much less does God need a ladder to lean on to speak to Jacob, the heir of the promise. The images and pictures suggested by this ladder have been explained in various ways, and it is not worthwhile to gather and recount them all.

Lyra says that the rungs refer to the patriarchs listed at the beginning of the Gospel of Matthew in the genealogy of Christ.[5] For both sides indicate that Christ descends from sinners, as well as from the righteous. The angels, he says, refer to the revelation of the incarnation of Christ—the revelation that took place through the fathers, the prophets, and the apostles. He interprets the ascent as the devotion of the saints when they pray. This thought is not inappropriate, but it does not seem to be the principal explanation of the allegory.

The *Glossa ordinaria* interprets the ascending angels as the blessed in heaven serving God.[6] From there they descend to minister to humanity, as in Hebrews [1:14], "Are not all angels spirits in the divine service, sent to serve for the sake of those who are to inherit salvation?" And in Daniel 7:10 we read, "A thousand thousands served him, and ten thousand times ten thousand stood attending him."

St. Gregory calls the angels preachers, who, as they ascend, contemplate Christ and afterward, when they descend to the church, serve the members of the church. But who could number all the speculations? While they are godly, yet, like many things in the fathers, they have not been expressed at the right time or at the right place. It is true that a preacher must first ascend in order to preach, to receive the word and teaching from God, and in the same way must study, learn, read, and meditate. Later the preacher should descend and teach others. These are the twin offices of the priests: to turn to God in prayer and to the people with teaching. But these matters should be left to their own proper place and time.

Because mention is made of this ladder in the first chapter of the Gospel of John, we should instead look at that text. For there the Lord himself seems to interpret this picture. When Philip brings Nathaniel to Christ [John 1:47], he says, "Here is truly an Israelite!" Here, as Augustine says, he reminds us of the ladder of Jacob, who is also called Israel. Christ thus says, "Do you believe because I told you that I saw you under the fig tree? You will see greater things than these." He added, "Very truly, I tell you, you will see heaven opened and the angels of God ascending and descending upon the Son of Man" [John 1:50–51]. We should believe and be content with the explanation of our Savior, because he understands better than all other interpreters, even though they agree properly that this dream signified the infinite, inexpressible, and wondrous mystery of the incarnation of Christ, who was to descend from the patriarch Jacob; as God says, "In your seed, etc." Therefore, it was revealed to Jacob by the very God that he would be the father of Christ and that the Son of man would be born from his seed. God did not speak this in vain. Indeed, God painted that picture of the ladder to comfort and console Jacob in faith in the future blessing, just as previously God gave the same promise to Abraham [Gen 22:17–18] and Isaac [Gen 26:24] in order that they might teach and transmit it to their descendants as certain and infallible and expect a savior from their own flesh. In this way God strengthens Jacob, who, like the useless trunk of a tree, is wretched and afflicted in a foreign land. By means of this new vision, God transfers to him all the blessings, to assure him that he is the patriarch from whom the seed promised to Adam will come.

Therefore, we must understand the angels in their proper meaning, as Christ describes them in John 1:51, where he speaks of them as "the angels of God," that is, the blessed ones. They ascend and descend on Christ or upon Christ. The ladder signifies the ascent and the descent that are made by means of the ladder and by means of the rungs. If you remove the ladder, it signifies nothing else than the ascent and the descent. Angels, however, do not use a physical ladder or an imaginary one. Nevertheless, there is an ascent and a descent, that is, an angelic ladder, so to speak. This is the principal meaning, just as Christ himself explains the descent and the ascent of the angels upon the Son of man without a ladder.

What is this ascent and descent? I answer that it is this very mystery: that in one and the same person there is true God and true human. Accordingly, the unity of the person fulfills this mystery. And we, believing, fulfill the word of Christ [John 1:51], "You will see the angels ascending and descending." For we believe in the one Lord, God's only-begotten son, born of the Virgin Mary, true God and human. This mystery is so great, so grand, so inexpressible, that the angels themselves cannot marvel at it enough, much less comprehend it. But, as is stated in 1 Peter 1:12, these are "things into which angels long to look." For angels cannot rejoice and marvel enough at that inexpressible union and unity of the most diverse natures that they do not reach either by ascending or by descending. If they lift up their eyes, they see the incomprehensible majesty of God above them. If they look down, they see God and the divine majesty subjected to demons and to every creature.

These are marvelous things, to see a man and the lowliest creature humbled below all, to see the same creature sitting at the right hand of the Father and raised above all the angels, and to see him in the bosom of the Father and soon subjected to the devil. As is stated in Psalm 8:5, "You have made him a little lower than the angels." Likewise in Ephesians 4:9, "He had descended into the lower parts of the earth." This is a wonderful ascent and descent of the angels, to see the highest and the lowest completely united in one and the same person, the highest God lying in the manger. Therefore, the angels adore him there, rejoice, and sing, "Glory to God in the highest" [Luke 2:14]. On the other hand, when they consider the lowliness of human nature, they descend and sing, "And on earth peace."

When we see the same thing in the life to come, we too shall feel and speak far differently from the way we feel and speak now. For now these are things such as the angels do not comprehend. Nor can they be satisfied. Indeed, they always desire to look into this inexpressible goodness, wisdom, and mercy, poured out upon us when that person who is the highest and is terrible in his majesty above all creatures becomes the lowest and most despised. We shall see this wondrous spectacle in that life, and it shall be the constant joy of the blessed, just as it is the one desire and joy of the angels to see the Lord of all, who is the same as nothing, that is, the lowest.

We carnal and ignorant human beings do not understand or value the magnitude of these things. We have barely tasted a drink of milk—not solid food—from that inexpressible union and association of the divine and human nature. This [union] is of such a kind that not only has the humanity been assumed [by the divine], but the humanity has been made liable and subject to death and hell. Yet in that humiliation [the divine] has devoured the devil, hell, and all things in itself. This is the communion of attributes.[7] God, who created all things and is above all things, is the highest and the lowest. Thus we must say, "That man, who was scourged, who was the lowest under death, under the wrath of God, under sin and every kind of evil, and finally under hell, is the highest God." Why? He is the same person. Although the nature is twofold, the person is not divided. Therefore, both things are true: The highest divinity is the lowest creature, made the servant of all humanity, yes, subject to the devil himself. On the other hand, the lowest creature, the humanity or the man, sits at the right hand of the Father and has been made the highest. He subjects the angels to himself, not because of his human nature, but because of the wonderful conjunction and union established out of the two contrary and unjoinable natures in one person.

This, therefore, is the article by which the whole world, reason, and Satan are offended. For in the same person there are things that are most contrary. He who is the highest, such that the angels do not grasp him, is not only comprehended but has been so comprehended, is so finite, that nothing is more finite and confined, and vice versa. But he is not comprehended except in that word, as in breasts in which milk has been set forth and poured. Faith takes hold of this word, namely, I believe in the Son of God, our Lord Jesus Christ, who was conceived by the Holy Spirit, born of the Virgin Mary (these are the breasts), suffered under Pontius Pilate, was crucified, died, and was buried; he descended into hell; the third day he rose from the dead; he ascended into heaven and sits at the right hand of God the Father Almighty, after subjecting all the angels to himself. Here there is God and man, the highest and the lowest, infinite and finite in one person, emptying and filling all things.

This surely is the ascent and the descent of the angels of God and of the blessed, who look on this, pay attention to it, and proclaim it, as can be seen on the day of nativity. They descend as though there were no God up in heaven. They come to Bethlehem and say, "Behold, I announce great joy to you; the Lord has been born for you" [cf. Luke 2:10–11]. In Hebrews 1:6 we read, "When [God] brings the firstborn into the world, he says, 'Let all God's angels worship him.'" They adore him as he lies in the manger at his mother's breasts. Indeed, they adore him on the cross, when he descends into hell, when he has been subjected to sin and hell, when he bears all the sins of the whole world. And they submit themselves forever to this lowest one. Thus, therefore, the angels ascend and see the Son of God, who is begotten from eternity. On the other hand, they descend when they see him born in the time of Mary. And whether ascending or descending, they adore him.

This is how Christ explains this ladder. I regard this as the chief and proper interpretation of this passage. And this is that great and indescribable dignity of humankind that no one can express, namely, that by this wonderful union God has joined human nature to God's self. Ambrose and especially Bernard take great pleasure in this passage, which is exceedingly delightful, and in this work of the incarnation.[8] And it is right and godly for them to do so. For this pleasure will be a joy above all joy and will be eternal blessedness when we truly behold there our flesh, which is like us in all respects in the highest, as well as the lowest, place. For he did this all for us. He descended into hell and ascended into heaven. This sight the angels enjoy forever in heaven, and this is what Christ means when he says (Matt 18:10), "Their angels continually see the face of my Father in heaven." They look constantly at the divinity. And now they descend from heaven, after he has been made human. Now they look upon Christ and wonder at the work of the incarnation. They see that he has been made man, humiliated, and placed on his mother's lap. They adore the man who was crucified and rejected, and they acknowledge him as the Son of God.

Bernard loved the incarnation of Christ exceedingly. So did Bonaventure.[9] I praise these men most highly for the sake of that article on which they reflect gladly and brilliantly, and which they practice in themselves with great joy and godliness. Bernard thinks and imagines rightly enough that the devil fell because of that envy by which he begrudged humanity so great a dignity that God would become human. For [Bernard] thinks that, when Satan was a good angel in the sight of God, he saw that one day the divinity would descend and take upon itself this wretched and mortal flesh and would not take upon itself the nature of angels. Moved by that indignity and envy, thinks Bernard, the devil raged against God, with the result that the devil was thrown out of heaven.

These thoughts of Bernard are not unprofitable, for they flow from admiration for the boundless love and mercy of God. The devil was a very handsome angel and a decidedly outstanding creature. Seeing that it had been predetermined that God would assume human nature and not the nature of the angels, the devil was inflamed with envy, anger, and indignation against God for not being willing to take him, a most handsome spirit, and because he could not be a participant with the divinity in such great majesty. The devil was pained that the wretched mass of human flesh had to be preferred to himself, thinking that all this became him better than it did sinful flesh, which is liable to death and all evils. And, what is most surprising, this opinion crept into the Qur'an, no matter who the author or what the occasion was. It certainly seems that the devil himself suggested to the author of the Qur'an that good angels became demons because they refused to adore Adam.[10] Satan could not conceal this sin of his. Therefore, he imposed it on this instrument of his to stir up hatred against God. He distorted the true cause of the Fall, as though the angels were compelled to adore Adam, that is, a creature, and, when they refused, were hurled headlong from heaven and became demons.

This is almost in agreement with what Bernard imagined, by what he himself points out the devil betrays and in what respect he sinned. [The devil] wanted to be like God. When he saw that it would come to pass that God would lower God's self in such a way that God would assume humanity, he thought that this honor most properly suited himself. Accordingly, the ladder is the wonderful union of the divinity with our flesh. On it the angels ascend and descend, and they can never wonder at this enough. This is the historical, simple, and literal sense.[11]

Later there is another union, a union between us and Christ, as John expresses it in a very beautiful manner: "I am in the Father and the Father is in me," says Christ (John 14:10). This comes first. Later he says, "You in me and I in you" (John 14:20). This is the allegorical meaning of the ladder. But the allegory should nourish faith and not teach about our affairs or our works. Therefore we are carried along by faith and become one flesh with him, as Christ says in John 17:21: "that they may all be one; even as you, Father, are in me, and I am in you, may they also may be in us." In this way we ascend into him and are carried along through the word and the Holy Spirit. And through faith we cling to him, since we become one body with him and he with us. He is the head; we are the members. On the other hand, he descends to us through the word and the sacraments by teaching and by exercising us in the knowledge of him. The first union, then, is that of the Father and the Son in the divinity. The second is that of the divinity and the humanity in Christ. The third is that of the church and Christ.

PART III

A New Path to Prayer

Editors' Introduction to Part III: This section represents Luther's devotional spirituality. There are no greater contributions by Luther to the devotional spirituality of his followers than the small and the large catechisms that he wrote in 1529 and his hymnody. Although other aspects are noted, the emphasis in this section is on Luther's teaching about prayer. We have included from the Large Catechism (1529) the Preface, the explanation of the first commandment, and the introduction to the Lord's Prayer. In the organization of both catechisms Luther moves from the commandments to the creed to prayer. The commandments drive us to the gracious God proclaimed in the creed, and prayer places our needs, such as they are, before the gracious God we have.[1] In Luther's spirituality the word is never separated from the sacraments but is embodied in baptism and the Lord's Supper. Luther consistently linked word and sacrament:

> When [Luther] was asked whether it was enough for a person to confess sin and believe in absolution and not use the sacrament [of the altar], he replied, "No! It is stated in the words of institution, 'Do this in remembrance of me' [1 Cor 11:25]. Everything that is required of a Christian must be in the sacrament: acknowledgement of sin (which we call contrition), faith, giving of thanks, confession. These things must not be separated from one another."[2]

Included also in this section is Luther's "Commentary on Psalm 118," his favorite psalm, written in the same period as the catechisms but at the Coburg Castle, which he referred to as his "desert" (1530). The themes in the commentary are "personal, devotional, political, exegetical, polemical."[3] In 1529 he had written some notes on this psalm, which he had asked the neoclassical poet Eoban Hess to put to verse. Later he told Hess that he read the poem every day.[4] Its exhortations to pray in thanksgiving for the gracious gifts from God to each person and his insistence on the sanctity of every household and vocation capture Luther's understanding of devotion, which moved away from its professionalization in the monastery into the home.

This movement is captured in his classic "A Simple Way to Pray, for Master Peter the Barber," also included in this section. Written in 1535, it is "a miniature instruction book, song book, confessional, and prayer book." Finally, Luther commended his message in hymns that were deeply catechetical. According to Ulrich Leupold, his hymns fell on fertile soil in the sixteenth century because "he introduced no innovations, but only allowed the German hymn—long existing—to come into its own and fulfil its destiny."[5] Luther's hymns are written with little adornment but with strong nouns and verbs, for they were intended to convey a biblical and theological message, not a mood. "They were a confession of faith."[6]

THE LARGE CATHECHISM:
PREFACE AND FIRST
COMMANDMENT

Our reasons for dealing so thoroughly with the catechism are not trivial, nor why we urge and plead that others promote the study of it. Seeing so many preachers and pastors being so neglectful is regrettable, because they thereby disdain their office and this teaching. Some do so out of high and lofty erudition, others from pure laziness and concern to fill their paunch. They act as if they were pastors and preachers only out of their concern for a full stomach and for the use of their properties as long as they live, as they were accustomed to under the papacy.[1]

Now they have easy access to many wholesome books that make quite clear to them how they should teach and preach. Before, all they had were manuals, called *Sermons That Preach Themselves, Sleep Soundly, Be Prepared,* and *Treasury of Sermons,*[2] but they are not upright or industrious enough to buy the books; nor, if they do have them, do they bother to look at them and read them. Oh, what altogether shameful hogs and gluttons they are,[3] who should more rightly be swineherds and dog-keepers than guardians of souls and pastors.

And now that they no longer have to chatter the troublesome [breviary's] seven hours, it would be much better if morning, noon, and night they would replace it by reading a page or two of the catechism, prayer book,[4] New Testament, or something else from the Bible and pray the Lord's Prayer for themselves and their parishioners! In this way they would again show some gratitude and respect for the gospel, which has relieved them of so many burdens and difficulties, and they might feel a little shame that, like pigs and dogs, they do not get more out of the gospel than this lazy, harmful, scandalous, fleshly freedom. Sad to admit, the rabble has too low a regard for the gospel, and, even when we have tried as hard as we can, we do not make much of a difference. What can we expect if we want to be as idle and lazy as we were under the papacy?

Add to that offensive vice the secret, evil plague of security and over-satiated, self-satisfied boredom that has come over us. Many think the catechism a simple, trivial teaching, and, after reading through it once, they think they fully understand it, throw the book into the corner, and then feel ashamed to read from it anymore. Indeed, one surely also finds among the nobility thugs and misers who profess that from now on they need neither pastors nor preachers, because now they have the books themselves, from which they can learn well enough on their own. Self-assured, they allow the parishes to fall into ruin, while the pastors and preachers far and wide suffer hunger and want.⁵ That's what these mad Germans consider the appropriate thing to do. Because we Germans are such scandalous folk, we have to bear it.

Let me say this for myself: I am a doctor and a preacher, yes, and experienced as all those might be, who are so pretentious and self-assured. Still, like a child learning the catechism, in the mornings and whenever else I have the time, I read and recite, even word for word, the Lord's Prayer, the Ten Commandments, the creed, the psalms, etc. I must read and study more of it every day, and I still cannot achieve the understanding that I would like, so I must remain a child and a student of the catechism, and I remain one gladly. These fine, finicky fellows after one cursory reading immediately want to be doctors above all doctors, knowing everything and needing nothing more. Well now, such a thing is a sure indication that they disdain both their office and the people's souls and God and God's word to boot. They do not need to fall; they have already taken a gruesome fall. What they really need is to become children again and learn the ABC's, and not think they have long ago outgrown these shoes.

So I ask these lazy-bellies or presumptuous saints, for God's sake, to let themselves be convinced and believe that they truly are not the educated and lofty doctors they think they are. Never, ever, should they think that they have completed learning these parts of the catechism or know them well enough, even though they think right away that they know them all too well. For even if they learned and knew all these things perfectly (which is, of course, impossible in this life), they would still, in any case, find it useful and profitable to read it daily and incorporate it into their meditations and conversation. For the Holy Spirit itself is present during such reading, conversing, and meditating and always gives more and new light and devotion. Thus it tastes better and better and is digested, as Christ also promises in Matthew 18[:20], "Where two or three are gathered in my name, I am there among them."

Besides, nothing helps more powerfully against the devil, the world, the flesh, and all evil thoughts than occupying oneself with God's word, having conversations about it, and contemplating it. Notice how the first psalm even praises that one as blessed who "meditates on the law day and night." Without a doubt, you will not be able to burn a stronger incense or fragrance against the devil than involving yourself in God's commandments and words and speaking, singing, or thinking about them. Indeed, this is the real holy water and sign from which the devil flees and can be chased away.[6]

Now certainly for this reason alone you should gladly read, recite, think about, and practice these articles, even if there were no other profit and use for them than to chase away the devil and evil thoughts. For the devil cannot stand to hear God's word or endure it. God's word is not like some idle chatter, such as the tale of Dietrich of Bern,[7] but, as St. Paul says in Romans 1[:16], it is "the power of God"—yes, surely, the power of God that burns the devil and strengthens, comforts, and helps us beyond measure.[8]

And why should I say more? If I were to relate all the utility and profit that God's word effects, where would I find enough paper and time for it? The devil is called a master of a thousand arts. What will one call God's word, which drives away and reduces to nothing this craft master of a thousand arts with all his skills and power? The word must be a hundred thousand times more crafty and cunning. And should we nonchalantly disdain such power, usefulness, strength, and fruit, especially if we want to be pastors and preachers? In such a case one should not only not feed us, but even have the dogs drive us out and throw horse manure at us. For not only do we need all these things as we do our daily bread, but we need it every day against the daily, ceaseless onslaughts and surveillance of that thousand-crafted devil.

If that were not admonishment enough to read the catechism daily, then it should suffice that God's command compels us. For in

Deuteronomy 6[:7–8] God makes the solemn demand that we should meditate on God's commandments while sitting, walking, standing, lying down, and getting up; so too we should have it as a constant marker before our eyes and as a sign for our hands. Certainly God did not order and require this so earnestly without reason. God knows our danger and need and knows the devil's constant, raging, storming assaults. Thus, God wants to warn, arm, and protect us with good "armor" against these "flaming arrows" [Eph 6:11, 16] and good medicine against this evil disease and poison. Oh, what mad, senseless fools we are that we should ever dwell or be embedded among such mighty enemies as these devils and then reject our weapons and defense, being too lazy to put them on or even remember them.

And what are those tiresome, pretentious saints doing who neither want nor desire to read and learn the catechism daily? They consider themselves far more learned than God and all the holy angels, prophets, apostles, and Christians. For God is not ashamed to teach it daily, knowing there is nothing better to teach, and God always teaches it the same way without proposing anything new or different. All the saints do not know what else to learn and cannot exhaust this learning. Then are we not the very finest ruffians who allow ourselves to think that, having read and heard it one time, we know it all and need no longer read and learn it? We can finish learning in one hour what God cannot finish teaching, indeed, even from the beginning to the end of the world. All the prophets and saints had to learn it and still had to remain its students and have to remain so until today.

For it is the case that whoever knows and keeps the Ten Commandments perfectly knows the whole scripture and thus is able to counsel, help, comfort, judge, and make decisions in all causes and cases, both spiritual and temporal. Such a person is likely to be a judge over all teaching, estates,[9] spirits, law, and everything else in the world. What is the whole psalter but meditations and exercises on the first commandment?[10] For I know and declare that such lazy bones or presumptuous spirits do not understand one psalm, let alone the complete holy scriptures, and yet they want to know and disdain the catechism, which is a brief excerpt and summary of the complete holy scriptures.

Therefore, I once again beg all Christians, especially pastors and preachers, that they would not try to be doctors too soon and delude themselves by thinking they know it all. (A span of new cloth and wishful thought shrink a great deal going through the wash.)[11] Thus they must study and practice the catechism daily and carefully and diligently guard against the poisonous contagion of such certainty or of such vain masters of wishful thinking. They must always take the time and never stop reading and teaching, learning, thinking, and meditating until they experience and are certain that they have taught and educated the devil to death and have learned more than God and all God's saints.

If they are that zealous, I assure them, they will also become aware of the kind of fruit they will bear and how God will make beautiful people out of them. In time they themselves will confess that the longer and the more they make use of the catechism, the less they know of it, and the more they will have to learn from it.[12] Then, like the hungry and thirsty, they will feel as if, for the first time, they are tasting something, where before they were so overstuffed and super-sated that they could no longer bear even to smell it. For this purpose may God's precious grace be given us! Amen.

Preface[13]

This sermon is designed and undertaken as an instruction for the children and the uneducated. That is why from of old to now it is called a catechism in Greek, that is, instruction for children. It contains what each and every Christian should know. Thus, whoever does not know it should not be counted as a Christian and should not be admitted to any sacrament. It is the same with artisans who lack the art and usage or skills of their craft; one throws them out and considers them incompetent. For that reason one should have young people take the articles that belong to the catechism or children's sermon and learn them thoroughly and well, diligently practicing and applying themselves to them.[14]

At least once a week, therefore, each and every head of household is responsible for asking and questioning closely the children and household workers, one at a time, as to what they know or are learning and, where they lack in knowledge, seriously to hold them to it.[15] For I still remember the time—indeed, even now it is all too common—that one daily found crude, ignorant, older, and age-worn people who knew absolutely nothing of these things. Yet, not knowing them even now, they go to baptism and the sacrament and use everything the Christians have, even though those who go to baptism should by right know more and have a more complete understanding of all Christian teachings than children and pupils chasing their ABC's. To be sure, for the common crowd, we have not gone farther than the three articles,[16] which has been the custom from ancient times in Christendom, but seldom rightly taught and practiced.[17]

Whoever wants to be a Christian in fact as well as in name, both young and old, should practice and become knowledgeable in the following, namely:

First of All: The Ten Commandments of God[18]

The First: You shall have no other Gods besides me.

The Next: You shall not take the name of the Lord your God in vain.

The Third: Remember to keep the day of rest holy.[19]

The Fourth: You shall honor your father and mother.

The Fifth: You shall not kill.

The Sixth: You shall not commit adultery.

The Seventh: You shall not steal.

The Eighth: You shall not bear false witness against your neighbor.

The Ninth: You shall not covet your neighbor's house.

The Tenth: You shall not covet your neighbor's wife, male or female servants, cattle, or anything that belongs to your neighbor.

Next: The Main Articles of Faith

I believe in God, the Father almighty, creator of heaven and earth. And in Jesus Christ, God's only Son, our Lord, who was conceived by the Holy Spirit, born of the Virgin Mary, suffered under

Pontius Pilate, was crucified, died, and was buried; he descended into hell. On the third day he rose again from the dead; ascended into heaven, and is seated at the right hand of God, the Father almighty, from where he will come to judge the living and the dead. I believe in the Holy Spirit, one holy Christian church,[20] the communion of saints, the forgiveness of sins, the resurrection of the flesh, and a life everlasting. Amen.

Third: The Prayer, or the Lord's Prayer, as Christ Taught It

Our Father, you who are in heaven, hallowed be your name. Your kingdom come. Your will be done on earth as in heaven. Give us today our daily bread, and forgive our sins as we forgive those who sin against us. And lead us not into temptation, but deliver us from evil. Amen.

Those are the necessary articles that one should learn first, reciting them word for word. One should admonish the children to say them by heart every day when they get up in the morning, when they are at the table, and in the evening when they go to sleep. Give them no food or drink until they have said it. Each and every head of a household is also responsible to do the same in regard to the workers in the household,[21] the servant men and women, and not keep them if they do not know it or want to learn it. Under no circumstances should a person be tolerated who is too coarse and wild to learn these things, since we have briefly summarized everything that is in the scriptures in these three parts in a plain and simple way. For the dear fathers or apostles (whoever they were)[22] have in this way put together in summary the teaching, life, wisdom, and learning by which Christians speak and act and with which they are concerned.

Now once these three articles are understood, it is also appropriate to know what to say about our sacraments (which Christ himself instituted): baptism and the holy body and blood of Christ, according to the texts of Matthew and Mark, who write at the end of their gospels how Christ bid the disciples farewell and sent them out.

Concerning Baptism

"Go and teach all nations, and baptize them in the name of the Father and of the Son and of the Holy Spirit" [Matt 28:19].[23] "The one who believes and is baptized will be saved; but the one who does not believe will be condemned" [Mark 16:16].

That is enough for a simple soul to know about baptism from scripture. The same is true for the other sacrament, using short and simple words, like the text of St. Paul.

Concerning the Sacrament

"Our Lord Jesus, on the night when he was betrayed, took the bread, gave thanks, broke it and gave it to his disciples, saying, 'Take and eat. This is my body, which is given for you. Do this in remembrance of me.' In the same way he also took the cup after supper and said, 'This cup is the new testament in my blood, which is shed for you for the forgiveness of sins. Do this, as often as you drink it, in remembrance of me.'"[24]

With that one would have altogether five articles for the whole of Christian teaching, which one should forever drive home. Require them to be able to recite these parts word for word, and listen to them carefully to test them. Do not let yourself depend upon the young ones' learning and remembering these things just from the sermon.

Now, when they know these articles, one can afterward teach some psalms or hymns, based on the same subjects,[25] as additional material for their strengthening, so that the youth are led into the scriptures and make daily progress.

It should not, however, be sufficient only to parrot the words and so be able to recite them. Let the young people also attend the sermon, especially at the times designated for preaching the catechism,[26] so that they can hear how it is interpreted and learn to understand what each and every article means. And when one asks them, they should also be able to say aloud what they have heard with fine and correct answers, so that preaching has fruit and is not useless. Thus we diligently present the catechism often in our preaching in order to inculcate the youth with it, not in a manner over their heads or too difficult, but briefly and very simply, so that they understand it well and it remains fixed in their memory. Therefore, we want to consider the designated articles one after another and in the clearest way say about them as much as needed.

The First Commandment

"You shall have no other gods."

That is, you should have me alone for your God. What does that mean, and how does one understand it? What does it mean to have a god, or what is God?

Answer: A "God" is that upon which one relies for all good things and in whom one takes refuge in all times of trouble. Thus, to have a God is nothing less than to trust and believe in that one from the whole heart. As I have often said, it is the trust and faith of the heart alone that makes both a God and an idol. If faith and trust are right, then your God is also right, and again, where faith is false and not right, then the right God is also not there. For the two belong together, faith and God. Now anything upon which you hang your heart and rely, I say, is really your God.

Therefore now, the meaning of this commandment is to require the right faith and trust of the heart, which embraces the right and only God and clings to this God alone. This is to say, "See to it that you let me be your God alone, and never search for another." That is, "Rely on me for whatever good you might lack, and seek it from me. And where you suffer misfortune and need, crawl to me and hold onto me. I, I myself, will give you enough and help you out of all trouble; just do not let your heart hang or rest on any other."

Let me explain that a little more clearly, because one can understand it by observing examples from everyday life that illustrate the very opposite. There are some who believe they have God and have enough of everything when they have money and possessions, upon which they rely and get an attitude that is so rigid and secure that they could care less about anybody else. Such persons certainly also have a god, and it is called mammon, or money and possessions, upon which they hang their whole heart. Money is indeed the most common idol on earth. Those who have money and good things know they are secure, happy, and unafraid, as if they were sitting in the middle of paradise. On the other hand, those who have no money doubt and despair, as if they knew of no God. For one will find very few people who have good spirits and do not grieve and complain when they do not have mammon. This desire for wealth clings and sticks to our nature until we are in the grave.

So, too, whoever trusts in and boasts of having a great education, cleverness, power, prestige, family, and honor, also has a god, but not the right and only God. Just observe how pretentious, secure, and proud people are with these good things and how much they despair when they are not present or they are taken away. Therefore, I say again that the correct interpretation of this article is that to have a God means having something upon which the heart trusts completely....For that reason, in order to see that God does not want us to take this commandment lightly but take it very seriously, God first poses a frightening threat and then a beautiful, comforting promise after it. We surely need to drive both of these home and emphasize and impress them upon young people, so that they can become mindful of them and remember them.

"For I the Lord your God am a strong and jealous God,[27] visiting the inequity of the parents upon the children until the third and fourth generation of those that hate me and showing mercy to many thousands who love me and keep my commandments."[28]

Even if these words refer to all the commandments (as we shall hear later),[29] they are still really attached to this main commandment heading the list, because it is most important that a person have the right head. For if the head goes the right way, then the whole life goes right as well, and vice versa. So learn from these words how angry God is against those who rely on something other than God, and, conversely, how good and gracious God is to those who trust and believe, from their whole heart, in God alone. God's wrath does not diminish until the fourth generation; in contrast, God's kindness and goodness flow over many thousands. One should not have a false sense of security and take risks in the face of this danger, as crude souls think, as if not very much depended on it. God is the sort that does not allow to go unpunished those who turn away from God and whose anger does not stop until the fourth generation, continuing until they are utterly uprooted and destroyed. Therefore, God wants to be feared and not despised.

God has proven it also in all the histories and stories, as scripture richly illustrates and our daily experience teaches us as well. For God completely uprooted all idolatry from the very beginning and, because of it, overthrew both heathens and Jews, as in our time today God causes all false worship to fall, so that ultimately all those who remain in it will have to perish. So therefore, if one now finds proud, mighty, and rich fat cats, who boast of their mammon without regard to whether God is angry or smiling, even if they think they can survive and endure God's wrath, they will still not succeed. Before they know it, they will break to pieces, together with all the things upon which they have trusted, just like all the others who have perished before them, who imagined themselves so secure and powerful.

And precisely because of these hardheads, who have the opinion that since God is looking on and allows them to sit tight and secure, God therefore does not care or does not observe their ways, God will strike hard and punish them, not being able to forget until their children's children, so that everyone will be upset by it and see that God is not joking. For these are also the ones meant when God says "those who hate me," that is, who remain obstinate in their spite and arrogance. Whatever one preaches or says to them they do not want to hear; if one rebukes them to make them recognize and understand themselves in order to improve before the punishment begins, they become mad and enraged. Then they truly deserve wrath, as we now daily experience with the bishops and rulers.

But as frightening as these threatening words are, there is so much more comfort in the promise that those who entrust themselves to God alone can be certain that God will show mercy upon them, proving it with acts of kindness and sheer blessings, not only for them, but also for their children for a thousand and more thousands of generations. It should move and drive us to trust in God with all the confidence of our heart, if we desire all good things in time and eternity, since such a great majesty approaches us with such favor, charms us so heartily, and gives us such rich promises.

Therefore, let each one of us take sincerely to heart that we not regard these words as if they had been said by a human being. For they bring to you either eternal blessing, fortune, and salvation or eternal wrath, misfortune, and sorrows of the heart. What more could you want or desire than that God promises to be yours in such a friendly way, to bring you all good things, protect you, and help you in all times of need? The problem is that the world believes nothing of the sort nor does it consider this to be God's word, so these words sadly fail to reach us. That is because the world sees that those who trust in God rather than mammon suffer sorrow and need. The devil opposes them and prevents them from having any money, favor, or honor, such that they can barely survive. On the other hand, those that serve mammon have power, favor, honor, possessions, and complete security before the world. For that reason one has to grasp these words, even in the face of contradiction. These words do not lie or deceive but will have to become true.

Think back yourself, or ask what happened to these people, and tell me: those who cared and hustled all their lives only to scrape a great deal of money and exorbitant possessions together, what did they finally achieve? You will find that they wasted their toil and trouble, or, even if they brought home great treasures, still it turned to dust and flew away. You will find that their wealth never made them happy, and afterward the inheritance did not even reach the third generation.[30] You will find enough of these examples in all the histories and also from elderly and experienced people, just pay attention and observe them. Saul was a great king, chosen by God, and an upright man, but, when he was established in his office, he let his heart sink, clutched his crown and power, and then had to perish with all he had, so that not even one of his children remained.[31] David, on the other hand, was a poor man, rejected, driven away, and shunned. His life was not at all secure, but he still survived Saul and became the king. For these words had to stand and become true, since God cannot lie nor deceive. So just let the devil and the world deceive you through their appearances; they endure, it is true, for a while, but finally amount to nothing.

Therefore, let us learn this first commandment well. We see how God will tolerate no pretensions or trust in anything else, requiring nothing loftier from us than heartfelt trust and the anticipation of all good things from God. Thus we can rightly proceed forward with rigor as God provides and use things just as a shoemaker uses needle, awl, and thread for work and afterward sets them aside, or as a guest uses an inn for food and lodging, using them solely for the need of the moment. Each one in his or her way of life should do the same according to God's order and allow none of these things to become his or her lord or idol.

That is enough about the first commandment. We have had to explain it comprehensively, because it is the most important;[32] everything depends upon it, because (as said before) where the heart is in the right place with God and this commandment is kept, all the other commandments will follow on their own.

THE LARGE CATECHISM:
THE LORD'S PRAYER

We have already heard what we should do and what we should believe;[1] in this the best and most blessed life exists. Now the third part follows: how one should pray. It is so with us that no one can fulfill the commandments completely, even if one has begun to have faith. The devil, the world, and one's own flesh resist the fulfillment of the commandments with terrible might. Thus there is nothing so vital as to hang always on God's ear, calling and pleading that God give, preserve, and increase in us faith and the fulfillment of the Ten Commandments and that God clear away everything that lies in the way and hinders the same. That we may know, however, what and how we should pray, the Lord Jesus himself taught the way and words, as we will see.

Before we explain the Lord's Prayer sequentially, we must first counsel and entice the people to prayer, just as Christ and the apostles did.[2] First, we are obligated to pray because God has commanded it. Thus, we heard in the commandment, "You shall not take God's name in vain," that God's holy name should be praised, called upon, or prayed to in every need. To call upon it is nothing other than praying. Slovenly people think that it is indifferent whether one prays or not, as they go about in their folly, thinking, What should I pray? Who knows if God pays attention or hears my prayer? If I do not pray, someone else will! For this reason prayer is as strictly and emphatically commanded as all the other commandments—to have no other God, not to kill, not to steal, etc. Nevertheless, they are in the habit of never praying and use as an excuse that we have rejected false and hypocritical prayers, as if we therefore taught that one should or need not pray at all.

This is certainly true for what was called prayer in the church up to now; speaking in monotones and braying are by no means prayer.

198

Such an external act, when it is done properly, can be an exercise for young children, students, and common people, and can be sung or read, but it is not prayer. This is prayer as the other commandment teaches: "Calling upon God in every need." This God wants from us, and it is not a matter of our choosing; we should and must pray if we want to be Christians, just as we should and must obey father and mother and the government. Through invocation and bidding we honor God's name and use it profitably. Beyond everything else you should note that one should quiet and repress whatever thoughts would prevent and intimidate us from praying. In other words, it is not appropriate that a son say to his father, "Why do I need to obey? I will go and do as I please; it is all the same to me!" On the contrary, we have the commandment: you should and must do it. That is, it is not in my discretion to do or not to do, but I should and must pray.[3]

Because prayer is so strictly commanded, you should consider and conclude that we should not despise our own prayer but hold it in the highest regard. Always take the other commandments as illustrations. A child should never despise being obedient to father and mother but should always think: This work is a work of obedience, and what I do has no other purpose than that it obeys God's commandment. I can ground myself on this, not because of my own worthiness, but because of the commandment. Similarly, in this case, we should consider what and for what we pray as requested by and done in obedience to God. We should therefore think, For my sake it counts for nothing, but it is most important that God commanded it. Therefore, each one of us should come before God in prayer for whatever we need in obedience to this commandment.

Therefore, we urgently entreat and admonish all people to take this to heart and in no way forsake their prayers. Up to now it was taught in the devil's name in such a way that no one respected the command to pray. Belief held that it was enough when the act of prayer was done. It did not matter if God heard or not. This makes prayer a matter of luck and random murmuring, and it is therefore wasted prayer.

We let ourselves be deterred and alarmed by thoughts such as these: I am not holy or worthy enough; if I were as holy as St. Peter or Paul, then I would pray. But away with such thoughts, because the same commandment that addressed Paul addresses me as well and is given as much for me as for him. He has no holier commandment to honor than I. Therefore, you should say, "The prayers that I make are as valuable, holy, and pleasing to God as those of St. Paul and the holiest of saints. The reason? In regards to the person, I am content to let him be holier, but not in regards to the commandment, because for prayer God is not a respecter of the person, but considers the word and obedience. Just as all the saints rest their prayers on the commandment, so also do I, and I pray for the same things for which they all pray and ever have prayed."

It is first and foremost that all our prayers are founded and stand on our obedience to God, irrespective of our person, whether we are sinners or righteous, worthy or unworthy. God does not want this commandment taken in jest. Indeed, God will be angry and punish when we do not ask in prayer, just as God punishes all other kinds of disobedience. Furthermore, we are to know that God will not let our prayers be in vain or lost. If God did not want to hear you, you would not have been asked and so strictly commanded to pray.

In addition, it should drive and entice us that God has also made and attached a promise that the answer will be "Yes, certainly!" to whatever we pray. As God says in Psalm 50[:15], "Call on me in the day of trouble; I will deliver you," and as Christ says in Matthew 7:7–8, "Ask, and it will be given you....For everyone who asks receives." This should certainly awaken our hearts and set them on fire to pray with desire and love. To this we have the witness of the word that God delights in our prayers.

In addition, our prayers will be granted and guaranteed, so that we should not despise prayer, cast our prayers to the wind, or pray without certainty. You can hold this over God and say, "I am coming before you, dear Father, and ask you not out of my own presumptuousness or out of my worthiness, but because of your commandment and promise that cannot remain unfulfilled and cannot lie." Whoever does not believe this promise should know that God is thereby angered, dishonored, and accused of lying.

Beyond this we should be enticed and drawn, knowing that, besides the commandment and the promise, God provides us in anticipation with the words and the way and puts into our mouths how and what we should pray. This is done in order that we may see how heartily God takes up our troubles and that we should not doubt that this prayer pleases God and is certainly heard.

This prayer therefore has a great advantage over other prayers that we might compose ourselves. In the latter case, the conscience would always doubt and say, "I prayed, but who knows if it is pleasing to God or if I achieved the right manner and method?" Therefore, no more noble prayer can be found on earth, for it has such an excellent witness that God hears it gladly, and we should not trade all the world's riches for it.

Thus it is also prescribed so that we may see and reflect on those troubles that ought to press and force us to pray without ceasing. Whoever wants to plead must present a petition, make a request, and name something that is desired; otherwise, it cannot be called a prayer. This is why we rightly rejected the prayers of the monks and priests, who howl and murmur fearfully day and night, but not one of them thinks of praying for the slightest thing.

If one were to gather all the churches together, including their clergy, they would have to confess that they never prayed from the heart even for a drop of wine. Not one of them took it upon himself to pray out of obedience to God or faith in the promise. Nor do they reflect on their troubles, but do not think any farther (to put the best construction on it) than to do a good work in order to pay God; they do not want to take anything from, but instead give to God.

If a prayer is to be prayer, it has to be done with earnestness, so that one feels one's need—and such a need that it squeezes and drives us to call out and scream. In this way the prayer happens by itself, the way it should, and requires no teaching as to how one should prepare oneself for it and prepare oneself for devotion. In the Lord's Prayer you will find sufficient need generously expressed that should be our concern as well as the concern of others.

Consequently, the prayer should also serve to remind us of such things, so that we consider them and take them to heart in order not to become lazy in our praying. We all have a sufficient amount of need, but it is our failure that we do not feel and see it. God wants you to bring to voice your needs and desires, not because God does not know them, but so that you set your heart on fire to long all the more and more strenuously and to spread out your arms to receive much.

From childhood on everyone should become accustomed to pray daily for every personal need, wherever one even begins to feel affected, and also for others in one's environment, among whom are preachers, the government, the neighbor, and always, as has been said, to remember and know God's commandment and promise, which are ignored at one's own peril. I say this because I want to return to the people the right way of praying, so that they do not go about it so crudely and coldly and thus daily become more incompetent in praying.[4] This is what the devil wants and tries mightily to achieve; for the devil rightly experiences suffering and damage when prayer is on the right course.

This we should know: that all our shelter and protection rests in prayer. We are far too weak against the devil and the devil's minions when they attack, because they can simply crush us under their feet. Consequently, we need to consider and take up the weapons with which Christians are to be armed to withstand the devil. What do you think has accomplished such great results in the past, parrying the counsels and plots of our enemies and checking their murderous and seditious designs by which the devil expected to crush us and the gospel as well, except that the prayers of a few upright people intervened like an iron wall on our side?[5] They would have otherwise had to witness a much different game, as the devil would have stained all of Germany in its own blood. They may want to laugh contentedly and mock now, but by prayer alone we will match both them and the devil, as long as we hold on diligently and do not become lax. Whenever an upright Christian prays, "Dear Father, let your will be done," God answers from above, "Yes, dear child, this will certainly be done, in spite of the devil and the world."

Let it be a warning that, above all, one should learn to revere and cherish prayer and to make the correct distinction between babble and asking for something. We do not despise prayer in any way, but we do reject all completely useless howling and murmuring, just as Christ himself rejects and forbids long empty phrases.[6] Now, we would like to consider the Lord's Prayer in a brief and clear fashion. In seven successive articles or petitions all needs are summed up with which we must struggle without end; each need is so great that it should drive us to pray our life long.

COMMENTARY ON PSALM 118—
THE BEAUTIFUL THANKSGIVING

To the most honorable Lord, Frederick, Abbot of St. Giles of Nuremberg, my dear Lord and patron.

Grace and peace in Christ, our Lord and Savior. Worthy Lord and patron, I wanted to express my thanks for your love and generosity. As far as the world is concerned, I am a poor beggar, but, even if I had much, your station in life is such that I would not be able to offer you much of anything. Thus, I have turned to my riches, that which I hold as my treasure, and have chosen to take up my dear psalm, "The Beautiful Thanksgiving" [Ps 118]. I have put my thoughts on paper, because I have to while away my time in this desert. Every so often I have to spare myself and take a break and have fun, away from my main and greater work of fully translating the prophets into German, which I also soon hope to finish.

I have wanted to write to you such thoughts and send them to you as a present. I have nothing better. Even if it may be considered by some to be empty, useless gossip, I nonetheless know that nothing evil or unchristian is in it. For it is my psalm, which I love. While the entire psalter and the holy scriptures altogether are also dear to me, as they are my sole comfort and life, nevertheless, I have struck up a very special relationship with this psalm, so that it must be mine and be called mine. It has worked quite diligently for me, deserving to become mine, and has helped me in some great emergencies, out of which no emperor, king, sage, clever person, or saint would have been able to help me. And it is dearer to me than any honor of the pope, Turks, emperor, and all the world's goods and power, and I would not want to trade this psalm for all of them put together.

Were someone to look askance at me for considering and boasting this psalm to be mine, since the psalm, of course, belongs to all

203

the world, that person should know that the psalm is not taken away from anyone just because it is mine. Christ is also mine, but he certainly remains for all the saints just the same. I will not be jealous but will share it joyfully. Would to God that the whole world would claim this psalm for themselves as I do. That would produce such a friendly quarrel that harmony or love could not compare. Sadly, there are all too few, even among those who rightly should instruct others, who would even once address the holy scriptures or a single psalm from the heart and say, "You are my dear book; you will be my little psalm."

It is certainly one of the greatest plagues on earth that the holy scripture is taken so lightly even among those responsible for it. Night and day people concern themselves endlessly with everything else, like art and other books. It is only the holy scripture that lies there, as if we do not need it. And those who wish to honor it by deigning to read it once think themselves smart enough to master it all on the first reading. There has never been art or book that has been studied like the holy scriptures. Nevertheless, in scripture are not, as some think, mere book words, but pure life words,[1] that are not there for mere speculation and intellectual thinking, but for living and doing.[2] Yet our complaining is of no use; they do not pay attention. May Christ our Lord help us by his Spirit so that we honor his holy word with sincere love and honor. Amen. Now I commend myself to your prayers.

Out of the Desert, July 1, 1530.[3]
Martin Luther

The Beautiful Thanksgiving

"O give thanks to the Lord, for he is good; his steadfast love endures forever! [Ps 118:1]."

This verse is a comprehensive thanksgiving for every blessing that God, the Lord of all, unceasingly provides on a daily basis for both good and wicked people. This is the style of the holy prophets. When they wish to thank and praise God for particular occasions, they begin in an expansive and lofty way and praise God generally for all God's wonders and good deeds. So it is here, because this psalm above all praises God for the greatest act of kindness that God gave the world, namely, Christ and his reign of grace, promised to the world and now revealed. It begins with all-inclusive praise, saying,

"O give thanks to the Lord," because God is a God who has a heart for us, a gracious, loving, compassionate God who is continually kind to us and pours one good thing on us after another.

You should not read the words *good* and *God's steadfast love* coldly and without emotion, racing over them the way the nuns read the psalter or as choirmasters and choristers bleat and bellow these precious words in the churches. On the contrary, you must think that these are living, striking, rich words that encompass everything and focus on one thing. They witness that God's goodness is not like that of humans; rather, from the bottom of God's heart, God is inclined to help and do good continually. God is slow to anger and punishment, except when compelled and driven by persistent, impenitent, and stubborn wickedness. A human being could never wait so long to grow angry and to punish but would punish a hundred thousand times earlier and harder than God.

God abundantly and powerfully proves friendly and gracious in daily and everlasting goodness. As the psalmist writes, "God's steadfast love endures forever!" That is, God unfailingly showers the best upon us. God creates body and soul, protects us day and night, and continually preserves our lives. God causes the sun and moon to shine on us; fire, air, water, and the heavens to serve us; the earth to yield wine, grain, fodder, food, clothing, and wood; and lets all that we need grow. God gives us gold and silver, house and home, spouse and children, cattle, birds, and fish. In short, who can count it all? And all this is bountifully showered upon us every year, every day, every hour, and every minute. Who can calculate the goodness of God in having and keeping a healthy eye or hand? When we are sick or must get along without one of these, then we know what a gift it is to have a healthy eye, hand, foot, leg, head, nose, or finger, and what grace it is to have bread, clothing, water, fire, a house, and other things.

If people were not so blind and did not take the goodness of God for granted and even scorn it, they would realize that, no matter how wealthy they were, they would be swindled were they to exchange these blessings for an empire or a kingdom. For what kind of treasure is a kingdom when one does not have one's health? What is the value of all the world's money compared to the new day given to us in each day's rising of the sun? If the sun failed to shine one day, one would rather be dead, and how could a person's possessions or authority help? What would the finest wine or malmsey in the world amount to if we had to go without water for one day?[4] How would our magnificent castles, houses, silk, satin, purple, golden jewelry, precious stones, all our pomp and glitter and show help us if we had to do without air for the length of one Lord's Prayer?

These are the greatest gifts from God and also the ones that we deride most, and, because they are so common, we do not give thanks for them. We take them and use them each day so thoughtlessly, as if it had to be so and we were entitled to them; thus, we do not need to thank God for them even once. In the meantime, we tear off and care only to worry, quarrel, wrangle, strive, and storm after unnecessary money and goods, honor and luxury—in short, after something that cannot hold a candle to the blessings mentioned above. Worse, it hinders our joyful and serene use of the common gifts, such that we do not recognize them as such, nor do we thank God for them. Behind all of this is the devil, who does not want us to use and acknowledge all of God's gifts to us and thus be happy.

Now, tell me how many persons there are on earth who understand this verse. The truth is that not even a worthless lout is so wicked that, when he sings or hears this verse in church, he does not imagine that he fully understands it and has plumbed the depths of its meaning. Yet he never gave it a thought in his whole life and never even gave thanks for the milk that he drank from his mother's breast, let alone all the countless, ceaseless gifts that God has given him throughout his life. Thus through his thanklessness he has sinned more hourly than there are leaves and grass in the forest, that is, if God were a lender and kept close account of the debt.

Therefore, this verse should be in the heart and mouth of everyone every day and every moment. Every time one eats or drinks, sees, smells, walks, stands; every time one uses one's limbs, body, belongings, or anything made, one should consider that, if God had not given these things to use and had not preserved them despite the devil, one would not have them. At the same time one is admonished and accustomed to give thanks for these everyday gifts today with a glad heart and a joyful faith in God, saying, "Truly you are a kind and good God, who eternally, that is, without end, gives to me, an unworthy and thankless one, so much good and blessedness. You are so good and bless me so you deserve thanks and praise."

This serves also as a comfort when things do not go well. We are such weaklings and suffering "martyrs" when even one leg hurts or a small sore swells that we can fill heaven and earth with cries and howls, grumbling and cursing. We do not see what a tiny evil such a small thing is, compared to the countless blessings that God provides. This is like a king who gets angry because he has lost a penny and forgets that he owns half the world's money and possessions and therefore begins to curse and swear violently, throws a tantrum, shouts profanities, denounces and blasphemes God with thunderous curses. In just the same way cursing thugs, today, try to prove their masculinity by using profanity.

Snorers that we are, God lets us experience these minor troubles so that we may be awakened from our deep sleep and be driven by knowledge and realization to consider what would happen if the great and countless blessings present to us disappeared because God's favor turned away from us. Thus the faithful Job declared, "Shall we receive the good at the hand of God and not the bad?" (Job 2:10). You see that Job was able to sing this beautiful confession well and said, "The Lord gave, and the Lord has taken away; blessed be the name of the Lord" (Job 1:21). He did not simply stare at the evil, as we would-be saints do, but he kept the goodness and favor of God in sight and comforted himself with it to overcome evil with patience.

Similarly, we should consider and accept all our fortunes in no other way than that God is lighting a lamp for us by which we can see and recognize God's goodness and favor in other countless things. Thus we should imagine that such tiny misfortunes are barely a drop of water in a big fire, or a little spark in a large body of water. In this way we would grow to know and love this verse: "Oh, give thanks to the Lord, for (yes indeed) he is good; his steadfast love endures forever." In German this means—because in translating I have tried hard to be faithful to the Hebrew—"Oh, what a faithful, heartwarming, loving Lord God you are, who provides for me and the whole world at all times such goodness and mercy. Thanks be to you!"

The Hebrew word *chesed*, which is *eleemosyne* in Greek and until now has been called "mercy," I have translated as "steadfast love"; for it really means "goodness in action." Christ himself uses the word when he says (Matt 12:7), "I desire mercy and not sacrifice." And St. Paul tells Timothy (1 Tim 6:2), "Servants should devote themselves to believing masters, since they are believers and beloved who devote themselves to good deeds."[5] In Matthew 6:1 Christ says, "Beware of practicing your good deeds"[6]—that which, according to custom, we call alms from the Greek *eleemosyne*. The word *alms* has also come into misuse, so that one understands *alms* as nothing but a piece of bread given to a beggar at the door, but *eleemosyne* really means *chesed* or "goodness in action," such as God grants us and we, in turn, should do for others.

The word *forever* is not to be understood to mean only the goodness in heaven after this life, but the Hebrew word *olam* means what in German we call "continually" or "always," whether here or hereafter. Thus one says of a restless person: "Why all this continual running around? What will all this everlasting running around be?" I had to exegete this word and explain it, so that we would really understand this verse. It is used often in the scriptures and especially in the psalms, and it teaches us the offering that pleases God most. We cannot do something greater or better in relation to God or serve God more nobly than to say thanks. As is said in Psalm 50:23, "Those who bring thanksgiving as their sacrifice honor me; to those who go the right way I will show the salvation of God." Such offerings please God more than all offerings, endowments, monasteries, and whatever is similar to them. As the psalmist says (Ps 69:30–31): "I will praise the name of God with a song; I will magnify him with thanksgiving. This will please the Lord more than…a bull with horns and hoofs."…

"Out of my distress I called on the Lord; the Lord answered me and set me in a broad place" [Ps 118:5].

Here you see where this little band is found. It does not move in open joy before the world. Anxiety is its dwelling or inn. The psalmist paints his whereabouts and his condition; namely, that he is stuck in all manner of suffering. As is proper when one begins to talk about something, he is brief; he sums up all kinds of troubles and calls them "distress." Later he will relate and explain more, just as if I might say how much St. Paul had to suffer but did not explain what he suffered. Even so, the psalmist first shows generally and briefly God's comfort and help, when he says, "the Lord answered me." As if he were saying, "I must always suffer, but I am always comforted." He will soon describe how this happens and wherein his comfort consists.

In Hebrew the word *hammetsar* means "something narrow," just as I would think the German word *angst* is derived from a similar image of "something narrow."[7] When one is afraid and hurting in trials and misfortunes, one feels trapped, squeezed, and pressed, as the proverb says, "The great wide world is too narrow for me."[8] In Hebrew the word *bammarachab*, meaning "in a large place," is used in contrast to *distress*.[9] Just as *narrow* implies distress, tribulation, and peril, *in a broad place* denotes consolation and help. Accordingly, this verse really says, "I called upon the Lord in my trouble; he heard me and helped me by comforting me." Just as distress is a narrow place, which casts us down and cramps us, so God's help is a large place that makes us free and happy.

Note the great art and wisdom of faith. It does not run back and forth in the face of trouble. It does not fill everyone's ears with complaints, nor does it curse and scold its enemies. It also does not complain against God by asking, "Why does God do this to me? Why not to others who are worse than I am?" Faith does not despair of God who sends trouble. Faith does not consider God angry or an enemy, as the flesh, the world, and the devil strongly suggest. Faith rises above all this and sees God's fatherly heart behind God's unfriendly face. Faith sees the sun shining through these thick, dark clouds and this gloomy weather. Faith dares to call from the heart on God, who assigns it destruction and who looks upon it with a sour face.

That is an art above all art and the work of the Holy Spirit alone, which is known only to righteous and true Christians and about which those who practice works righteousness know nothing. They prattle on much about good works, although they have never known or done any; nor can they perform any. This ability is impossible for human nature. As soon as God sends distress, it becomes afraid and despairs, thinking that it is at an end and that God has nothing but wrath for it. Then the devil performs his tricks with all his power and might in order to drown it in doubt and sadness. In addition, when it observes the aggravating and overly generous gifts that God gives to the other three groups, it thinks that God provides grace to them and no wrath. Then the poor conscience becomes weak; it would collapse were it not for the help and comfort that come from God through righteous pastors or by righteous Christian words. Some there are who hang, drown, or stab themselves, or otherwise perish, shrivel, and wither.

Thus, let the one who wishes to learn, learn. Let everyone become a falcon and soar above distress and know with certainty and not doubt that God does not send a person distress for destruction. As we will hear later, in verse 18, God wants to drive a person to pray, to call, to struggle, and to practice faith and to learn to know God from a different perspective than before. God wants a person to become accustomed to do battle even with the devil and with sin, and by grace to be victorious. If there were only peace and no tribulations, we would never learn the meaning of faith, the word, spirit, sin, death, or the devil. Nor would we ever really come to know God, and, in brief, we would never be true Christians, nor could we remain Christians. Trouble and distress drive us there and keep us in Christendom. Crosses and troubles, therefore, are as necessary for us as life itself and much more necessary and useful than all the possessions and honor in the world.

It says, "I called upon the Lord" (118:5). You must learn to call. (You have heard that well.) Do not sit by yourself or lie on your bed hanging and wagging your head and devouring yourself with your thoughts by worrying. So do not strive and struggle to free yourself, and do not dwell on how badly it is going for you, how miserable you are, and how much you are suffering as a person. But get up, you lazy scoundrel, get down on your knees, lift your hands and your eyes to heaven, recite a psalm or the Lord's Prayer, and place your trouble with tears before God. Complain and call upon God, as this verse teaches, as well as Psalm 142:2: "I pour out my trouble before God, I tell God my trouble." Similarly, Psalm 141:2: "Let my prayer be counted as incense before you, and the lifting up of my hands as an evening sacrifice." Here you learn that praying, taking your troubles to God, and lifting your hands are the most pleasing offerings to God. God longs for you, wants you to bring your troubles, and does not want you to multiply your troubles by letting them weigh on you having you carry them around, torture yourself, and be the martyr. God wants you to be too weak to carry these troubles and overcome them by yourself so that you learn to find your strength in God. Thus you will glorify God's strength in you. In this way people become real Christians. Otherwise, they are only babblers, who prattle about faith and spirit but do not know what it is all about or what they themselves are saying.

You must also not doubt that God sees your troubles and hears your prayer. You must not pray haphazardly or simply shout into the wind. In doing so you mock and tempt God. It would be better not to pray at all than to pray like the priests and monks. You need to learn how to praise this point in this verse: "The Lord answered me and set me free." The psalmist declares that he prayed and cried out and that he was certainly heard. And if the devil tries to convince you that you are not as holy, worthy, and righteous as David, and thus you cannot be certain that God will hear you, then make the sign of the cross and say: "Let those be righteous and worthy who will! I know for sure that I am a creature of the same God as David was. No matter how holy David was, he did not have another, better, or greater God than I."

There is only one God of both saints and sinners, of the worthy and the unworthy, of the great and the small. In summary, no matter how unequal we are among one another, God is, nevertheless, the one and equal God of us all, who wants to be honored, called upon, and prayed to by all. What more did the saints and the worthy ones have than I before they became saints and worthy ones? Did they become saints and worthy by themselves? As unworthy sinners, did they not receive it from the same God from whom I seek to receive it, as a poor, unworthy sinner? The God who gave it to David has also promised it to me and commanded me to demand, seek, pray, and knock (Matt 7:7). Because of this promise and command I kneel down, lift my eyes to heaven, and beg for comfort and help. Through this God is honored as the true God from whom I ask for help and comfort. Through this God regards me as worthy and is revealed as the true God that I believe in. God will not place the divine name and honor in jeopardy on my account. This I know for sure. The one who does not pray or call upon God in the time of trouble does not know God to be God and does not ascribe the divine honor that we owe as God's creatures, about which much is said elsewhere.[10]

"I shall not die, but I shall live" [Ps 118:17].

The seventeenth verse of this song ("I shall not die, but I shall live") addresses and confesses the trouble out of which God's hand delivers the righteous, namely, death. They truly experience death when they are in death's grip. Meeting death face to face is not a pleasant experience for the flesh. Death does not come alone; it always brings sin and the law with it. Therefore, one can see why the righteous ones become martyrs, for they must live under the fear of, and wrestle and fight with, death. If it does not occur through tyrants and the godless by fire, sword, prison, and similar persecutions, then it occurs through the devil himself. The devil cannot suffer the word of God or all of those who uphold and teach it, but he attacks them, whether in death or life. In life it is with severe attacks of temptation over faith, hope, and love for God. The devil can attack the heart with such terror, death, and despair that a person avoids God, becomes God's enemy, and commits blasphemy. As a result, the troubled conscience can think only to consider God, the devil, death, sin, and hell, and all creation as one, for it has all become a perpetual enemy. Neither the Turk nor an emperor could besiege a city with such force as the devil can besiege a conscience.

While one is dying or at death's door, the devil can also do this, if God permits. Thus the devil is a master at magnifying our sins and accusing us of God's wrath. The devil is an amazingly powerful spirit who can cultivate fear and construct hell from the tiniest of sins. It is true that no one can really see the primary sins, namely, unfaith and blasphemy of God and similar sins of the heart, where these sins reside; that is, one does not fear, trust, and love in God as God intended one to do. On the other hand, it would not be good for one to be able to see these sins. I do not know if any faith exists on earth that could withstand them and not fall into despair.

Thus God provides space for sins of action, from which the devil can produce hell and damnation quickly, just because you had one drink too many or overslept, and soon you become ill and want to die from your guilty conscience and sadness.

Even more upsetting, the devil can take your best works and reduce them to such dishonorable and worthless things and render them so damnable before your conscience that your sins scare you less than your best good works. In fact, you wish you had committed grievous sins rather than done such good works. Thus, the devil causes you to deny these works, as if they were not done through God, so that you commit blasphemy. Thus hell is not far away, and neither is death. Who can count all the devil's abilities to generate sin, death, and hell? This is his handiwork; the devil has practiced it over five thousand years and can do it better than any master. And the devil has been a prince of death for just as long and has certainly explored and rehearsed how he might imbue a poor conscience with a foretaste of death. The prophets, especially the dear David, felt this and experienced it. They truly lament, teach, and speak of it as if they regularly experienced these things. One speaks of being at death's door, another of hell, and then of the wrath of God.

Now, however this comes about, that we hear that the saints must unquestionably wrestle with the devil and contend with death. The devil provides persecutions, plague, sickness of all sorts, and life-threatening dangers. In that conflict nothing is better and more vital for victory than learning to sing this little song of the saints, so as to look away from self and cling to the hand of God. By this the devil is swiftly betrayed, such that he finds only empty straw to beat: "I want to be as nothing. The Lord is all my strength," as stated above. When I say this, I am completely empty with regard to myself and all that is mine. I can say: "Devil, what do you seek? If you are looking for works and my holiness before God, I do not have any. My strength is not my own. The Lord is my strength. You cannot squeeze blood out of a turnip! If you are seeking to accuse me of my sins, yes, I do not have any of them either. Here is only God's strength. You can blame that until you are satisfied. I do not know of sin and holiness in me. I know of nothing whatever, except God's power in me."

It would be wonderful, I say, if one could mock oneself and the devil with empty pockets, as a certain poor householder mocked a thief whom he caught in his home one night. He said, "You silly thief, do you expect to find something here in the dark when I can't find anything in broad daylight?" What can the devil do when he finds a soul so empty that it will not respond to him as regards sin or holiness? There he must abandon all his skill even at magnifying sin and denigrating good works. He is referred to the right hand of God. Those who do this he leaves in peace. If you abandon this song and the devil catches you in your sin and good works, if you deal with the devil such that you pay attention and listen to him, then he can do with you as he wishes. Then you forget God's right hand and lose everything.

Nevertheless, as we have heard, it is an art to deny one's self. We must keep learning this as long as we live, just as all the saints before us, with us, and after us must do. Therefore, just as we experience sin, so we also have to experience death, just as we must fight to be free from sin and cling to the right hand of God until we become completely free. Just so, we must also contend with death and the prince of death, or, better, its chief, until we are completely free. See how the verse depicts this fight. The devil or the persecutor closes in on the saints even to the point of death. But what do they do? They turn away their eyes, yes, their entire bodies. They step entirely outside of themselves and cling to the hand of God and say: "Devil and tyrant, I shall not die, as you pretend. You lie! I shall live! I shall not speak of my works or any human works. I know nothing of myself and my holiness, but I have the works of the Lord before my eyes. I will speak of these. These will I praise. On these I will rely. God is the one who helps in times of sin and death. Only if you can topple these works can you conquer me."

This verse then emphasizes the two points mentioned above in verses six and seven: comfort and help, with which God blesses the righteous and the just....

Here you see this comfort and help is eternal life, which is the true, everlasting blessing of God. The entire psalm has this theme. The psalmist separates the righteous from the other three groups[11] and yet allots to those groups everything belonging to this life on earth, that is, temporal government and spiritual rule, the benefit of goods, and use of every creature. Therefore, the blessing of this small and righteous group must necessarily be another life, namely, eternal life. Since the three groups begrudge and deny them their blessings in this life, their consolation must be eternal and their help everlasting. How can it be otherwise, since the psalmist glories in the Lord above all human and princely possessions that the other groups have. The Lord is an eternal possession; therefore, everyone must conclude that, where the heart recognizes a gracious God, there must be forgiveness of sins. If sins are forgiven, death is gone.

Without fail there must be the comfort and confidence of eternal righteousness and everlasting life.

We should recognize this verse as a masterpiece. How powerfully the psalmist banishes death from sight! He will know nothing of dying and sin. At the same time he visualizes life most vividly and will hear nothing but life....[12]

At this point we should learn the rule that, whenever in the psalter and the holy scripture the saints deal with God concerning comfort and help in their need, eternal life and the resurrection of the dead are involved.[13] All such texts belong to the doctrine of the resurrection and eternal life, in fact, to the whole third article of the creed with its doctrines of the Holy Spirit, the holy Christian church, the forgiveness of sins, the resurrection, and everlasting life. It all flows from the first commandment, where God says, "I am your God" (Exod 20:2). The third article of the creed constantly emphasizes this. While Christians deplore the fact that they suffer and die in this life, they comfort themselves with another life beyond this, namely, that of the very God who is above and beyond this life. It is not possible that they should utterly die and not live again in eternity. For one thing, the God on whom they rely and in whom they find their consolation cannot die, and thus they live in God....For this little group, therefore, death remains no more than sleep.

But if it is true that they live in God, then it must first be true that they have forgiveness of sin. If they have no sin, they surely have the Holy Spirit, who makes them holy. If they are holy, they are the true holy Christian church, the little flock, and they rule over all the power of the devil. Then one day they will rise again and live forever. These are the great and lofty works of the right hand of God....

Now saints live not only in the life to come; they begin life now by faith. And wherever there is faith, everlasting life has begun. And the texts in scripture regarding faith also belong to all the doctrines listed above. The three groups we have discussed have no need of faith for this life, since the ungodly have this life most of all. Nor can faith attach itself or cling to anything that counts in this life; it breaks away and clings to that which is above and beyond this life, that is, to God. This verse teaches that the saints begin this eternal life here and live even while dying....

This is the worst and most discouraging text for tyrants and for murderers of the saints. I hardly know of another verse in scripture to the effect that the saints, whom they believe to be silenced and suppressed, are just beginning to speak. "What the devil! There is no use in arguing with the saints if after death they actually begin to do that for which they were killed! They will never cease or desist. They remain unkilled and unsilenced and proclaim forever the works of the Lord...."

"You are my God, and I will give thanks to you; you are my God; I will extol you" [Ps 118:28].

The psalmist now concludes this psalm with a strong declaration against all the offenses and examples of unbelievers. He would say, "They will not accept you as God. You are the rejected stone, a malefactor crucified among malefactors. Your word and service are held to be the devil's word and service. For this I must suffer all manner of disgrace and danger. But let it pass; you are nevertheless my God. I will still believe in you, and I know for a certainty that you are my God. Let the law, temple, altar, and all services at Jerusalem be gone. Let friend and foe pass away. Let there be no more wisdom, holiness, strength, goods, honor, and whatever else will pass away. I desire you alone; in the place of all these, you will be more than enough. I will be your poor little parson and priest and offer the true sacrifices and services of God, namely, the thank offering and the hymns of praise. This will be my mighty office, my feast of the tabernacles, that I preach or praise nothing but you, the rejected Cornerstone, the crucified God. This is my resolution. By this I will abide. This shall be the long and short of it. This is what I sought and meant with this psalm. Let no one tell me anything else. Let me not be confused. As St. Paul says (Gal 6:17), "I carry the marks of Jesus branded on my body." Amen. Hosanna. Amen....

A SIMPLE WAY TO PRAY, FOR MASTER PETER THE BARBER

How One Should Pray,[1] for Peter, the Master Barber[2]

Dear Master Peter, I will impart to you as much as I can as to how I relate myself to prayer.[3] May our Lord God grant that you and everyone do it better than I. Amen.

First, when I feel that I have become cold and ill-disposed to pray because of other business or thoughts (insofar as the flesh and devil always prevent and hinder prayer), I take my dear psalter and run into my room (or, if it is day and the right time, I run into church among the people) and begin saying the Ten Commandments, the creed, and, if I have time, several verses of Christ, St. Paul, or the Psalms aloud to myself, just as children do.

That is why it is good to let prayer be the first thing in the morning and the very last work in the evening that you do. Diligently watch out for the false, treacherous thought that says, "Wait a while. I will pray in an hour. I first have to finish this or that." For by such thoughts one abandons prayer for other matters, which then arrest and absorb a person, and the prayer for the day comes to nothing.

Certainly, some works can actually appear to be as good as or better than prayer, especially when need requires them. Thus a saying attributed to St. Jerome goes, "All the work of believers is prayer," and there is a common saying, "Whoever works faithfully prays twice." This is said because, in one's work, a believing person fears, honors, and reflects on God's command not to do injustice to anyone, to steal, to take advantage, or to cheat. And it is without doubt that such thoughts and faith make a prayer out of one's work and a praise offering as well....

To be sure, concerning this kind of a constant prayer, in the eleventh chapter of Luke, Jesus says, "One should pray without ceasing."[4] That is because one should unceasingly be on guard against sin

217

and injustice, and this cannot happen when one does not fear God and keep the divine command before one's eyes, as Psalm 1[:2] says, "Blessed is the one who meditates on the law of the Lord day and night," etc.

One must see to it, however, that we do not gradually lose the habit of true prayer and begin to imagine that a great many works are necessary for our salvation and that doing them is ultimately better than prayer, and then interpret them to be necessary when they are not. In the end, as a result, we will become lax and lazy, cold, tired, and weary of prayer. For the devil, all around us, is not lazy or lax, and our flesh is still all too alive and ready to sin and inclined against the spirit of prayer.

Now when the heart has come to itself and become warm by such heart-to-heart conversation, then kneel down or stand with folded hands, and with your eyes to heaven, speak or think as briefly as you possibly can:

"Ah, heavenly Father, my dear God, I am a poor, unworthy sinner, not even worthy to lift up my eyes or hands to you and pray to you. But you have commanded us all to pray and also have promised to hear us, and through your dear Son, our Lord Jesus Christ, you have taught us both the words and the way. Therefore, I come, responding to your command to be obedient to you and trusting in your gracious promise, and, in the name of my Lord Jesus Christ, I pray with all your holy Christians on earth, just as he taught me, 'Our Father, you who are,'" etc., the whole of it, word for word.

After that, repeat a portion or as much as you wish, for instance, the first petition, "Holy be your name," and say, "Oh, yes, Lord God, dear Father, do make your name holy, both in us ourselves and in all the world....They use it all instead to strive against your kingdom. They are great, many and mighty, thick, fat, and sated, and they plague, hinder, and destroy the meager number in your kingdom, who are weak, despised, and few. They do not want to tolerate them on earth, and they think that in such a way they are doing you a 'divine service.'[5] Dear Lord God and Father, convert, guard, and defend those who are still going to become children and members of your kingdom, that they with us and we with them may serve you in true faith and authentic love in your kingdom, that from this reign begun, we might enter your eternal kingdom come. But deter those who will not cease and desist from destroying your kingdom. Let them be cast down from their thrones and humiliated, so they have to stop. Amen."

The third petition: "Your will be done on earth as it is in heaven." Say, "Ah, dear Lord God and Father, you know how the world is. Where it cannot completely reduce your name to nothing and entirely destroy your kingdom, they go around day and night with evil thoughts and devious plots. They devise many snares and strange assaults, take counsel and conspire, comfort and strengthen themselves, rant and rave, and proceed full of evil intentions against your name, word, kingdom, and children as they murder them. Therefore, dear Lord God and Father, deter and convert them. Convert those who will yet come to recognize your good will, that they with us and we with them may obey your will and, further, that they may patiently and gladly suffer all evil, the cross, and adversity, and thereby recognize, explore, and consciously experience your good, gracious, and perfect will. Deter those, however, who will not cease and desist from their raving, ranting, hating, threatening, and evil will, for the sake of doing harm. Make their counsel, evil assaults, and tricks come to nothing and end in shame and be turned against them, as Psalm 7[:16] sings. Amen."

The fourth petition: "Give us this day our daily bread." Say, "Ah, dear Lord God and Father, give your blessings also for these bodily needs of our daily lives. Graciously give us lovely peace; guard us from war and unrest. Give our dear emperor skill and victory over his enemies; give him wisdom and knowledge that he may rule his earthly realm peacefully and most blissfully. Give all kings, rulers, and lords good will and counsel to keep their land and people in tranquility and justice. Especially help and lead the dear sovereign of our country (named...) under whose guard and protection you preserve us, so that he might rule securely and blessedly, protected from all evil, lying tongues, and unfaithful people. Give all subjects the grace to serve faithfully and to be obedient. Give all estates,⁶ burghers and peasants, a way to become righteous, and let them show each other love and faithfulness. Graciously give good weather and fruitful harvest. I commend to you also house, land, wife, and child. Help me to oversee them well and nourish and raise them in a Christian way. Deter and direct the destroyer and all evil angels who wish to hinder and harm us in these things. Amen."

The fifth petition: "Forgive us our debts as we forgive our debtors." Say, "Ah, dear Lord God and Father, spare us from your going into judgment against us, because in your sight no living person is justified. Ah, in addition, do not count it against us as sin that we are, unfortunately, so ungrateful for all your inexpressible benefits, both spiritual and physical, and that we so often each day stumble and sin, more than we can notice and even know [Psalm 19:12]. Do not look upon how righteous or evil we are, but upon your bottomless mercy, in Christ your dear Son, given as a gift for us. Also, forgive all our enemies, and all those who do us harm and injustice, just as we forgive them from our hearts. They do the greatest harm to themselves in that they make you angry because of the way they deal with us. It is no help to us if they are ruined, but we would much prefer to see them saved with us. Amen." (And whoever in this situation feels unable correctly to forgive might here pray for the grace to forgive. But this belongs in a sermon.)

The sixth petition: "and lead us not into temptation." Say, "Ah, dear Lord God and Father, keep us alert and fresh, passionate and busy in your word and service, so that we do not become complacent, lazy, and sluggish, as if we now had it all. Otherwise, the raging devil may surprise and fall upon us and again take away from us your precious word, or cause division, conflict, and schism among us, or otherwise lead us into sin and shame, both spiritually and physically. Rather, give us through your Spirit wisdom and strength, so that we can offer valiant resistance and keep the victory. Amen."

The seventh petition: "but deliver us from evil." Say, "Ah, dear Lord God and Father, this wretched life is really so full of sorrow and tragedy, so full of danger and insecurity, so full of faithlessness and malice (as St. Paul says, the times are evil [Eph 5:16]) that we are right to be tired of life and to yearn eagerly for death. But you, dear Father, know our weakness. Therefore, help us move through such manifold evil and wickedness safely, and, when the time comes, give us a gracious hour and a blessed departure from this veil of tears, that we do not become terrified by death or despair, but, with a firm faith, commend our souls into your hands. Amen."

Notice, at last, that you have to make the "Amen" strong every time and not doubt. God is surely listening to you with every grace and is saying yes to your prayer. Do not think to yourself that you are kneeling or standing there alone, for all of Christendom, all upright Christians, are with you and you among them in a unanimous, harmonious prayer, which God cannot disdain. And do not leave the prayer unless you have said or thought, "All right, God has heard my prayer, and truly I know this for certain, for that is what *Amen* means."

You should also know that I do not intend you to recite all these words in your prayer. Then it would turn at last into chatter and idle, empty babble, like reading out of a book or going by the letter, the way it was when laypeople read the Rosary or clerics and monks read the prayers of the breviary.[7] Instead, I want your heart to be stimulated and instructed as to what thoughts should be grasped in the Lord's Prayer. The heart can, however (when it has become warm and longingly in the mood for prayer), express such thoughts well in many different ways, with more words or just a few. For I do not even bind myself to such words and syllables; I speak the words one way today and another tomorrow, according to my feelings and what mood I am in. Nevertheless, I stay as close as I possibly can to the same thoughts and ideas. Often it happens that, in one part or petition, I lose myself in such rich thoughts that I let the other six petitions go. And when such rich, good thoughts come, then one should forego the other prayers and give room to those thoughts and listen in silence. Then, on pain of death, make no hindrance, because there the Holy Spirit's divine self is preaching, and when the Spirit preaches, one word is better than a thousand of our prayers. In this way I have sometimes learned more in one prayer than I could ever have gotten from much reading and thinking.

Therefore, it is of the greatest importance that the heart free itself to get into the right mood.[8] As Ecclesiasticus [Sir 18:23] says, "Prepare your heart for prayer in order that you do not tempt God." What else is it but tempting God when the mouth is chattering and the heart is strangely absent elsewhere? As the cleric prayed,[9] "Be pleased, O God, to deliver me.[10] Stable boy, have you hitched up the horses? O Lord, make haste to help me![11] Maid, go milk the cows! Glory to the Father and to the Son and to the Holy Spirit.[12] Run, boy, and may a fever catch you, etc." These are the prayers that I often heard and experienced in my day under the papacy; almost all of their prayers are of this kind. God is only blasphemed by them, and it would be better if they played instead, if they cannot or will not do any better. For I myself in my day prayed many canonical hours, and, sad to say, the psalm or the hours were done before I became conscious about whether I had started them or was in the middle.

And while not all of [these people] let themselves go and speak like the above-mentioned cleric, mixing business and prayers together, they certainly do so with the thoughts in their hearts going from one thing to another.[13] When they are done, they do not know what they did or what they touched and brushed against; they begin with "Praise,"[14] and, snap, they are in dreamland, only God knows where. In my opinion, if you could see their thoughts, they would appear like a juggling act more ridiculous than you ever saw, as these cold, devotionless hearts juggle all their mixed-up thoughts together in prayer. But now I see quite well, praise God, that it is not a fine prayer when one forgets what one has said. For a true prayer gives careful consideration to all the words and thoughts from the beginning to the end of the prayer.

So, as a diligent and good barber, you must keep your thoughts, senses, and eyes precisely on the hair and the scissors or razor and not forget where you trimmed or shaved, for, if you want to talk a lot or become distracted thinking about something else, you might well cut someone's nose or mouth or even his throat. Therefore, if a thing is to be done well, it requires the full attention of a person's senses and members, as it is said, *"Pluribus intentus minor est ad singula sensus"*[15]—Who thinks about many things thinks about nothing and does nothing well. How much more does a prayer need to have the undivided attention of the whole heart alone, if it is to be a good prayer!

That is briefly what can be said about the Lord's Prayer or prayer [in general] and the way I myself am accustomed to pray. To this day I suckle from the Lord's Prayer like a child,[16] and as an old man eat and drink from it and never get my fill. It is the very best prayer for me, even greater than the psalter (and I love the psalter very much). Truly, it was composed and taught by a real master, and it is lamentably remiss that such a prayer from such a master is mindlessly chattered and blabbered throughout the world with no real devotion. Each year many pray perhaps several thousand Lord's Prayers, and, if they would pray that way a thousand years, they still

222

would not have tasted or prayed one dot or letter of it.[17] In summary, the Lord's Prayer is the greatest martyr here on earth (along with the name and word of God), because everyone plagues and abuses it, and few take comfort and joy in its correct use.[18]

If now, however, I have had time and space for the Lord's Prayer, then I also do the same thing for the Ten Commandments. I take one part after another, making myself as completely free of distractions from praying as is possible, and I wind each command into four parts—like a fourfold woven wreath. That is, I first take up each command as a teaching, the way it intends itself to be, and I ponder what it is in the command that our Lord God requires of me in such earnest. Next, I make a thanksgiving out of it; third, a confession; and fourth, a prayer. This I do with thoughts and words such as these: "I am the Lord your God," etc. "You shall have no other gods before me," etc. Here I first think that God requires and teaches heartfelt trust in all things, because God wants to be our God in complete earnest. Thus, I should cling to God on pain of losing eternal salvation, and I should not let my heart build upon or trust in any other thing, whether goods, honor, wisdom, power, holiness, or any single creature. Next, I thank God for having such unfathomable compassion toward me; for deigning to come in so fatherly a way to me, a lost person; for offering to be my God [even when] unasked, unsought, and undeserved; for giving me divine acceptance; and for wishing, in all my needs, to be my comfort, protection, help, and strength. We poor, blind people have sought after many a god and would still be looking for one if God did not allow us to hear so openly in our own human language God's offer and desire to be our God. Who could ever and eternally thank God enough for it? Third, I confess and acknowledge my great sin and ingratitude, that through my whole life I so shamefully scorned such beautiful teaching and such a precious gift. With countless idolatries I have grimly provoked God's wrath, for which I am sorry and beg for grace. Fourth, I petition and say, "Ah, my God and Lord, help me by your grace that every day I might learn and understand this commandment better and act according to it with heartfelt trust. Protect my heart, lest I become so forgetful and thankless that I search for other gods. Let me not seek such comfort on earth or in any creature, but let me cling to you alone, pure and fine, knowing that you are mine and you remain my one true God.[19] Amen, dear Lord God and Father. Amen."

Thereafter, if I have the will and the time, the next commandment can be turned into four parts as follows: "You shall not take the name of the Lord your God in vain," etc. First of all, I learn that I should glorify God's name, keep it holy, and make it beautiful, and not swear, curse, and lie with it. I should not be arrogant or seek my own prestige and honor, but in humility call upon God's name to worship, honor, and praise it, letting it be my only glory and honor that the Lord is my God and I, a poor creature and God's unworthy servant. Next, I thank God for such glorious gifts, that God's name has been revealed to me, that I myself can boast of God's name, and that I am allowed to be called God's servant and creature, etc., that God's name is my refuge, like a mighty fortress to which the righteous flee and find protection, as Solomon says [Prov 18:10]. Third, I confess and acknowledge my shameful and weighty sin, in that I have acted against this commandment all the days of my life. I have not only left God's holy name uncalled upon, unglorified, and unhonored, but also have been ungrateful for such gifts and then misused them to commit scandal and sin by swearing, lying, and deceiving, for which I am sorry and beg for grace and forgiveness. Fourth, I ask for help and strength, that from now on I might be able to learn such a commandment well and be protected from such shameful thanklessness, sins, and misuse of God's name and allowed to be found thankful and in rightful awe and honor of this name.

What I already said about the Lord's Prayer, I advise once more: If the Holy Spirit comes from under such thoughts and begins to preach in your heart with rich, enlightening thoughts, accord the Spirit the honor. Let the determined thoughts you were pursuing pass; be quiet, and listen closely to the one who can do it better than you. Take notice of what the Spirit preaches, and write it down. Then, as David says [Ps 119:18], you will behold the wonders of the law of God.

The third commandment, "Remember the sabbath day,[20] to keep it holy." Herein I first learn that the sabbath day is a law. It is not for being idle or for worldly pleasantries and amusements, but we are supposed to make it holy. However, it is not through our actions and works that it becomes holy, because our works are not holy. It is through the word of God, which is completely pure and holy, that the day is made holy, the way it makes all things holy that relate to it, whether time, place, person, work, rest, etc. So it is through the word that even our works become holy, as St. Paul says, 1 Timothy 4:5, that all creatures are made holy through the word and prayer. Therefore, I learn in this commandment that on the sabbath I should, first of all, hear and reflect on the word of God, thereafter thank and praise God in the same word for all divine good deeds, and pray for myself and the whole world. Whoever keeps the sabbath in this way makes the sabbath holy. Whoever does not, does worse than those who work on the sabbath.

Next, I thank God in this commandment for God's good deeds and grace, which are great and beautiful, giving us the preaching of the divine word and commanding us, especially upon the sabbath day, to make use of it. This is a treasure no human heart can ponder enough, because God's word is the one single light in the darkness of this life: a word of life, a consolation, and complete blessedness. And in the absence of the dear word, pure, terrifying, dreadful darkness, ignorance, and schism, every misfortune and death are there, and the devil's own tyranny, as we see before our eyes on a daily basis.

Third, I confess and acknowledge my great sin and shameful thanklessness, that I have used the sabbath day so slanderously all the days of my life, that I so pathetically disdained God's dear and precious word, that I was too lazy, resistant, tired, and weary to hear it; not to mention that I never heartily yearned for it or ever gave thanks for it. Thus I have let my dear God preach to me in vain, have allowed the noble treasure to pass me by, and have trampled it under foot, all of which God endured patiently from me with pure divine goodness, and did not, because of it, stop constantly preaching to me and calling me, filled with fatherly and divine love and faithfulness, for the sake of the salvation of my soul. For that I am sorry and beg for grace and forgiveness.

Fourth, I pray for myself and the whole world that the dear Father would keep us in the divine, holy word and not take it away from us because of our sin, ingratitude, and laziness. May God protect us from schismatics and false teachers and send for us true and faithful laborers into the harvest [Matt 9:38], that is, true and righteous pastors and preachers, and also give all of us the grace humbly to hear, accept, and honor their word as God's own word and to thank and praise God from the heart for it as well.

The fourth commandment, "Honor your father and your mother." First of all, in this command, I learn to recognize God my Creator and how wonderfully God created me with body and soul, gave me life through my parents, and gave them the heart out of which they served me as the fruit of their bodies with all their strengths, brought me into the world, nourished me, waited on me, cared for me, brought me up with great diligence, concern, danger, toil, and tears. And even up to this hour God has protected me and often helped me, God's creature, out of crises and innumerable dangers to body and soul, as if creating me anew each hour. For the devil begrudges that we are alive for a moment.

Next, I thank the rich and goodly Creator for myself and the whole world, that in this commandment God founded and sustained the reproduction and survival of the human species, that is, of households, and states.[21] For without these two institutions or authorities the world could not exist for a year, since without worldly government there is no peace, and where there is no peace there can be no households,[22] and where there are no households, there children can neither be begotten nor brought up, and the estate of a mother and father would have to cease completely. So this commandment concerns, keeps, and preserves both household life and city life, commands obedience to children and subjects, and also watches over them so that obedience takes place and violence does not go unpunished. Otherwise, the children out of disobedience and the subjects out of rebellion would long ago have torn up and laid waste household life and city life, because they far outnumber the parents and authorities. Hence, such benefits are also inexpressible.

Third, I confess and acknowledge my troubling disobedience and sin against this commandment of my God, because I did not honor my parents, nor was I obedient. I often angered and insulted them, took their parental discipline with impatience, murmured against them, and disdained their faithful admonishment, much rather preferring to follow loose company and evil rogues. But God curses such disobedient children and denies them a long life, for very many go under and perish shamefully even before they have grown up. For "whoever does not obey their father and mother must obey the executioner," or otherwise have their life take an evil end because of God's wrath. I feel sorry for all of these things and beg for grace and forgiveness.

Fourth, I pray for myself and all the world that God would bestow divine grace and pour out rich blessings, both over household life and city life, that from this time forward we become devout, honor our parents, obey authorities, resist the devil, and not follow devilish enticement into disobedience and unrest. Indeed, help that we better households and country, maintain the peace, praise and honor God, and, for our own benefit and all good, recognize such gifts and give thanks for them.

At just about this place we should pray for parents and higher authorities, that God bestow upon them knowledge and wisdom to stand before us and govern us peacefully and blessedly. May God shield them and turn them away from tyranny, raging, and fury, so that they honor God's word and do not persecute it or do injustice to anyone. For one must appropriate such great gifts with prayer, as St. Paul teaches; otherwise, the devil becomes the head abbot of the court, and everything heads for evil and chaos.

And if you happen to be a parent, this is the time that you should not forget yourself or your children and workers. Rather, pray earnestly that the dear Father, who placed you in the honor of his name and office and also wants you to be called and honored as a father and mother, will bestow upon you the grace and blessing to govern and nourish your spouse, child, and worker in a godly and Christian way, give you wisdom and strength to bring them up well and give them a good heart and will to follow and be obedient to your will. For both are God's gifts: the children and their well-being, so they are well counseled and remain good. Otherwise, a house becomes nothing other than a pigsty, a rogue school, as one sees among godless, vulgar people.

The fifth commandment: "You shall not kill." Here I learn, first, what God would have from me: That I shall love my neighbors in such a way that I do them no bodily harm, either with words or actions, not through anger, impatience, envy, hate, or any kind of arrogance. Neither should I take revenge on them or do them any harm but know that I am responsible to help and counsel them in all their bodily needs. For with this commandment God ordered me to preserve my neighbor's body and, on the other side, ordered my neighbor to preserve my body, and, as Jesus Sirach says, God has committed to each of us our neighbor [Sir 9:14].

Next in this place I thank God for the inexpressible love, care, and faithfulness for me, that God has built up such a great and strong watchtower and wall around my body, that all people should be responsible not to harm me and to protect me. On the other side, I have to watch out over what happens to all people. God keeps watch where this does not happen and orders the sword for punishment of those who do not act accordingly. Where such a fine commandment and foundation did not otherwise exist, the devil would instigate such murder among the people that no one could live safely for an hour, as it can happen when God gets angry and punishes the disobedient and unthankful world.

Third, I confess and complain in this place about my malice and that of the world, that we are not only so dreadfully ungrateful for such fatherly love and concern for us, but it is also even more especially shameful that we do not even know such commands or want to learn them. We disdain them as if they did not concern us or as if nothing was in them for us. We go along on our self-satisfied way, having no bad conscience about the way we treat our neighbor and break this commandment. We scorn, abandon, indeed, persecute and hurt or even kill our neighbor in our thoughts. We follow our anger, fury, and all malice, as if we were doing right and did well by it. Truly, here is the time for screaming and complaining, because we ourselves are evil rogues, blind and wild, ill-natured people, who, like the raging animals here, trample on, knock down, scratch, tear, bite, and devour each other, and do not at all fear the severity of such a commandment of God.

Fourth, I beg that the dear Father would help us learn to understand this holy commandment, so that we also keep it and live according to it. That God protect us one and all from that murderer who is the master and example of all murders and injuries and grant such rich and divine grace that we and all others become friendly toward one another, gentle, good-natured, forgiving each other heartily, bearing each other's failures and brokenness in a Christian, brotherly and sisterly way, and therewith living in true peace and unity, as this commandment teaches and requires.

The sixth commandment, "You shall not commit adultery." Here I learn once again about what God intends and requires from me, namely, that I should live in a chaste, disciplined, and moderate way, both with thoughts and words and deeds. In no way should anyone use a wife, daughter, or maid shamefully, but much more help, save, and protect them and do everything that serves to maintain their honor and chastity.[23] Also help to shut the useless mouths of those who want to take away or steal their honor. For I am responsible for all these matters, and God requires of me not only that I not abuse my neighbor's wife and those belonging to him, but also that I be responsible for maintaining and preserving his chastity and dignity, just as I would want my neighbor to act with me, according to this commandment, in relation to me and to mine.

Next, I thank the dear and faithful Father for such grace and blessed kindness that, in this commandment, God shields and protects my husband, son, servant, wife, daughter, and maid and so earnestly and sternly forbids anyone to bring them down in shameful scandal. For God assures protection and keeps watch not to leave this sin unpunished, even if it is God that must punish the one who trespassed and broke this command and safeguard. No one will escape from God. They will have either to pay the price here or finally to quiet such lust in hellfire. For God demands chastity and will not tolerate adultery, as we see every day among the unrepentant, dissolute people, who are finally seized by God's wrath and shamefully run into the ground. Otherwise, it would be impossible to sustain the chastity and honor of one's wife, child, and help from the unclean devil for an hour. It would become a veritable, promiscuous dog-marriage and a reversion to animal nature, as happens when God in anger removes the divine hand and lets such evil exceed all measure.

Third, I confess and acknowledge my sin and that of all the world, how I have sinned against this commandment, whether through thoughts, words, or deeds all the days of my life. I was not only unthankful for such beautiful teaching and gifts but also probably murmured against God, who would command such discipline and chastity and did not allow all manner of promiscuity to go free and unpunished, or allow the institution of marriage to be disdained, ridiculed, and considered damned. How indeed the sins against this command compared to all the others are the coarsest, most noticeable, can have no cover or whitewash. For all of which I am sorry, etc.

Fourth, I pray for myself and all the world that God would give us grace to keep this commandment with pleasure and love, that we not only live chastely, but also help and counsel others to do so as well.

In the same way, I continue with the other commandments, while I have time or am in the mood. For, as I have said, I would not want anyone to feel bound to these words or thoughts of mine. I merely want to offer you my example. Whoever wants can follow it or improve it, whoever can, and it is possible to take all the commandments at once or as many as wished. For the soul, when it focuses on one thing, whether good or bad, and takes it seriously, can think more in one moment than the tongue can speak in ten hours or the pen write in ten days. There is something so adept, subtle, and powerful about the soul or the spirit that it can get through all the ten commandments in their four parts very quickly, if it wants to and takes it seriously.

The seventh commandment: "You shall not steal." First of all, I learn in this place that I am not to take my neighbors' possessions, or want to have them against their will, whether secretly or openly. I learn not to be unfaithful or dishonest in business, service, or work, so that I do not win what I receive like a thief, but I shall earn my living with the sweat of my brow and eat my own bread with complete honesty. Likewise, I should help my neighbors and not allow what belongs to them to be taken away by the devious means I mentioned above, just as I wish for myself. I also learn that God, out of fatherly concern and with great sincerity, puts a fence around my possessions and protects them by this law. By threat of punishment, God forbids others to steal from me, and, if they do, God exacts a penalty for it, committing to Jack, the executioner, the gallows and the rope. Where it is impossible for him, divine punishment follows that will reduce them to beggars in the end. As one says, "Who likes to steal as a youth will go begging when old." Likewise, "Ill-gotten gain does not remain," and "Evilly come, speedily go."

Next I thank God's faithfulness and goodness for giving me and the world such good teaching and the shield and protection derived from it. For, where God does not protect, not a nickel or a piece of bread would be able to remain in anybody's house.

Third, I confess all my sin and ingratitude where I short-changed others or dealt with them dishonestly in my life, etc.

Fourth, I pray that God would bestow grace that I and the whole world might still learn, meditate, and become better by this commandment, so that the stealing, robbing, loan sharking, faith-lessness, and injustice decrease and soon, by the last day, entirely come to an end, for which the prayers of all the saints and creatures have aimed, Romans 8[:20–23]. Amen.

The eighth commandment: "You shall not bear false witness," etc. This teaches, first, to be genuine with one another and avoid every kind of lie and slander, gladly speak and hear the very best about others. With that a wall and defense is established around our reputation and integrity, against disparaging mouths and false tongues, which God will also not leave unpunished, as said about the other commandments.

Then we should thank God both for the teaching and the pro-tection, which are here given us so graciously by God.

And third, making confession and yearning for grace that we have spent all our lifelong days being so ungrateful and sinful by lying, falsifying, and bad mouthing the person next to us, for whom, by the way, we are responsible. We are to rescue the honor and innocence of our neighbors, just as we would gladly have them do for us.

Fourth, we beg for help in order to keep this commandment in the future and for a helpful tongue, etc.

The ninth and tenth commandments: "You shall not covet your neighbor's house, spouse," etc.

This first teaches us that, under the false pretense of legality, we should not try to take away our neighbors' goods or possessions, nor should we coax them away, estrange them, or extort anything from them, but help our neighbors keep what belongs to them, as we would like to see happen to us. And it is also a protection against the subtle devices and devious moves of the worldly wise, who will also in the end receive their punishment. Next we should give thanks; third, confess our sin with sorrow and remorse;[24] and fourth, pray for help and strength to become righteous and keep this commandment of God.[25]

These are the Ten Commandments treated in a fourfold way, namely, as a miniature instruction book, song book, confessional, and prayer book. Through them a heart should be able to get in touch with itself and warm up for prayer. But watch out that you do not attempt everything or too much for yourself, so that you do not weary your spirit. Likewise, a good prayer should not be long or drawn out, but frequent and hefty. It is enough if you can get one part or a half a part, by which you can make a spark in your heart and get a little fire going.[26] Now that will be and must be given by the Spirit, further teaching you in your heart, when it is in harmony with God's word and has become free of alien business and thoughts.

About faith and the holy scripture nothing should be said here, for that would become an endless thing. Someone who is practiced could well complete the Ten Commandments in one day, in another a psalm or a chapter out of the scripture in order to strike a match and get the fire in the heart burning.

[In an expanded edition Luther continues:][27] Now whoever has time left over or otherwise is in the mood can also take the creed and with it make a fourfold interwoven wreath. The Confession of Faith, however, has three main parts or articles according to the three persons of the Godly Majesty, the same way that they were also previously divided in the catechism.

The First Article about the Creation

"I believe in God, the Father almighty, Creator of heaven and earth."

Here, firstly, a great light shines into your heart, if you let it, and teaches you in short words what cannot be exhausted by the spoken words of all tongues or the writing of many books, namely, what you are, where you come from, where heaven and earth come from. For you are God's creation, especially made,[28] God's creature and work; that is, of yourself and in yourself you are nothing, can do nothing, know nothing, have power for nothing. For what were you a thousand years ago? What were heaven and the earth six thousand years ago? They were completely nothing as well, just as that which will never be created is nothing. What you are, know, can do, and are capable of is called God's creation, as [in this creed] you confess with your mouth, which gives you nothing to boast about before God, except that you are completely nothing and God is your Creator, who at any moment can make you nothing. Of such a light reason knows nothing. Many extraordinary people have searched into what heaven and earth, human beings and creatures are and have not discovered [their meaning]. But here it states, faith asserts, God has created all things out of nothing. Here is the pleasure garden of the soul taking a walk in God's works. But it is too much to write about here.

Next, we should thank God that, through divine goodness, we have been created from nothing and are sustained on a daily basis from out of nothing, and are such fine creatures, who have a body and soul, reason, five senses, etc., and that God set us to be sovereign over earth, fish, birds, animals, etc. Genesis, chapters 1, 2, and 3 belong here.

Third, one should confess and complain about our unbelief and ingratitude, that we have not taken all this to heart, believed, meditated on, and understood it, worse than the irrational animals, etc.

Fourth, we pray for a true and certain faith, that we will sincerely believe and hold our dear God to be our creator from now on, as this article states.

The Next Article about the Redemption

"And in Jesus Christ, God's only begotten Son, our Lord," etc.

A very great light is shining here again and teaches us how we are redeemed from death through Christ, God's Son. After the creation, we have fallen [into death] because of Adam's sin and had to be lost for eternity. And this is the time; as, in the first article, you had to count yourself to be one of the creatures of God and not doubt it, here you also have to count yourself as one of the redeemed and not doubt it. And before all words, place the word

233

our, as in Jesus Christ, our Lord, thus also our suffering people, our dead, our risen ones, so that all of it is ours and concerns us. You are there the same way, included among ours, the way the word itself brings about.

Next, be heartily thankful for such grace and rejoice in this redemption.

Third, complain bitterly and confess your shameful unbelief or doubt about such grace. Ah, what will all come to mind here! How much idolatry you have again practiced with all the worship of the saints and innumerable works of your own, by which you have striven against this redemption.

Fourth, now pray that God keep you from now on until the end, in the true and pure faith in Christ your Lord.

The Third Article about Sanctification

"And in the Holy Spirit," etc.

That is the third great light, which teaches us where this Creator and Redeemer are to be found and encountered outwardly on earth, and the way everything is going to turn out in the end, about which much could be said. Here in short is the summary: Wherever the holy Christian church is, there one finds God the Creator, God the Redeemer, and God the Holy Spirit, the one who daily makes us holy by forgiveness of sins, etc. The church, however, exists where God's word by such faith is rightly preached and confessed. Here once again you have much to think about concerning all the things that the Holy Spirit practices on a daily basis in the church, etc.

Therefore give thanks here that you have also come and been called into this church.

Confess and complain about your unbelief and ingratitude, that you have not paid attention to all of this, and pray for a right and firm faith that waits and endures, until you come to the place where all things will stay eternally, which is after the resurrection from the dead in eternal life. Amen.

THE TEN COMMANDMENTS (LONG VERSION)

These are the holy Ten Commands,
A gift from God through Moses' hands.
God's servant true, he carried them
From high on Sinai Mountain. Lord have mercy.

The Lord your God am I alone;
No other gods besides me own.
To me shall you your trust impart;
Love me with all of your heart. Lord have mercy.

Do not misuse or take in vain
The Lord your God's most holy name.
On good and right heap not your praise,
Unless it is what God says. Lord have mercy.

The seventh day for you is blessed
That you and all may take your rest.
Let go the work you need to do,
That God may work within you. Lord have mercy.

To father, mother—all parents—
Give honor and obedience.
Where you can serve them by your hand
Long is the life you'll command. Lord have mercy.

Though angry, you must never kill;
Revenge and hate are not God's will.
Be patient and let mercy show,
And, what's more, treat well your foe. Lord have mercy.

Be faithful to your marriage vows;
Let no one else your heart arouse.
Aspire that you be chaste and pure,
Modest, respectful, mature. Lord have mercy.

No goods or money shall you steal.
In unjust profits do not deal.
You should assist with generous hand
The poor who live in your land. Lord have mercy.

You shall not lie or cause deceit.
Malicious words do not repeat.
Instead, defend your neighbor's name,
And hide away all their shame. Lord have mercy.

Do not long for your neighbor's house
Or goods or property or spouse.
But wish your neighbor all things good,
Just as for yourself you would. Lord have mercy.

God gives these great commandments so
You, human one, your sins may know
And that you clearly can perceive
How before God you should live. Lord have mercy.

Lord Jesus Christ, we seek your aid;
Come mediate for us, we pray.
Without you are our works in vain,
Deserving naught else but pain. Lord have mercy.

THE TEN COMMANDMENTS (SHORT VERSION)

Oh, friends, would you live blessedly
And stay with God eternally?
Then hold the Ten Commandments dear
That God has given us here.
Lord, have mercy.

I alone am your God and Lord;
No other gods should you look toward.
Your heart should only trust in me.
My own dear realm shall you be.
Lord, have mercy.

My name respect in word and deed,
And call on me in time of need.
Without fail keep the sabbath day—
I can work in you that way.
Lord, have mercy.

Give honor and obedience
To me first, then to your parents.
Do not kill or become enraged.
In marriage pure be engaged.
Lord, have mercy.

You shall from others nothing take.
Against them no false witness make.
Another's spouse do not pursue,
And gladly yield what they're due.
Lord, have mercy.

THE LORD'S PRAYER, BRIEFLY INTERPRETED AND BROUGHT TO SONG

Creator God in heaven above,
You've called us children in your love.
As family, then, we call on you
In prayer, as you would have us do.
Let no words from our lips depart
Save they come from the inmost heart.

Most holy is your sacred name.
Now help us your pure word retain
That, holding to your name aright,
We may be holy in your sight.
Keep all false teachings from our head;
Save all poor souls who are misled.

Your kingdom come, both in our time
And in eternity sublime.
The Holy Spirit in us dwell
And many a spiritual gift as well.
Break Satan's rule and cruel rage,
And shield your church from age to age.

And let your will, Lord God, be done
On earth as in your heavenly home.
Grant that we patient may remain,
Obedient in love and pain.
All flesh and blood with shame instill
That act against your holy will.

A NEW PATH TO PRAYER

Give us this day our daily bread
And all by which we're truly fed.
Protect us from unrest and strife,
Disease and poverty in life.
May wholesome peace become our lot,
That fear and greed may be forgot.

And please, dear Lord, our debts forgive
That we no more in shame must live.
So gladly too let us release
Those in our debt and grant them peace.
To serve you always us prepare,
With love and unity to share.

And save us from the time of trial,
When evil spirits come with guile;
Equip us to resist and stand
When set upon on either hand.
Make firm our faith, well fortified,
The Holy Spirit at our side.

From evil, Lord, may we be spared,
Though we by wicked times are scared.
Release us from eternal death,
And comfort us at our last breath.
Grant each of us a blessed end;
We put our souls into your hand.

Amen, that is, it will be so.
Our faith through you will ever grow,
And, trusting you, we have no doubt
Concerning what we've prayed about.
Upon your word and in your name,
We say amen as our refrain.

Christ Jesus to the Jordan Came

A spiritual song about our Holy Baptism in which is finely and briefly summarized what it is, who instituted it, and its use

Christ Jesus to the Jordan came
To do as God was willing,
To be baptized by John his aim,
His ministry fulfilling.
    He gave to us a bath so good
    To wash away our sinning,
    And by his own dire wounds and blood
    A victory o'er death winning,
    It meant for us a new life.

So all should hearken and conceive
What God means by baptism
And what a Christian should believe
To elude heresy's schism.
    God's will is that the water bear
    Much more than just plain water;
    God's holy Word is also there
    With Spirit beyond measure.
    This is the true baptizer.

Through words and pictures has God been
These things plainly relaying,
As at the Jordan River, when
We heard the father saying,
    "This is my child, my own, my dear,
    On whom my favor's resting.

A NEW PATH TO PRAYER

My wish is that his words you hear
To find in them a blessing
And follow all his teachings."

And God's own Son is standing here
As fragile human being.
The Holy Spirit too comes near,
The dove that we are seeing,
    In order that we never doubt,
    When we are to be baptized,
    That all three Persons are about
    On earth with us to abide,
    For all have been our baptists.

Lord Christ his children calls again,
"Go to the world, proclaiming
That everyone is lost to sin,
From sin should be abstaining.
    But who believes and is baptized
    Is saved by that forever.
    So as a newborn person rise,
    For death has lost its terror.
    A heavenly home is waiting."

But who cannot believe such grace
Is slave to sin unbounded,
Condemned eternal death to face,
By powers of hell surrounded.
    One is not saved by piety;
    Good works can only bring scorn.
    The Fall makes all futility,
    Wherein we all have been born;
    One cannot save one's own self.

It's only water to the eye
When from our hands it's flowing.
The power that's in the blood of Christ

LUTHER'S SPIRITUALITY

Is what faith is beholding.
    For faithful ones a river flows,
    By Christ's own blood red tinted,
    With healing power for human woes
    That from Adam descended
    And we ourselves committed.

God Be Exalted! Sing God's Praise in Chorus

Wittenberg 1524

God be exalted! Sing God's praise in chorus,
For a feast is spread before us
Of God's own body and God's blood most precious.
Grant, Lord, that this meal refresh us.
O Lord, have mercy.
Lord God, through your own holy body
That came from your dear mother, Mary,
And your blood, holy spilled,
Keep us, Lord, from every ill.
O Lord, have mercy.

Your holy life to death for us was given
That we might have life in heaven.
No greater good could be among your presents;
Thus we eat in your remembrance.
O Lord, have mercy.
Your love, Lord, has so greatly moved you,
Your blood did great wonders for us do—
Paid for our guilt and shame,
Giving God the sweetest name.
O Lord, have mercy.

Lord, grant to us your blessings and your favor,
That we may walk with the Savior.
In mutual love and union keep us planted,
Lest we take this meal for granted.
O Lord, have mercy.

LUTHER'S SPIRITUALITY

Lord, your holy spirit keep near us,
And upon a proper course steer us,
So your poor Church may be
Kept in peace and unity.
O Lord, have mercy.

WERE GOD NOT WITH US AT THIS TIME (PSALM 124)

Were God not with us at this time,
Let Israel be declaring—
Were God not with us at this time,
We would be lost, despairing,
 So poor and small a group are we,
 Despised by much humanity,
 Who endlessly attack us.

Such anger did they toward us show
That, if God had permitted,
They would have swallowed us up whole,
Our life and limb quite forfeit.
 We would as in a flood be drowned
 By raging waters all around,
 As victims of their violence.

All praise and thanks to God on high
We've not become their captives.
As tethered birds escape to fly,
Our soul free from its snares lives.
 The cord is snapped, and we are free,
 God's name stands by us faithfully,
 The God of earth and heaven.

LORD GOD, I CRY FROM DEEPEST NEED (PSALM 130)

Lord God, I cry from deepest need
To you. Please hear my pleading.
In mercy bend your ears toward me
That they my prayers are heeding.
 If you, O Lord, would look upon
 The wrongs and harms that we have done,
 Then who could stand before you?

Only by your goodwill and grace
Are you our sins forgiving.
We are not fit to see your face,
However well we're living.
 Before you none at all can boast;
 We fear our arrogance the most
 And live in your grace only.

Therefore, in God is all my hope
And not on my deserving.
My heart will find a sweet repose
In God with trust unswerving
 Addressing me, the precious word
 My comfort and my true treasure,
 Whom I will trust forever.

And should it last all through the night
And even into morning.
My heart will cling to God's great might
Despairing not, nor worrying.

A NEW PATH TO PRAYER

So you, O Israel, heir decreed,
Who by the spirit was conceived,
Keep watch; your God is coming.

Though manifold the sins we see,
God's grace is more abundant.
However great our trials be,
God helps with hand omnipotent.
    God is alone the good shepherd,
    Who Israel's freedom has assured
    From all its sin and sorrow.

Jesus Christ, Our Lord and Savior

Wittenberg 1524

Jesus Christ, our Lord and Savior,
Turned God's anger into favor
And, through his own agony,
Saved us all from hell's misery.

Lest this ever be forgot, he
Offers to us his own body
In a bit of bread to eat
And in the wine his blood so sweet.

Are you to this meal proceeding?
Then these holy things be heeding.
Who unworthy comes to dine
A taste of death, not life, will find.

Give to God the glory, therefore,
That you are completely cared for,
While for your misdeeds and sin
God's only son to death was giv'n.

So believe with faith unfailing
This meal is for all the ailing,
Those whose hearts are sore distressed
By weighty sin and anxiousness.

For such kindness and compassion
Hearts should seek with dedication;

A NEW PATH TO PRAYER

Are you well? Then watch your step,
Lest evil be the pay you get.

"Come to me," invites the savior,
"Let me care for you forever.
Strong ones need not see my face;
A doctor's skills would be a waste.

"Were there something that you could do,
Then why had I to die for you?
This meal's not for you been spread,
If you can help yourself instead.

"From your heart you must profess this;
From your mouth you must confess this.
Then may you be fully fit
And may this food your soul equip.

"There will be a harvest surely:
You should love your neighbors purely,
That unto them you will do
Just as your God has done for you."

WE PRAISE YOU, JESUS, THAT YOU'VE COME

We praise you, Jesus, that you've come
As a human to our home.
Of a young maiden was your birth,
As angel choirs announced to earth.
Lord, have mercy!

Eternal Father's only child
Now we find in manger mild.
Our God, the everlasting Good,
Is clothed in our poor flesh and blood.
Lord, have mercy!

Asleep in Mary's lap has lain
One the world cannot contain—
Our God a little child so small,
Who nonetheless sustains us all.
Lord, have mercy!

The light eternal enters time,
Gives this world a whole new shine.
It brightens up the darkest night
And makes us children of the light.
Lord, have mercy!

God's only child, by nature God,
Lives as guest in earth's abode.
He leads us out of tears and strife
To make us heirs of heavenly life.
Lord, have mercy!

A NEW PATH TO PRAYER

He came to earth as poor as dust
To have mercy upon us
And give to us, like angel host,
The richest blessings heaven can boast.
Lord, have mercy!

God did all this to indicate
That God's love for us is great.
Rejoice, O Christendom, therefore,
And thank our God forevermore.
Lord, have mercy!

CONCERNING THE TEMPTATION IN PREDESTINATION TO DOUBT ONE'S OWN ELECTION[1]

Dr. Martin Luther said, "What an unquenchable fire it is to begin [such] a disputation, for the more one disputes it, the more one will despair. Our dear Lord God is such an enemy to this disputation that, against it, God has set baptism, the Word, and the sacraments as certain signs and pledges from which we should in no way back down, asserting, 'I am baptized, I believe in Jesus Christ. What does it matter to me if I am elected or not?' God has laid a foundation for us on which we can gain a footing, Jesus Christ, and through him we climb into heaven. Christ is the way and the door to the Father. Yet, in the devil's name, we first begin to build at the roof and have contempt for the foundation, and that is why we fall. If we could only believe the promises of faith that God has spoken, regarding that one alone who is speaking, then we would magnify this word. But, when we look to the mouth of the other, accepting the human word, then for us it is the same as if a cow had flashed its teeth at us."

NOTES

Part I—Luther's Spirituality in a Late-Medieval Context

Editors' Introduction to Part I

1. For a partial catalog of historic images of Luther, see Eric W. Gritsch, *Martin—God's Court Jester: Luther in Retrospect* (Philadelphia: Fortress Press, 1983), vii, viii.

2. "Spirituality refers to a lived experience and a disciplined life of prayer and action, but it cannot be conceived apart from the specific theological beliefs that are ingredients in the forms of life that manifest authentic Christian faith." Don E. Saliers, "Spirituality," in *A New Handbook of Christian Theology*, ed., D. Musser and J. Price (Nashville, TN: Abingdon, 1992), 440.

3. See Theodore G. Tappert, ed. and trans., *Luther: Letters of Spiritual Counsel*, Library of Christian Classics, vol. 18 (Philadelphia: Westminster Press, 1955), 13–24.

4. Heiko A. Oberman, *Luther: Man between God and the Devil* (New Haven, CT: Yale Univ. Press, 1989).

5. For a definition of apocalyptic spirituality, see Bernard McGinn, *Apocalyptic Spirituality: Treatises and Letters of Lactantius, Adso of Montier-En-Der, Joachim of Fiore, The Spiritual Franciscans, Savonarola*, Classics of Western Spirituality (New York: Paulist Press, 1979), 1–16.

6. Scholars have shown that the late-medieval period was not one of religious and spiritual decline but a blossoming of devotion and interest in spirituality. Luther's decision to enter a monastery and his lifelong quest to understand the relationship between God and humanity is thus not an exception but an example of his late-medieval context. In his great biography of Luther, Roland Bainton describes him as the "Homo Religiosus." See *Here I Stand: A Life of Martin Luther* (Nashville, TN: Abingdon, 1950), 16. See also Scott Hendrix, "Martin Luther's Reformation of Spirituality," in *Harvesting Martin Luther's Reflections on Theology, Ethics, and the Church*,

ed. Timothy J. Wengert, 240–60 (Grand Rapids, MI: William B. Eerdmans, 2004); Marc Lienhard, "Luther and the Beginnings of the Reformation," in *Christian Spirituality: High Middle Ages and Reformation*, ed. Jill Rait (New York: Crossroad, 1989), 268–99; and in Otto Gründler, "Devotio Moderna," in Rait, *Christian Spirituality*, 190, 191.

Letter to George Spenlein

1. George Spenlein was an Augustinian monk who had transferred from Wittenberg to the monastery in Memmingen. Luther reports to Spenlein how he settled the affairs of the property he had left behind. More important, he deals with a pastoral issue. See Martin Brecht, *Martin Luther: His Road to the Reformation 1483–1521*, trans. James L. Schaaf (Philadelphia: Fortress Press, 1981), 156, 157. George Spenlein later became an evangelical pastor at Arnstadt.

2. *D. Martin Luthers Werke: Kritische Gesamtausgabe, D. Martin Luthers Briefwechsel*, 18 vols. (Weimar: Hermann Boehlaus Nachfolger, 1930–85), 1:33–36. Hereafter WABr. See also LW 48:11–14.

3. A book of logic by Luther's teacher at the University of Erfurt, Jodokus Trutfetter of Eisenach. See Martin Brecht, *Luther: His Road to Reformation 1483–1521*, trans. James L. Schaaf (Philadelphia: Fortress Press, 1981), 34–36. While the explanation accounts for only two and a half guilders, Luther notes three and a half.

4. Baptista Montuanus, who died in 1518, was a valued Latin poet of that day. The book was his *Eclogues*.

5. *Pater Vicarius:* Johannes von Staupitz, who was Luther's superior in the Reformed Congregation (Observants) of the Hermits of St. Augustine. The Observants, in contrast to the Conventuals, insisted on a strict adherence to the rule of the order. Staupitz was also Luther's predecessor in the chair of Bible at the University of Wittenberg. See David C. Steinmetz, *Reformers in the Wings* (Grand Rapids, MI: Baker, 1971), 18–29. See also Steinmetz, *Misericordia Dei: The Theology of Johannes von Staupitz in Its Late Medieval Setting*, vol. 4 of *Studies in Medieval and Reformation Thought* (Leiden: Brill, 1968). According to Luther, Staupitz was his spiritual adviser *(Seelsorger)*, helping him understand temptation, predestination, and penance. For a discussion of the order's spirituality, see Adolar Zumkeller, "The Spirituality of the Augustinians," in *Christian Spirituality: High Middle Ages and Reformation*, vol. 17 of *World Spirituality: An Encyclopedic History of the Religious Quest*, ed. Jill Raitt, Bernard McGinn, and John Meyendorff (New York: Crossroad, 1989), 63–74.

6. This theme of "the happy exchange and struggle" that Luther inherited from the church's tradition is more fully developed in "The Freedom of a Christian" in Part II of this volume.

Letter to the Elector, Frederick the Wise

1. WABr 2:448–49. While Luther was in hiding at the Wartburg, his colleague, Andrew Carlstadt, incited disturbances by his radical reforms of the liturgy. Against the prince's wishes Luther announced that he would return to Wittenberg. He wanted to console the prince in the pain caused by the riots by noting that he possessed a real relic, namely, the cross. See Theodore G. Tappert, ed. and trans., *Luther: Letters of Spiritual Counsel*, vol. 18 of Library of Christian Classics (Philadelphia: Westminster Press, 1955), 139.

2. Frederick III, "the Wise," (1463–1525) was the elector of Saxony, whose political acumen, power, and religious and humanistic interests were critical to Luther's survival. He was fairly learned, understanding Latin and some French, and was devoted to the church and passionate in his devotion to relics. He had gathered a huge collection. He was the founder of the University of Wittenberg, brought the Augustinian Order of Hermits there, including Staupitz—the first professor of Bible and its first dean—and the young star professor, Luther. Frederick had been instrumental in discreetly rescuing Luther after the Diet of Wittenberg in 1521. See Martin Brecht, *Martin Luther: His Road to the Reformation 1483–1521*, trans. James L. Schaaf (Philadelphia: Fortress Press, 1981), 107–23.

3. This is the theme in Eric W. Gritsch, *Martin—God's Court Jester: Luther in Retrospect* (Philadelphia: Fortress Press, 1983).

Letter to Jerome Weller: On the Devil

1. WABr 5:518–20. The dating of this letter is uncertain.

2. Under Luther's influence Jerome Weller (1499–1572) changed his course of study from law to theology and resided in Luther's home (1527–35) as a tutor to the children. From 1539 to his death he was professor of theology in Freiberg, Saxony. See Theodore G. Tappert, ed. and trans., *Luther: Letters of Spiritual Counsel*, vol. 18 of Library of Christian Classics (Philadelphia: Westminster Press, 1955), 84, and LW 54:203.

3. Luther was also a regular victim of *Anfechtungen (tentationes)*, "temptations," or "attacks of the devil." According to Eric Gritsch, "Literally, *Anfechtung* means to be fought at, if not fenced at (from *fechten,*

'fencing'), and is often rendered as 'temptation,' from the Latin term *tentatio*, which Luther sometimes used." This is the word he used in this context. See Eric W. Gritsch, *Martin—God's Court Jester: Luther in Retrospect* (Philadelphia: Fortress Press, 1983), 225 n. 35.

4. This story also appears in *D. Martin Luthers Werke: Kritische Gesamtausgabe, Tischreden*, 6 vols. (Weimar: Hermann Boehlaus Nachfolger, 1912–21), 1, no. 223. Hereafter WATR.

Letter to Matthias Weller: The Mutual Consolation of the Faithful

1. WABr 7:104–6. Matthias (1507–63) was Jerome Weller's brother. He was employed in the chancellery of Duke Henry of Saxony. He was also a musician. See Theodore G. Tappert, ed. and trans., *Luther: Letters of Spiritual Counsel*, vol. 18 of Library of Christian Classics (Philadelphia: Westminster Press, 1955), 96–97.

2. *Anfechtung der Traurigkeit.*

3. Luther's word is *regal*, a small portable organ.

4. *Saitenspiel.*

Letter of Comfort to His Dying Father

1. WABr 5:238–41; LW 49:267–71. As demonstrated in this letter, Luther's relationship with his father was much closer and warmer than some modern accounts would claim. See Erik H. Erikson, *Young Man Luther: A Study in Psychoanalysis and History* (New York: W. W. Norton, 1962), 49–97. Hans Luther died on June 5, 1530, three months after this letter of consolation was written. On June 5 Luther wrote to Melanchthon: "John Reineck wrote me today that my beloved father, the senior Hans Luther, departed this life at one o'clock on Exaudi Sunday. This death cast me into deep mourning, not only because of the ties of nature but also because it was through his sweet love to me that my Creator endowed me with all that I am and have. Although it is consoling to me that, as he writes, my father fell asleep softly and strong in his faith in Christ, yet his kindness and the memory of his pleasant conversation have caused so deep a wound in my heart that I have scarcely ever held death in such low esteem." WABr 5:351, quoted in Theodore G. Tappert, ed. and trans., *Luther: Letters of Spiritual Counsel*, vol. 18 of Library of Christian Classics (Philadelphia: Westminster Press, 1955), 30.

2. An apparent reference to an epidemic called English Sweat.

3. Cyriac Kaufmann was a nephew of Martin Luther and was a student in Wittenberg. Tappert, *Luther* 18:30 n. 16.

Luther Counsels Weller: The Greater the Saint before God, the Greater the Temptations

1. WATR 3, no. 3798.

2. See Letter to Jerome Weller in this volume, and LW 54:203, *Table Talks* for information on Dr. Jerome Weller.

About Fleeing into Solitude

1. WATR 2, no. 1329.

2. Luther is probably referring to a Gnostic sect of the second century.

Commentary on Psalm 82: Secular Saviors

1. *D. Martin Luthers Werke: Kritische Gesamtausgabe*, 65+ vols. (Weimar: Hermann Boehlaus Nachfolger, 1883–), 31/1:183–218. Hereafter WA. See also LW 13:41–72.

2. According to *Luther's Works*, "A letter written by Lazarus Spengler on March 17, 1530, indicates that Luther was already working on the commentary. Luther's preface to Justus Menius's book on the Anabaptists, dated April 12, 1530, refers to the book as a finished product." LW 13:x.

3. There was, of course, a long tradition of debate and conversation among medieval theologians and philosophers about the naturalness of human political community. See, for example, Brian Tierney, *The Crisis of Church and State 1050–1300* (Englewood Cliffs, NJ: Prentice-Hall, 1964).

4. "Whoever wants to learn and become wise in secular government let that one read the heathen books and writings. They have truly painted it and portrayed it quite beautifully and generously, with both verses and pictures, with teachings and examples; and they became the source for the ancient imperial laws. I am convinced that God gave and preserved such heathen books as those of the poets and the histories, like Homer, Vergil, Demosthenes, Cicero, Livy, and afterwards the fine old jurists—as God has also given and preserved other temporal goods among the heathen and godless at all times—that the heathen and godless, too, might have their

prophets, apostles, and theologians or preachers for the secular government." LW 13:109.

5. "…God willed to give temporal dominion to the heathen or to reason. God had to provide people who had wisdom and courage, who had the necessary inclination and skill, and who would preserve it…. The heathen, for their part, have their heathen books; we Christians, for our part, have the books of the holy scriptures. The former teach virtue, laws, and wisdom with respect to temporal goods, honor, and peace on earth; the latter teach faith and good works with respect to eternal life in the kingdom of heaven. How could a prince or king on earth be portrayed any better than the heathen have portrayed their Hercules?" LW 13:199.

6. See John Tonkin, *The Church and the Secular Order in Reformation Thought* (New York: Columbia Univ. Press, 1971), 56. See also Brian Gerrish, *Grace and Reason: A Study in the Theology of Luther* (Oxford: Clarendon Press, 1962).

7. The canon reads, "If anyone, at the instigation of the devil, incurs the guilt of laying violent hands upon a cleric or a monk, let him lie under the bond of anathema." *Decreta*, Part II, causa 17, quaestio 4, canon 29 in *Corpus Iuris Canonici*, ed. Emil Richter and Emil Friedberg, 2 vols. (Leipzig, 1879–81), 1, 822. Cited in LW 13:42 n. 1.

8. *Stande*. The word *estate* refers to the medieval status groups: priests, princes, peasants, and burghers, each of which had a mutual responsibility to the others. They are similar to classes, but, while classes develop from the principle of production, estates develop from those of consumption. Traditionally, the estates were those of princes, peasants, and priests. In this division of labor the princes (or nobility) protected and the priests prayed for the others, while the peasants plowed the fields and provided bread.

9. The NRSV reads, "God has taken his place in the divine council; in the midst of the gods he holds judgment." Luther's wording is kept here, since the commentary refers to it repeatedly.

10. For Luther, Christian instruction cannot occur at home without good government. This is the opposite of a modern view that Christian family values depend upon the home and not on a well-ordered and just government that protects the poor. For Luther, the Christian household depends on just government.

11. This is a commentary on the Peasants' War.

12. Here, in part, one can see how Luther could be misunderstood in relation to obeying authorities without questioning them, but he turns to a critique of unjust rulers later in the psalm.

13. These examples of God bringing down the mighty are recited by Luther in his comments on the Magnificat (Luke 1:52). See LW 21:343–45.

14. The German word Luther uses here is *Gemein*. It can mean either "assembly" in the sense of "local church" or "community" in the sense of "town." See LW 13:46. See also Gordon W. Lathrop and Timothy J. Wengert, *Christian Assembly: Marks of the Church in a Pluralistic Age* (Minneapolis: Fortress Press, 2004), 3–16.

15. The biblical text indicates "an exceedingly large city."

16. This spirituality of the giftedness of creation and the human need to be grateful is a common theme for Luther. See especially his commentary on Psalm 118 in this volume.

17. Thomas Müntzer (1489–1525), an Anabaptist reformer, was both iconoclastic and millenarian. He was a leader for the peasants in the Peasants' War and was beheaded after the defeat at Frankenhausen. Andreas Carlstadt (1480–1541) was a leader early in the reformation movement, but Luther eclipsed him after the Leipzig debate. He led the liturgical and social reforms in Wittenberg that Luther returned from the Wartburg to repudiate. He did not support Luther's views on secular authority.

18. The Latin phrase used here is *iudicio et iure*.

19. Luther adopted his own versification on this point.

20. *Pater patriae* and *Servator patriae*. It is important to notice that the importance of good government, just laws, regulations, and social justice would have a profound impact on the development of a spirituality of Lutheran social justice in Europe. A deregulated society is one in which the poor and defenseless are oppressed.

21. In the omitted paragraph Luther compares the vocation of justice that the prince exercises to the lives of the saints, which are usually celebrated for their spirituality.

22. This proverbial expression was already in Walther von der Vogelweide (d. ca. 1230). See WA 31/1:202.

23. Suetonius *Augustus* 25.

24. This is verse 4 of the psalm, but it is the third verse in the portion of the psalm under current discussion.

25. The etymological derivation is not accurate. Although the selection ends on a note that may appear to glorify the role of princes and lords, Luther, in the next section, not included in this volume, is sharply critical of the abuse of the office given by God to the rulers of his time.

An Admonishment to Pastors to Preach against Usury

1. WA 51:403–24. Written in 1540.

2. See Karlfried Froehlich, "Luther on Vocation," in *Harvesting Martin Luther's Reflections on Theology, Ethics, and the Church*, ed. Timothy J. Wengert (Grand Rapids, MI: William B. Eerdmans, 2004), 123.

3. Ibid.

4. For a comprehensive treatment of this issue, see Carter Lindberg, *Beyond Charity: Reformation Initiatives for the Poor* (Minneapolis: Fortress Press, 1993). This introduction is dependent upon his analysis. See also David Crowner and Gerald Christianson, eds. and trans., *The Spirituality of the German Awakening* (New York/Mahwah, NJ: Paulist Press, 2003).

5. See the Commentary on Psalm 82 in this volume, where the prince could turn the whole principality into a hospital or a place of care for all the people.

6. See Carter Lindberg, "Luther on Poverty," in Wengert, *Harvesting Martin Luther's Reflections on Theology*, 146: "The medieval ideology of poverty had been entrenched for centuries, but the acceptance of the idea that money can make money was a relatively recent development with the rise of cities from the twelfth century on. Usury, the taking of interest where there is no production, had long been condemned. Already Pope Leo I in the mid-fifth century had stated that 'Taking interest is the death of the soul' and usury had been prohibited by numerous councils from Lateran II (1139) to Lateran V (1535). But by all accounts, the entrepreneur was well established by Luther's time." See also Hans-Jürgen Prien, *Luthers Wirtschaftsethik* (Göttingen: Vandenhoeck and Ruprecht, 1992).

7. Lindberg, "Luther on Poverty," 140–44.

8. *Pfaffen.*

9. Luther is not speaking figuratively; the possibility of being beheaded was real.

10. Ambrose, *Exposition of the Psalm*, 118, Sermon 12, 44, *Partrologia cursus completes*, Series latina, 221 vols. ed. J. P. Migne (Paris, 1844–90), 15:1449. Hereafter MPL. For a discussion of the accuracy of Luther's use of this citation, see Martin Luther, *Studienausgabe*, 6 vols., ed. Hans-Ulrich Delius (Berlin: Evangelische Verlagsanstalt, 1979–99), 2:85 n. 764.

11. See WA 51:397: A saying that "ill-gotten gain can never be inherited as far as the third heir."

12. *Zinskauf.* For an explanation of how a field was mortgaged and by productivity and regular payments repaid, see Prien, *Luthers Wirtschaftsethik*, 62–63.

NOTES

Preface to the Revelation of St. John (1522)

1. For a full discussion of apocalyptic spirituality, see Bernard McGinn, *Apocalyptic Spirituality: Treatises and Letters of Lactantius, Adso of Montier-En-Der, Joachim of Fiore, The Spiritual Franciscans, Savonarola*, Classics of Western Spirituality (New York: Paulist Press, 1979), 1–16.

2. Heiko Oberman, "'Iustitia Christi' and 'Iustia Dei': Luther and the Scholastic Doctrines of Justification," in *The Dawn of the Reformation* (Edinburgh: T. and T. Clark, 1986), 120–21. A similar judging Christ was seated above the entrance to the City Church in Wittenberg.

3. Although medieval iconography of the Last Judgment inspired fear and guilt, it was never without hope. See Bernard McGinn, "The Last Judgment in Christian Tradition," in *The Encyclopedia of Apocalypticism in Western History and Culture*, ed. Bernard McGinn, vol. 2 (New York: Continuum, 1998), 394–95. See also the introduction to Carolyn Walker Bynum and Paul Freedman, eds., *Last Things: Death and the Apocalypse in the Middle Ages* (Philadelphia: Univ. of Pennsylvania, 2000), 5–10.

4. For an extensive discussion, see Philip D. W. Krey, "Luther and the Apocalypse: Between Christ and History," in *The Last Things: Biblical and Theological Perspectives on Eschatology*, ed. Carl E. Braaten and Robert W. Jenson (Grand Rapids, MI: William B. Eerdmans, 2002), 135–45. See also Bernard McGinn, "Revelation," in *The Literary Guide to the Bible*, ed. Robert Alter and Frank Kermode (Cambridge, MA: Harvard Univ. Press, 1987), 534.

5. "Letter to Paulinum, concerning the Study of the Scriptures," MPL 22:548–49.

Preface to the Revelation of St. John (1530 and 1546)

1. SA 2:390.

2. See Luther's February 25, 1530, letter to Nicholaus Hausmann in Margaret A. Currie, *The Letters of Martin Luther* (London: Macmillan, 1908), 204.

3. See Jane Strohl, *Luther's Eschatology: The Last Times and the Last Things* (Ph.D. diss., Univ. of Chicago, 1989), 228–33. See also Heiko A. Oberman, *Luther: Man between God and the Devil* (New Haven, CT: Yale Univ. Press, 1989), 62–82. See also Hans-Ulrich Hofmann, *Luther und die Johannes-Apokalypse* (Tübingen: J. C. B. Mohr, 1982). Luther's lively doctrine of the devil and the heritage of the Franciscan/Joachite interpretation of the Apocalypse seem to come alive in this second preface.

4. Robert Barnes, "Images of Hope and Despair: Western Apocalypticism, ca. 1500–1800," vol. 2 in *The Encyclopedia of Apocalypticism in Western History and Culture*, ed. Bernard McGinn (New York: Continuum, 1998), 152. Barnes also notes, "His reading of Scripture and revision of prophetic truth became the key source of inspiration for a long tradition of Protestant apocalypticism" (151).

5. See Philip D. Krey, "Many Readers But Few Followers: The Fate of Nicholas of Lyra's 'Apocalypse Commentary' in the Hands of His Late-Medieval Admirers," *Church History* 64, no. 2 (June 1995), 185–201. See Philip D. Krey and Lesley Smith, *Nicholas of Lyra: The Senses of Scripture* (Leiden: Brill, 2000). See also, Bernard McGinn, "Revelation," in *The Literary Guide to the Bible*, ed. Robert Alter and Frank Kermode (Cambridge, MA: Harvard Univ. Press, 1987), 534. Like Nicholas before him, it is hard not to conclude that Luther is sometimes interpreting this commentary with tongue in cheek. Consider his interpretation of the three frogs below.

6. See Philip D. Krey, "Nicholas of Lyra: The Apocalypse Commentator, Historian, and Critic," *Franciscan Studies* 52 (1992), 53–84.

7. See Jaroslav Pelikan, "Some Uses of the Apocalypse in the Magisterial Reformers," in *The Apocalypse in English Renaissance Thought and Literature*, ed. C. A. Patrides and Joseph Wittreich (Ithaca, NY: Cornell Univ. Press, 1984), 81.

8. Ibid.

9. 1 Cor 12:10, 28–29; 14:1, 3–6, 22, 24, 29, 31–32, 37.

10. See St. Augustine's distinction of three kinds of visions: corporeal, spiritual (imaginative), and intellectual in the *Literal Commentary on Genesis* (12.6.15–12.7.16; 12.24.51) and Letter 147. See also Bernard McGinn, *The Foundations of Mysticism: Origins to the Fifth Century* (New York: Crossroad), 254.

11. Dan 2:31–45 and 7:16–27.

12. Luther uses the version from Acts 2:17.

13. For a history of its interpretations, see McGinn, "Revelation," 523–41. See also Luther's preface to the "Commentarius in Apocalypsin ante centum annos editus," WA 26:121, 123f. See also Philip D. Krey, "Luther and the Apocalypse: Between Christ and History" in *The Last Things: Biblical and Theological Perspectives on Eschatology*, ed. Carl E. Braaten and Robert W. Jenson (Grand Rapids, MI: William B. Eerdmans, 2002), 135–45.

14. Eusebius, *The Ecclesiastical History* 3, 25, 2–4.

15. See the preface of 1522.

16. This method of interpreting the Book of Revelation follows the tradition of Nicholas of Lyra, who popularized the historical sequential method that had been used by Alexander Minorita (d. 1271) and Peter Auriol (1280–1322). It had also been used by John Wyclif (1330–84?) in his *Apocalypse Commentary* (1371). Nicholas writes, "For in the spirit under certain images he saw the course of history from the time of the apostles to the end of the world, with respect to tribulations, consolations, and notable changes, of which some have already occurred and others are in the future." See Krey, trans., *Nicholas of Lyra's Apocalypse Commentary*, TEAMS: Commentary Series, ed. E. Ann Matter (Kalamazoo, MI: Medieval Institute Publications, 1997), 18. Also see Philip D. Krey, "Many Readers but Few Followers," 189.

17. This is a standard interpretation for chapters four and five in the Lyra tradition.

18. Luther will return to this theme at the very end of the preface.

19. Bishop of Cyprus, b. 270. He suffered in the persecution under Diocletian. A legend had him attending the Council of Nicea in 325.

20. Athanasius (ca. 300–373), bishop of Alexandria (328–373) and the most famous and steadfast champion of the Council of Nicea (325).

21. Hilary of Poitiers (ca. 315–ca. 367), bishop of Poitiers, France, in 353. He defended the doctrine of the Trinity, proclaimed at Nicea against the Arians.

22. Tatian (second-century Syrian) was a student of Justin Martyr. His Encratitism or ascetic beliefs about abstaining from marriage, wine, and meat were associated with Gnosticism by Eusebius *The Ecclesiastical History* 4, 28–29.

23. Pelagius (350–ca. 425), more than likely a Briton, was an ascetic and the founder of a movement emphasizing free will and good works. For the Pelagian movement the gift of grace was human freedom, namely, the God-given ability to decide between good and evil. The controversies between St. Augustine and Pelagius and his followers were formative for the Western theological tradition concerning nature and grace.

24. Marcion (d. ca. 154) was born in Sinope on the Black Sea in Pontus. See Eusebius, *The Ecclesiastical History*. He insisted upon a radical dichotomy between the Old and the New Testaments, between the law and the gospel. He put his own canon together, which included only a portion of the Gospel of Luke, and a limited number of Pauline epistles that he contended were authentic.

25. The Cataphrygians are really associated with the Montanists, but Luther races through the list indiscriminately.

26. Religious movement founded by Mani (216–76), who was born in southern Mesopotamia. His religion combined influences of Christianity, Zoroastrianism, and Buddhism. Its followers were divided into two groups. The "elect" were ascetic; that is, they did not eat meat and were celibate. The "hearers" were followers who did not need to take up an ascetical lifestyle. One of its most famous, although temporary, adherents was St. Augustine of Hippo.

27. The Montanists were followers of Montanus, a Phrygian apocalyptic and charismatic prophet who began to prophesy in Asia Minor about the year 172 (Eusebius *The Ecclesiastical History*). It was rigorously ascetic and valued martyrdom and rejection of the world's values.

28. *Geysterey.*

29. Thomas Müntzer (ca. 1490–1525), an apocalyptic prophet, was one of the leaders of the Thüringian peasants in revolt.

30. Origen (ca. 185–ca. 251) was a great Alexandrian theologian, exegete, and father of monasticism.

31. Novatian, a rigorist and schismatic Roman presbyter (mid-third century), opposed the lenient policies of the church toward those who had lapsed by committing grievous sins and had asked for readmission to communion. The movement required rebaptism and held that Catholic baptism was invalid.

32. Later Novatians took the name Cathars, meaning "pure."

33. A schism that broke out in the church in North Africa after the great Diocletian persecution in 303–5. The Donatists emphasized the values of purity and holiness against the Catholic stress on universality as a mark of the Christian community. This apocalyptic movement valued suffering and martyrdom, in contrast to compromise, in reaction to the persecuting Roman Empire. With claims to sanctity also went a proclamation of apostolic poverty.

34. The Hebrew is *Abaddon* and the Greek is *Apollyon*.

35. As early as 1518 Luther had used the *Fortalicium Fidei* of Alphonsus de Spina. Its fourth book was entitled, "De bello saracenorum." WA 40/3:670 n. 3.

36. Here Luther substitutes *Chor* or "choir" for what the Vulgate had as *foris templum* (outside the temple). For a fuller discussion, see LW 35:405 n. 54. Thus he is contrasting inner and external piety.

37. The "scroll" or "book" *(Buch)* is for Luther the canon law. Luther had learned about the two swords from the bull of Boniface VIII of 1302, "Unam Sanctam." See Denzinger, *The Sources of Catholic Dogma*, no. 469.

NOTES

38. Luther is referring to the Holy Roman Empire of the German Nation, established with papal blessing at the time of Charlemagne (800) and continuing to Luther's day. Luther also discusses the *translatio imperii* from Byzantium to Charles the Great in his preface to Daniel, written in the same year. LW 35:295.

39. This is actually 14:14–20.

40. After 1541 editions say, "in the fifteenth and sixteenth chapters."

41. Three important Reformation figures. Johann Faber (1478–1541), a lifelong friend of Erasmus, was once sympathetic to Luther's cause and then became an ardent opponent. Johann Eck (1486–1543) was a theologian and professor in the University of Ingolstadt. He was Luther's opponent at the Leipzig debate in 1519 and helped to cause Luther's excommunication from Rome in 1520. Jerome Emser (1478–1527), a former friend of Luther's, turned against him after the Leipzig debate.

42. This is a reference to the sack of Rome in 1527 by the troops of Emperor Charles V, who was a defender of the papacy.

43. The *letze trank* or "stirrup cup" is the parting draught of wine; here the cup of God's wrath.

44. See Andrew Colin Gow, *The Red Jews: Antisemitism in an Apocalyptic Age, 1200–1600* (Leiden: Brill, 1995).

45. In other places he sets this at the same time as Albrecht I (1298–1308). See his "Supputatio annorum mundi," WA 53:161f.

46. Dan 7:7, 9f. As noted above, Luther wrote his preface to Daniel in the same year that he wrote this preface.

47. That is, the counterfeit church has all its outward form, external trappings.

48. The beginning of the third article of the Creed.

49. The golden year is a papal year of jubilee, in which pilgrims to Rome receive a special indulgence.

50. See also WA 18:652, "Abscondita est Ecclesia, latent sancti."

51. Cf. Phil 3:20; Col 3:1.

Part II—Teaching the New Spirituality

Scholia on Psalm 5: On Hope

1. Martin Luther, *Evangelium und Leben*, ed. Horst Beintker (Berlin: Evangelische Verlagsanstalt GmbH, 1983), 20–31. See also Martin Luther, *Operationes in Psalmos*, ed. Gerhard Hammer, vol. 1 of *Archiv zur Weimarer Ausgabe der Werke Martin Luthers*, ed. Gerhard Ebeling, Ulrich Köpf, Bernd Moeller, and Heiko A. Oberman (Cologne: Bohlau Verlag, 1991), 542–52.

2. The NRSV reads, "But let all who take refuge in you rejoice."

3. *Flesh* and *spirit* each refers to the total person, turned away from God and neighbor in the first case, turned toward them in the second. Thus one can be spiritually turned away and thus be in the flesh, and physically turned toward and thus be in the Spirit.

4. In the NRSV Psalm 49:18 reads, "for you are praised when you do well for yourself."

5. This is not meant in a psychological sense or in terms of our self-confidence before others, but for our assurance and certainty of salvation.

6. *Einstellung*.

7. *Infusa virtus*.

8. *Tentatio*.

9. *Probatio*.

10. If we are good, we cannot know it.

11. Cf. Augustine *Sermon* 359A, 3–4.

12. The NRSV reads, "through faith for faith."

13. This was the original late-medieval definition of *hope* that Luther challenged above.

14. Cf. Ps 68:35.

15. Cf. NRSV: "But know that the Lord has set apart the faithful for himself."

16. Cf. Ps 4:3; 68:35.

17. Bishop of Poitiers who died in 367. See MPL 23:52.

18. Pope from 678 to 681.

The Freedom of a Christian

1. WA 7:20–38. There is disagreement among scholars as to which version was written first, but Stolt argues persuasively that the Latin was

first and the German is a translation. See B. Stolt, *Studien zu Luthers Freiheitstraktat mit besonderer Rucksicht auf der Verhältnis der lateinischen und der deutschen Fassung zueinander und die Stilmittel der Rhetorik* (Stockholm: Almquist and Wiksell, 1969).

2. See Peter Krey, "Sword of the Spirit, Sword of Iron: Word of God, Scripture, Gospel, and Law in Luther's Most-Often Published Pamphlets (1520–1525)" (Ph.D. diss., Graduate Theological Union, 2001). Luther could summarize or concentrate meaning, often even in a single word (e.g., *testament*). Readers know Luther today from his massive volumes and do not realize how much he was a pamphlet writer in the polemical fray of his time.

3. It is the Latin version that is translated in LW 31.

4. See Bernard McGinn, "The Changing Shape of Medieval Mysticism," *Church History* 65 (June 1996), 2.

5. Martin Marty offers other ways of translating *fröhlich:* "joyful," "fortunate," "cheerful," "glorious," or "blessed." See Martin Marty, *Martin Luther* (New York: Viking Penguin, 2004), 65. Luther also includes the word *Streit* (battle). It refers to the cosmic conflict, which Luther does not develop in this popular version as much as in the Latin one.

6. *Extra nos.* Luther safeguards his theology and faith from subjectivism by insisting on the external word, as opposed to an inner voice or inner light.

7. Marty, *Martin Luther,* 65.

8. Cf. Luke 2:34; 1 Cor 1:22–23.

9. Luther divides this work into three parts and a conclusion. Part I refers to the inner person, points 1–19 (WA 7:20.1—29.31); Part II, to the external body, points 20–25 (WA 7:29.31—34.23); and Part III, to relating to others, points 26–29 (WA 7:34.23—38.5).

10. *Herr* means "lord" or "Mr." or "gentleman." The meaning here is "an entitled self." To avoid sexist language, we have used *sovereign*.

11. Luther mistakenly wrote "1 Corinthians 12."

12. Or "preached about Christ."

13. Cf. Amos 8:11–14.

14. Luther mistakenly wrote "Psalm 104."

15. Hos 13:9. The NRSV says, "I will destroy you, O Israel; who can help you?"

16. Cf. Isa 10:22. Luther either translates or interprets the Hebrew to refer to words rather than people and thus has a "summing up" rather than "remnant." The NRSV says, "Destruction is decreed, overflowing with righteousness."

17. This saying is Luther's rewriting of Mark 16:16: *Glaubstu so hastu/glaubstu nit/so hastu nit.*

18. The LW translation of the Latin is, "So the word imparts its qualities to the soul," which is a free translation of *quale est verbum, talis ab eo fit anima.* Also, see Kenneth Hagen's translation in *A Theology of Testament in the Young Luther* (Leiden: E. J. Brill, 1974), 89: "One who hears the word becomes like the word, pure, good, and just."

19. Luther has *der eynige glaub.* It means "faith standing by itself."

20. Or when God sees that the soul "lets God be true."

21. That is, it is true and right that God is regarded as truthful.

22. Eph 5:30. The NRSV says "because we are members of [Christ's] body."

23. Hans-Ulrich Delius argues that *hürlein* did not have the pejorative connotation of "harlot" at that time. SA 2:277 n. 70. In the Latin version, however, Luther cites Hosea 1—3, in which Gomer is described as a harlot.

24. "Honor and praise" in German.

25. For Luther, the dog has "a piece of meat" in its mouth. The story comes from Aesop's fables.

26. Luther uses three Latin words: *ministros, servos, oeconomos.*

27. Luther uses the word *spear* here for "sting."

28. Cf. Rom 8:23.

29. *Seligkeit.* This word has been translated elsewhere as "salvation."

30. Sir 10:12. The NRSV says, "The beginning of human pride is to forsake the Lord."

31. The German has *und den selben gutt setzen,* "set it well."

32. Luther seems to personify faith or to see faith as identical with the person of Christ.

33. The three parts of the medieval sacrament of penance.

34. Phil 2:1–4, according to Luther. See the completely different translation of this text by Luther in 1522, *D. Martin Luthers Werke: Kritische Gesamtausgabe, Deutsche Bibel,* 12 vols. (Weimar: Hermann Boehlaus Nachfolger, 1906–61), 7:216. Hereafter WADB.

35. See no. 12 or no. 16 above.

36. The NRSV says, "And the life I now live in the flesh I live by faith in the Son of God."

37. In the Latin version Luther uses the word *raptus/rapi,* meaning that by faith the Christian is enraptured into God: *per fidem sursum rapitur supra se in deum.* See Heiko A. Oberman, *The Dawn of the Reformation: Essays in Late Medieval and Early Reformation Thought* (Edinburgh: T. and T. Clark, 1986), 149–54.

NOTES

The Magnificat Put into German and Explained

1. WA 7:545–46.

2. John Frederick (1503–54), the nephew of Frederick the Wise, succeeded his uncle and became elector of Saxony in 1532. From the fall of 1520 he was in correspondence with Luther, whom he called his spiritual father (WABr 2:237, 238).

3. "The Virgin Mary and her song of thanksgiving stand as models of true *pietas*, a word which, in its original sense that was still operative at the end of the Middle Ages, designated the mutual affection between parents and children. The praise of Mary is part of the Christian joy." George Tavard, "Medieval Piety in Luther's *Commentary on the Magnificat*," in *Ad fontes Lutheri: Toward the Recovery of the Real Luther: Essays in Honor of Kenneth Hagen's Sixty-Fifth Birthday*, ed. Timothy Maschke, Franz Posset, and Joan Skocir (Milwaukee: Marquette Univ. Press, 2001), 300.

4. "Luther, however, was not doing mere exegesis as he commented on the Magnificat. He made himself the bearer of a tradition he had inherited, which had a literary and a spiritual dimension. The literary dimension carried forward the medieval fondness for interweaving strands, as when two directions combined with three points of view bring about six considerations, that they may be followed, as in Bonaventure's *Itinerarium*, by a concluding seventh, so that the writing can, however, evoke the sevenfold sacramental system and the seven gifts of the Holy Spirit" (Ibid., 293).

5. Ibid., 292–96.

6. Luther and others frequently identified themselves this way in their correspondence with the princes.

7. See also 2 Sam 14:17; 19:27.

8. See "Commentary on Psalm 82" in this volume.

9. See also Jer 51:34; Ezek 32:2.

10. Luther made frequent references to Bias, a Greek sage (ca. 620–540 BC). See SA 1:315 nn. 17–18.

11. See ibid., 316 nn. 22–23.

12. *Er habs denn on mittel von de(m) heyligen geyst.*

13. Cf. 1 Sam 2:6–8; Job 22:29; Ps 75:8; Ezek 21:26; Matt 23:12; Luke 14:11, 18:14.

14. The American edition notes, "An apparent allusion to the old axiom, *Ex nihilo nihil fit.*"

15. *Du sitzest über de(n) Cherubin/und sihest ynn die tieffe oder abgrund.* The NRSV includes this in the apocryphal additions to Daniel, verse 32.

16. *Caro, anima, spiritus.*

17. Exod 26; 36:3–38; 40:1–16.

18. *Vorstandt.*

19. *Wissen.*

20. *Erkentnisz.*

21. The NRSV reads, "God gives the desolate a home to live in."

22. For a full discussion with a comprehensive bibliography of the influence of monasticism on Luther, especially the spirituality of the Augustinian Order, and Luther's reluctant break with monastic vows, see Heiko A. Oberman, "Luther contra Medieval Monasticism: Friar in the Lion's Den," in Maschke, Posset, and Skocir, *Ad fontes Lutheri*, 183–213.

23. The "Treatise on Good Works" (1520) appears in LW 44:21–114.

24. For the use of the Magnificat in evening payer, see SA 1:314 n. 6, 1:315 n. 22.

25. *Mein seel macht yhn grosz das ist mein gantzes leben weben synn und kraft halten viel von yhm alszo das sie gleich ynn yhn vorzuckt und empor erhebung fuelet ynn seinen gnedigen gutten willenn wie der volgend versz weyszet* (Luke 1:47).

26. Ps 49:18. The NRSV says, "For you are praised when you do well for yourself."

Preface to the Epistle to the Romans

1. How Luther's concept of faith continues to develop can be seen in his pamphlet "Sermon about Unrighteous Mammon" (untranslated), delivered August 17, 1522. It had fifteen editions in Luther's lifetime and was also included in three editions of sermon collections. Luther writes: "The real faith of which we speak will not allow itself to be made out of our thought, because it is a pure work of God in us without our being able to add anything we do to it. Thus St. Paul says in Romans 5:15: 'It is God's gift of grace won for us through Christ.' That is why it is such a mighty, active, restless, and busy thing, which immediately renews the person, gives a second birth, and leads the person into new ways and into new being. It is impossible for this same self not to do good works, continuously, [spontaneously] without interruption" (WA 10/3:285). See also Peter Krey, "Sword of the Spirit, Sword of Iron: Word of God, Scripture, Gospel, and Law in Luther's Most-Often Published Pamphlets (1520–1525)" (Ph.D. diss., Graduate Theological Union, 2001), 167.

2. In the Preface to the New Testament Luther blames Jerome for this clouding of the epistle. WADB 6:8.

3. See 1 Sam 16:7.

4. The NRSV reads, "the law is holy."

5. This is a formulation of the late-medieval theologian, Gabriel Biel, who argued that God would reward one with grace if "one did what is in one" *(Facere quod in se est).*

6. Here he means the Scholastics.

7. Rom 3:25; 4:25; 10:9.

8. See David C. Steinmetz, "Calvin and the Divided Self of Romans 7," in *Calvin in Context* (Oxford: Oxford Univ. Press, 1995), 114, 115.

9. Luther's concept of *totus homo* was first referenced in the Galatians Commentary of 1519 and the pamphlet against Latomus in 1521. This anthropological concept is more holistic than the dualism of mind and body.

10. An obvious printing error in the text reads *lebet* (lives), but it was corrected to *leret* (teaches) in 1530.

11. Cf. Heb 9:5; Rom 3:24–25.

12. The text indicates Psalm 13, but Romans 4:6–8 cites Psalm 32:1–2. The text was corrected in later editions.

13. This word is in the text twice and drops out in 1524.

14. The 1546 edition reads "under" rather than "in."

15. This stark statement by Luther that human nature is sinful and evil is problematic for the tradition. It is clear by inference that Luther is referring to the old self, or "flesh," as defined by him above, which needs the other side of the story, namely, that at the same time humans are created good. Thus, this literal translation needs to be balanced with Luther's theological anthropology.

16. The struggle goes on until the person comes out of "self-absorption" and becomes completely oriented toward God and neighbor. A creative tension exists between the spirit and the flesh (a coincidence of opposites), and because we belong to Christ, the victory belongs to the Spirit.

17. There are similar admonitions in 1 Cor 3:1–2 and Heb 5:12–14.

18. This use of Christ as example becomes less prominent in the later Luther. See the Galatians Commentary (1535), LW 26:313–16, 372–73.

Preface to the German Writings

1. There had been previous attempts at collecting Luther's works from the early 1520s.

2. This is a different order and set of practices from the medieval practices of *lectio divina*. See Timothy Wengert's Preface in this volume.

3. *Weise.* This can also mean a rule. A fund of oral, customary rules or laws were called *Weistümer,* "custumals" in English.

4. Markolf is a folk hero from a book of tales. See "Solomon and Markolf," in Felix Bobertag, *Narrenbuch* (Book of Fools) (Darmstadt: Wissenschaftliche Buchgesellschaft, repr. 1964), verses 1785ff.

Psalm 117: The Art That Cannot Be Mastered

1. WA 31/1:223–57.

2. "At the end of the thirteenth century and the early decades of the fourteenth century, Meister Eckhart repeatedly insisted that God could be found, directly and decisively, anywhere and by anyone." Bernard McGinn, "The Changing Shape of Late Medieval Mysticism," *Church History* 65, no. 2 (June 1996), 199. McGinn cites Eckhart: "Truly, when people think that they are acquiring more of God in inwardness, in devotion, in sweetness and in various approaches than they do by the fireside or in the stable, you are acting just as if you took God and muffled his head up in a cloak and pushed him under a bench. Whoever is seeking God by ways is finding ways and losing God, who in ways is hidden."

3. Ibid. See Bernard McGinn's description of this development in mystical writings.

4. See also the Magnificat.

5. Hans von Sternberg was Luther's caretaker at the Coburg fortress and was involved in the church visitation in Franconia and participated in the "secularization" of the monasteries of Franconia.

6. Thomas Müntzer, who was executed in 1525, symbolized for Luther the religious and political anarchism of the left-wing reformers. See also LW 13:61 n. 33.

7. Luther frequently reminisced about his early trip to Rome in 1510. See, for example, LW 1:7 n. 15.

8. In his second printing or edition (B¹) of "Psalm 117 Interpreted," Luther expanded his first one (A), which appears at the top of the WA pages with (B¹) at the bottom. In essence, the latter includes an introduction or dedication to Hans von Sternberg and adds another

three paragraphs, beginning on page 239. Then in the middle of WA, page 247, a paragraph from Luther's handwritten manuscript is added for the purposes of comparison with (A), and a paragraph from (B) is added to (A) on page 250. Last of all, six hefty paragraphs from (BC) are inserted before the very last paragraph of (A). At this point, having come to the end of the dedication of (B1), we return to the beginning to pick up (A).

9. Luther makes the same observations about the importance of the catechism in the Introduction to the Large Catechism and "A Simple Way to Pray."

10. The prophecy section has been omitted.

11. Here Luther identifies the monastic vocation and the Anabaptist call to separation from society.

12. Luther targets the Carthusians because they were especially rigorous in their spirituality.

13. (BC) insertion here for three paragraphs. WA 239:17.

14. See also "Judgment of Martin Luther on Monastic Vows (1521)," in LW 44:243–400 (see especially the introduction). See also the "Apology to the Augsburg Confession," written by Philip Melanchthon, on Monastic Vows, Article XXVII. See also the Address to the Christian Nobility.

15. See also LW 13:223 n. 89.

16. *Gray coat* symbolized the monks and the Anabaptists, whom Luther sometimes calls the new monks (LW 22:190). The gray coat was a sign of poverty. *Long face (sauren geberden)* here really means "against the world."

17. This is the essence of Luther's understanding of the legitimate vocation of government through reason and apart from Christ.

18. The Scholastics.

19. Luther means works that are alien to or unfamiliar Christian works, which are mindful of grace.

20. "And hope does not disappoint us" in the NRSV. The German translation is stronger and closer to the Greek.

21. See Luther's Heidelberg Theses, numbers 19 and 20, for his theology of the cross (WA 1:353–374 and LW 31:40).

22. See WA 8:166 or 37:411.

23. The NRSV reads, "as to a lamp shining in a dark place."

24. Luther now carries on a sustained dialectic for paragraphs.

25. This paragraph is inserted in pamphlet B (p. G ija).

26. The NRSV reads, "Those who bring thanksgiving as their sacrifice honor me; to those who go the right way I will show the salvation of God."

27. In pamphlet BC (p. H ij), Luther inserts six paragraphs here before the last paragraph.

28. Luther uses alliteration to effect in this sentence: *"Und das sonst kein ander weg noch steg, kein ander weise noch werk uns dazu helffen müge."*

29. *Schwärmer.*

Sermon at Coburg on Cross and Suffering

1. WA 32:28–39.

2. There is another transcript by Stoltz. The original text is in German. See LW 51:197.

3. See Phil 3 and Rom 12.

4. *"Christopher* is derived from the Greek contraction of the name of Christ *(Christos)* and the verb *pherein* (to bear)." LW 51:202 n. 1.

5. *Evangelisch*, a gospel believer.

Lectures on Galatians 3:6—"Thus Abraham Believed God"

1. WA 40/1:359–73.

2. Thus, Karl Barth took umbrage with Luther for both of these assertions, while Gerhard Ebeling defended Luther. Feuerbach earlier translated Luther's theology into anthropology and declared that human beings created God per se, while Luther strictly limited it to God in us; and Sigmund Freud went further, saying the heavenly Father was merely an illusionary projection of a human father into the heavens. See Gerhard Ebeling, *Luther: An Introduction to His Thought* (Tübingen: J. C. B. Mohr, 1964), 242–67.

3. See LW 13:88.

4. For Luther, unbelief is the chief sin.

5. A quotation from the first section of Book I of the *Institutes of Justinian*. See LW 36:357 n. 17.

6. That is, a good intention would make a neutral work good; it would not make an evil work good. See Thomas Aquinas, *Summa Theologiae*, I-II, Q. 18, Art. 8.

7. See LW 26:113 n. 32, "Both the affinities and the contrasts of Luther's thought with traditional mysticism are evident in his use of 'darkness' in passages like this."

8. This is a favorite idea of Luther, derived from Romans 8:23 and passages like Numbers 18:12–24.

9. See Thomas Aquinas, *Summa Theologiae*, I-I, Q. 48, Art. 5.

10. This is a *meritum de congruo*, which is a merit meeting the standard of God's generosity. It is a "half merit," which is an act performed in a state of sin, in accordance with natural or divine law *(facere quod in se est)*, and therefore accepted by God as satisfying the requirement for the infusion of first grace *(ex natura rei debita)*. In contrast with the *meritum de condigno*, the *meritum de congruo* has no other grounds on which reward is based than the mere generosity *(liberalitas)* of God. See Heiko A. Oberman, *The Harvest of Medieval Theology: Gabriel Biel and Late Medieval Nominalism* (Cambridge, MA: Harvard Univ. Press, 1963), 471–72.

11. Luther is thinking of the hydra of classical mythology.

12. The NRSV reads, "The mind that is set on the flesh is hostile to God."

13. *In eo enim ut sunt.* LW substitutes *et* for *ut*.

14. The Latin, which has become a classic Lutheran saying, is *Sic homo Christianus simul iustus et peccatur, sanctus, prophanus, inimicus et filius Dei est.*

15. Note this autobiographical account.

16. Here, Luther alludes to his teaching about the marvelous or joyful exchange between the soul as the bride and Christ as the bridegroom, most poignantly featured in "The Freedom of a Christian" in this volume.

17. The Old Testament reference is Exod 29:38–41.

18. *Imputatio seu reputatio.*

19. See the *Nicomachean Ethics*, Book V. Aristotle defines *justice* as "that moral disposition which renders one apt or having the capacity to do just things, and which causes them to act justly and to wish what is just." Aristotle, *Nicomachean Ethics*, trans. H. Rackham, Loeb Classical Library (Cambridge, MA: Harvard Univ. Press, 1934), 253. Thus, contrary to Luther's argument that it is divine grace from the outside that justifies the human being, who then does just actions, Aristotle had argued that "moral virtues...must be gained by practice and effort; morally, one becomes virtuous by performing virtuous acts." See Steven Ozment, *The Age of Reform 1250–1550: An Intellectual and Religious History of Late Medieval and Reformation Europe* (New Haven, CT: Yale Univ. Press, 1980), 235.

Jacob's Ladder

1. WA 43:575–83.
2. LW 5:xi.
3. See LW 26:127–29, where Luther explains his opposition to formal righteousness.
4. The NRSV reads, "You make the winds your messengers, fire and flame your ministers."
5. Nicholas of Lyra, Franciscan commentator (1270–1349). For a discussion of Lyra's Genesis Commentary, see H. Hailperin, *Rashi and the Christian Scholars* (Pittsburgh: Univ. of Pittsburgh Press, 1963); see also C. Patton, "Creation, Fall and Salvation: Lyra's Commentary on Genesis 1–3" in *Nicholas of Lyra: The Senses of Scripture*, ed. Philip Krey and Lesley Smith, Studies in the History of Christian Thought 90, ed. Heiko Oberman (Leiden: Brill, 2000), 19–43.
6. The standard medieval library reference work for the Bible. A collection of interlinear and marginal scriptural interpretations mostly from patristic sources, the "normal tongue" *(glossa ordinaria)* exerted tremendous influence on exegesis to the Reformation. For a complete discussion of its origin and use, see Karlfried Froehlich and Margaret T. Gibson, "Introduction to the Facsimile Reprint of the Editio Princeps Adolph Rusch of Strassburg 1480/81," in *Biblia Latina Cum Glossa Ordinaria* (Brepols-Turnhout: 1992), v–xxvi.
7. Or the communion of properties. See LW 22:492 n. 176.
8. See, for example, Ambrose, *De excessus fratris satyri*, II, 100, *Patrologia, Series Latina*, XVI, 1402; Bernard of Clairvaux, *Sermones de tempore*, Sermon I, *Patrologia, Series Latina*, CLXXXIII, 36 (cf. LW 22:103).
9. Bonaventure, *De Incarnatione verbi*, *Breviloquium*, IV, Opera omnia, VII (Paris, 1866), 282–95.
10. On this conception of the fall of Satan, see Qur'an, II, 36; VII, 12; XVII, 60.
11. *Hic est historicus, simplex et literalis sensus.*

Part III—A New Path to Prayer

Editors' Introduction to Part III

1. See Timothy Wengert, "Forming Faith Today through Luther's Catechisms," *Lutheran Quarterly* 11, no. 4 (1997), 383.
2. LW 54:563.

3. See Jaroslav Pelikan, "Introduction," LW 14: ix.

4. Ibid., x.

5. LW 53:195.

6. Ibid., 197, 198. See also, Robin A. Leaver, "Luther's Catechism Hymns," *Lutheran Quarterly* 11, no. 4 (1997), 397–421. Leaver writes, "The catechetical function of hymns has been fundamental to Lutheran theology and practice which, at least until the eighteenth century, ensured that every hymnal would have a substantial section of specific 'Catechism Hymns,' because through catechesis Christian experience is both created and interpreted" (398).

The Large Catechism: Preface and First Commandment

1. Luther is referring to the benefice system: properties given to the clergy for income. This arrangement did not yet include a conception of clergy being paid a salary.

2. In 1524 Luther described these kinds of works as "mad, useless, harmful books written by monks." They are "devil-introduced donkey dung" (WA 15/50:9–11). The collection of sermons named *Sleep Soundly, Sermons of the Time, Of the Saints,* and *For Sundays* were by the Minorite John von Werden of Cologne (ca. 1450–1500) and had twenty-five printings. The sermon repository, *Overpowering Sermons of the Time and of the Saints,* was printed seventeen times, and *The New Treasury of Lenten Sermons* existed in forty printings. See Johannes Geffcken, *Der Bildercatechismus des fünfzehnten Jahrhunderts und die catechetischen Hauptstücke in dieser Zeit bis auf Luther* (Leipzig: T. O. Wiegel, 1855), 13; and Rudolf Cruel, *Geschichte der deutschen Predigt im Mittelalter* (Hildesheim: G. Olms, 1966), 474–80.

3. *Fresslinge* and *Bauchdiener:* those who eat like animals and are servants of their stomachs or appetites. See Rom 16:18.

4. Luther published a prayer book in 1522 to marginalize Catholic prayer and devotional books (WA 10/2:375ff.).

5. In 1541 Luther writes, "We do not only fast, but we suffer hunger (along with St. Paul in 1 Cor 4:11), which we certainly see on a daily basis with our poor parsons, their dear wives, and little children, and many other poor, from whom the hunger stares out of their eyes. They hardly have bread and water, and further, have to walk about 'finger-naked,' having nothing of their own. The farmer and the burgher give nothing; the nobility takes, so that very few of us have anything, and we certainly cannot help everybody." WA 51:486.27–33; cf. 590.25ff.; cf. also Robert Kolb and Timothy Wengert, eds., *The Book of Concord: The Confessions of the Evangelical Lutheran Church* (Minneapolis: Fortress Press, 2000), 408–9.

6. Holy water served to put demons to flight and was used, among other things, in exorcisms.

7. Luther often uses the Saga of Dietrich of Bern—which was based on historical facts and legends about Theodoric the Ostrogoth (died 526)—to illustrate lies and fables. See Kolb and Wengert, *The Book of Concord*, 381 n. 12.

8. Ibid. n. 13. Kolb and Wengert translate this as "the power of God that burns the devil's house down." The German means "to cause damage to someone by means of arson."

9. See Psalm 82 in Part 1 n. 8.

10. Cf. WATR I (no. 751): "For what are the psalms other than syllogisms of the first commandment?" Luther could not be referring to the rational structure of syllogisms, but perhaps a performative structure of faith, moving from lamentation to praise through answered prayer.

11. A saying describing how, as a new taut tension-spanned cloth loses elasticity because of shrinkage, so human plans also suffer shrinkage when they are put into practice. WA 51:652, ll. 1–3 and 690 (no. 185). See Theodore Tappert, *The Book of Concord* (Philadelphia: Fortress Press, 1959), 361: "Vain imaginations, like new cloth, suffer shrinkage!"

12. This seems to be a version of the Socratic paradox: the more you know, the more you know you don't know; the less you know, the more you think you know.

13. This preface is based on Luther's sermon of May 18, 1528 (WA 30/1:2).

14. Kolb and Wengert translate this as "drilled in their practice." Kolb and Wengert, *The Book of Concord*, 383.

15. Cf. Hermann Werdermann, *Luthers Wittenberger Gemeinde wiederhergestellt aus seinen Predigten: zugleich ein Beitrag zu Luthers Homiletik und zur Gemeinde predigt der Gegenwart* (Gütersloh: C. Bertelsmann, 1929), 48, 62.

16. The Ten Commandments, creed, and Lord's Prayer. After 1525 the material of the catechism was expanded by two articles, namely, baptism and communion. WA 30/1:440–41.

17. Johann Mathesius, *D. Martin Luthers Leben in siebenzehn Predigten dargestellt* (Berlin: Der Verein, 1855), 129.13–16 (in German): "In the pulpit during my youth (I regret that I was in the captivity of the papacy until the age of twenty-five), I cannot remember ever having heard the Ten Commandments, creed (symbols), Lord's Prayer, or baptism. In school one lectured in Lent about confession and receiving the sacrament in one kind." Luther said this in 1529. Also found in other sources, e.g., WA 30.1:466–67.

18. Exod 20:2–17; cf. Deut 5:6–21.

19. *Feiertag* in German is literally "day of celebration," not "sabbath." Kolb and Wengert, *The Book of Concord*, 384.

20. Luther followed the common usage of his time here.

21. When the house was the center of productivity, servants, apprentices, and other household help were additional to the children, and the responsibility of the head of the household. After industrialization, the center of productivity became the factory, business, and office, separated from the household, so that now Luther would have to speak of teaching the employees.

22. Luther did not bother to trace the precise apostolic authors of the parts of the creed.

23. The NRSV reads, "Go therefore and make disciples of all nations, baptizing them in the name of the Father, etc."

24. 1 Cor 11:23–25 (Luther's translation).

25. Luther wrote songs based on the Ten Commandments, the Lord's Prayer, the creed, etc., as another way to learn the words by heart.

26. Kolb and Wengert note that "in Wittenberg preaching on the catechism was required four times a year according to the Ordinance of 1533." Kolb and Wengert, *The Book of Concord*, 386. See *Die Bekenntnisschriften der evangelisch-lutherischen Kirche*, 11th ed. (Göttingen: Vandenhoeck and Ruprecht, 1992), 559 n. 5.

27. Cf. Exodus 34:14, "For you shall worship no other God, because the Lord, whose name is Jealous, is a jealous God."

28. This text is Luther's translation of Exodus 20:5–6. It diverges a great deal from the one that Luther later uses in the conclusion of the Ten Commandments in this catechism.

29. Not in this short selection, but see Kolb and Wengert, *The Book of Concord*, 429, lines 321–22; 430, lines 326–27.

30. Luther is alluding to a Latin saying: Ill-gotten gains will not last to the third generation.

31. His sons Jonathan, Abinadab, and Malchishua all died in the battle against the Philistines (1 Sam 31:2; 1 Chr 10:2). His youngest son died at the hands of foul assassins (2 Sam 4:7).

32. "Luther believed that the Ten Commandments were arranged in decreasing order of importance." Kolb and Wengert, *The Book of Concord*, 392 n. 51.

The Large Catechism: The Lord's Prayer

1. Luther is referring to his explanations of the Ten Commandments and the creed.

2. For example, Matt 7:7; Luke 18:1; 21:36; Rom 12:12; Col 4:2; 1 Thess 5:17; 1 Tim 2:1; 1 Pet 4:7.

3. In the 1529 and later editions of the catechism, Luther inserted another paragraph here. See Kolb and Wengert, *The Book of Concord*, 441–42.

4. See "A Simple Way to Pray."

5. The rendering of this sentence has been taken from Kolb and Wengert, *The Book of Concord*, 444.

6. Matt 6:7; Mark 12:40.

Commentary on Psalm 118—The Beautiful Thanksgiving

1. Luther here plays on the words *lesewort* and *lebewort*.

2. Compare with Meister Eckhart's "Lesemeister and Lebemeister." See Bernard McGinn, *The Mystical Thought of Meister Eckhart: The Man from Whom God Hid Nothing* (New York: Crossroad, 2001), 1–19.

3. This commentary was written from the Coburg Castle during the Diet of Augsburg. Exposition of "Das Schöne Confitemini" (Give thanks to the Lord) (1530). WA 31/1:65–182 and LW 14:45–182.

4. An allusion to the increasingly prevalent custom of importing wines from Southern Europe into Germany.

5. This is the alternate reading in the NRSV.

6. The NRSV reads, "Beware of practicing your piety."

7. The English words *anguish* and *anger* are similarly rooted in the Latin *angustus*, "narrow," and *angere*, "to strangle."

8. The Weimar refers to similar sayings in 30/2:31 n. 1 ("heaven and earth are too narrow").

9. The Hebrew word may be found in LW 14:59 n. 25.

10. "Luther regularly explains the term 'god' as a reference, not primarily to the sovereign power or majesty of the Almighty but to God's love." LW 14:61 n. 26.

11. In the omitted section Luther has alluded to the priesthood, which has spiritual authority; the nobility, which has temporal authority; and the peasantry, which grows the crops and provides labor.

12. In the balance of the paragraph, omitted here, Luther cites John 8:51 and 1 Cor 15:55.

13. See Ps 90 in LW 13:81–82.

A Simple Way to Pray, for Master Peter the Barber

1. WA 38:351–73.

2. Peter Beskendorf, one of Luther's best friends and his barber. In those days a barber could also act as a surgeon. Luther wrote this for him in early 1535. See LW 43:189–91.

3. Literally, "I'll give you as good as I've got and how I hold with prayer."

4. Jesus teaches the disciples to pray and offers a parable encouraging prayer in Luke 11:1–13. However, the injunction to "pray constantly" is 1 Thessalonians 5:17.

5. *Gottes dienst.*

6. For *estate*, see note 8 for "Commentary on Psalm 82: Secular Saviors," herein. The estate of burghers developed when peasants gathered together to form towns and cities.

7. *Pfaffen* is the German word translated as "clerics."

8. Luther uses the words *ledig und lüstig.*

9. *Pfaff* is the German word translated as "cleric."

10. Latin: *Deus, in adiutorium meum intende* (Ps 70:1).

11. Latin: *Domine, ad adiuvandum me festina* (Ps 70:2).

12. Latin: *Gloria patri et filio et spiritui sancto.*

13. German idiom: They throw hundreds into the thousands.

14. Latin: *Laudate.*

15. Latin: "To be intent on many things is less than to have a single mind."

16. In these paragraphs Luther refers to the Lord's Prayer in the Latin: *Pater noster.*

17. Cf. Matt 5:18.

18. Luther relates to the Lord's Prayer as if it were a person, a martyr, a best friend, much as he does with the commentary "Das Shöne Confitemini." See note 3 of "Commentary on Psalm 118—The Beautiful Thanksgiving," herein.

19. Luther sometimes rhymes words and uses assonance in his prose, here: *sondern allein, rein und fein an Dir, meinem einigen Gotte bleibe.*

20. Luther uses *Feiertag*, literally, "day of celebration," not "sabbath."

21. *Oeconomiam und Politiam.*

22. *Haus wesen* in German, Carl Schindler in the LW translates "family."

23. LW 43:206 reads *ehren* as *ehen* and includes guarding their marriages. *Ehre* also means the "honor of a virgin," and *zu ehre helfen* meant "to have a wedding."

24. *Zerknirscht*, used especially for the confession at a deathbed. WA 38:372 n. 12.

25. In editions that came out right after the first ones, Luther added the section for the creed and left out the next two paragraphs.

26. Some of Luther's early editions insert Psalm 51 in this place.

27. This is the ending of an expanded edition of this pamphlet WA 38:352 Dff. The first three editions were shorter; all the rest had this section for the creed added.

28. *Gemechte*.

Concerning the Temptation in Predestination to Doubt One's Own Election

1. WATR 2:562, no. 2631b.

BIBLIOGRAPHY

Aland, Kurt. *Hilfsbuch zum Lutherstudium.* 4th rev. and exp. ed. Bielefeld: Luther-Verlag, 1996.

Beintker, Horst, ed. *Martin Luther: Evangelium und Leben.* Vol. 4 of Martin Luther *Taschenausgabe,* edited by Horst Beintker, Helmar Junghans, and Hubert Kirchner. Berlin: Evangelische Verlagsanstalt, 1983.

Benzing, Josef, and Helmut Claus. *Lutherbibliographie: Verzeichnis der gedruckten Schriften Martin Luthers bis zu dessen Tod.* Bibliotheca Bibliographica Aureliana. 2nd ed. 2 vols. Baden-Baden: Verlag Valentin Koerner, 1989, 1994.

Borcherdt, H. H., and George Merz, eds. *Martin Luther: Ausgewählte Werke.* 2nd ed. Vol. 5. Munich: Chr. Kaiser Verlag, 1936.

Bornkamm, Karin, and Gerhard Ebeling. *Martin Luther: Ausgewählte Schriften.* 6 vols. Frankfurt am Main: Insel Verlag, 1983.

Clemen, Otto, and Albert Leitzmann, eds. *Luthers Werke in Auswahl.* Vols. 1–8. Berlin: Verlag von Walter de Gruyter and Co., 1929.

Curie, Margaret A. *The Letters of Martin Luther.* London: Macmillan and Co., 1908.

Die Bekenntnisschriften der evangelisch-lutherischen Kirche. 10th ed. Göttingen: Vandenhoeck and Ruprecht, 1986.

Ehwald, Rudolf, ed. *Sendschreiben an Pabst Leo X und sein Büchlein von der Freiheit eines Christenmenschen (Widergabe der Reichsdruckerei).* Weimar: Verlag der Gesellschaft der Bibliophilen, 1917.

Köhler, Hans-Joachim. *Bibliographie der Flugschriften des 16. Jahrhunderts, Teil 1: Das frühe 16. Jahrhundert: Druckbeschreibungen.* 3 vols. Tübingen: Bibliotheca Academica Verlag, 1991–96. For Luther's pamphlets, see Vol. 2.

Köhler, Hans-Joachim, H. Hebenstreit, and Chr. Weismann. *Flugschriften des frühen 16. Jahrhunderts,* ca. five thousand pamphlets in German or Latin originally published 1501–30. (Microform). Interdocumentation Co., 1978–87.

Kolb, Robert, and Timothy J. Wengert, eds. *The Book of Concord: The Confessions of the Evangelical Lutheran Church.* Minneapolis: Fortress Press, 2000.

Lull, Timothy, ed. *Martin Luther's Basic Theological Writings*. Minneapolis: Fortress Press, 1989.

Luther, Martin. *The Bondage of the Will*. Translated and edited by J. I. Packer and O. R. Johnston. Grand Rapids, MI: Fleming H. Revell, 1957.

———. *D. Martin Luthers Werke, Kritische Gesamtausgabe*. 97 vols. Weimar: Hermann Boehlaus Nachfolger, 1883– .

Werke. 61 vols. Weimar, 1983– .

Briefwechsel. 18 vols. Weimar, 1930–85.

Deutsche Bibel. 12 vols. Weimar, 1906–61.

Tischreden. 6 vols. Weimar, 1912–21.

———. *Studienausgabe*, edited by Hans-Ulrich Delius. 6 vols. Berlin: Evangelische Verlagsanstalt, 1979–99.

Pauck, Wilhelm, ed. and trans. *Luther: Lectures on Romans*. Library of Christian Classics. Ichthus ed. Philadelphia: Westminster Press, 1961.

Pelikan, Jaroslav, and Helmut Lehmann, eds. *Luther's Works*. 55 vols. St. Louis: Concordia; Philadelphia: Fortress, 1955–86.

Schulz, Frieda, ed. *Die Gebete Luthers*. Quellen und Forschung der Reformationsgeschichte. Vol. 44. Gütersloh: Verlagshaus Gerd Mohn, 1976.

Smith, Preserved, and Charles M. Jacobs, eds. *Luther's Correspondence and Other Contemporary Letters (1507–1530)*. 2 vols. Philadelphia: The Lutheran Publication Society, 1918.

Strauss, Gerald. *Manifestations of Discontent in Germany on the Eve of the Reformation*. Bloomington: Indiana Univ. Press, 1971.

Tappert, Theodore G., ed and trans. *Luther: Letters of Spiritual Counsel*. Vol 18 of The Library of Christian Classics, edited by John Baillie, John T. McNeill, and Henry P. van Dusen. Philadelphia: The Westminster Press, 1955.

Woolf, Bertram Lee. *Reformation Writings of Martin Luther*. 2 vols. London: Lutterworth Press, 1952, 1956.

Select Bibliography for Luther's Spirituality

For a more comprehensive bibliography, see Marc Lienhard, "Luther and the Beginnings of the Reformation," in *Christian Spirituality: High Middle Ages and Reformation*, ed. Jill Raitt with Bernard Mc Ginn and John Meyendorff, 268–99 (New York: Crossroad, 1988).

BIBLIOGRAPHY

Aurelius, Carl Axel. "Luther on the Psalter." In *Harvesting Martin Luther's Reflections on Theology, Ethics, and the Church*, edited by Timothy Wengert, 226–39. Lutheran Quarterly Books, edited by Paul Rorem. Grand Rapids, MI: William B. Eerdmans, 2004.

Bainton, Roland. *Here I Stand: A Life of Martin Luther.* Nashville, TN: Abingdon, 1950.

Barnes, Robert. "Images of Hope and Despair: Western Apocalypticism, ca. 1500–1800." In *The Encyclopedia of Apocalypticism in Western History and Culture.* Vol. 2, edited by Bernard McGinn, 151–52. New York: Continuum, 1998.

Bayer, Oswald. *Living by Faith: Justification and Sanctification.* Translated by Geoffrey W. Bromiley. Lutheran Quarterly Books, edited by Paul Rorem. Grand Rapids, MI: William B. Eerdmans, 2003.

Bonhoeffer, Dietrich. "Martin Luther and the Holy Spirit." Vol. 9 in *Dietrich Bonhoeffer's Works*, edited by Wayne Whitson Floyd, Jr., 325–69. Minneapolis: Fortress Press, 1996.

Bynum, Carolyn Walker, and Paul Freedman. "Introduction." In *Last Things: Death and the Apocalypse in the Middle Ages*, edited by Carolyn Walker Bynum and Paul Freedman, 5–10. Philadelphia: Univ. of Pennsylvania Press, 2000.

Ebeling, Gerhard. *Luther Studium.* Vol. 3. Tübingen: J.C.B. Mohr (Paul Siebeck), 1985.

———. *Luther: An Introduction to His Thought.* Philadelphia: Fortress Press, 1970.

———. *Umgang mit Luther.* Tübingen: J.C.B. Mohr (Paul Siebeck), 1983.

Erikson, Erik H. *Young Man Luther: A Study in Psychoanalysis and History.* New York: W. W. Norton, 1958, 1962.

Erlander, Daniel. *Baptized, We Live: Lutheranism as a Way of Life.* Chelan, WA: Holden Village, 1981.

Forde, Gerhardt. *Justification by Faith: A Matter of Death and Life.* Philadelphia: Fortress Press, 1983.

Forell, George Wolfgang. *Faith Active in Love.* Minneapolis: Augsburg Publishing House, 1954.

Froehlich, Karlfried. "Luther on Vocation." In *Harvesting Martin Luther's Reflections on Theology, Ethics, and the Church*, edited by Timothy Wengert, 121–34. Lutheran Quarterly Books, edited by Paul Rorem. Grand Rapids, MI: William B. Eerdmans, 2004.

Haile, H. G. *Luther: An Experiment in Biography.* Princeton, NJ: Princeton Univ. Press, 1980.

Hamel, Adolf. *Der Junge Luther und Augustine.* Hildesheim: Georg Olms Verlag, 1934, 1980.

Hendrix, Scott. "American Luther Research in the Twentieth Century." *Lutheran Quarterly* 15, no. 1 (2001): 1–23.

———. *Luther and the Papacy: Stages in a Reformation Conflict*. Philadelphia: Fortress Press, 1981.

———. "Martin Luther's Reformation of Spirituality." In *Harvesting Martin Luther's Reflections on Theology, Ethics, and the Church*, edited by Timothy Wengert, 240–60. Lutheran Quarterly Books, edited by Paul Rorem. Grand Rapids, MI: William B. Eerdmans, 2004.

Hoffman, Bengt Runo. *Luther and the Mystics: A Re-examination of Luther's Spiritual Experience and His Relationship to the Mystics*. Minneapolis, Augsburg Publishing, 1976.

Hoffman, Bengt Runo, and Pearl Willemssen Hoffman. *Theology of the Heart: The Role of Mysticism in the Theology of Martin Luther*. Minneapolis: Kirk House Publishers, 2003.

Holl, Karl. *Gesammelte Aufsätze zur Kirchengeschichte: Luther*. Vol. 1. Tübingen: J.C.B. Mohr (Paul Siebeck), 1932.

Krey, Peter D. S. *Sword of the Spirit, Sword of Iron: Word of God, Scripture, Gospel, and Law in Luther's Most Often Published Pamphlets (1520–1525)*. Ph.D. diss. Graduate Theological Union, 2001.

Krey, Philip D. W. "Luther and the Apocalypse: Between Christ and History." In *The Last Things: Biblical and Theological Perspectives on Eschatology*, edited by Carl E. Braaten and Robert W. Jenson, 135–45. Grand Rapids, MI: William B. Eerdmans, 2002.

———. "Many Readers But Few Followers: The Fate of Nicholas of Lyra's 'Apocalypse Commentary' in the Hands of His Late-Medieval Admirers." In *Church History* 64, no. 2 (June 1995): 185–201.

Leaver, Robin A. "Luther's Catechism Hymns." *Lutheran Quarterly* 11, no. 4 (1997): 397–421.

Lindberg, Carter. "Luther on Poverty." In *Harvesting Martin Luther's Reflections on Theology, Ethics, and the Church*, ed. Timothy Wengert. Lutheran Quarterly Books, ed. Paul Rorem, 134–51. Grand Rapids, MI: William B. Eerdmans, 2004.

McGinn, Bernard, trans. and introduction. *Apocalyptic Spirituality: Treatises and Letters of Lactantius, Adso of Montier-en-Der, Joachim of Fiore, The Franciscan Spirituals, Savonarola*. Classics of Western Spirituality. New York: Paulist Press, 1979.

———. "The Changing Shape of Medieval Mysticism." In *Church History* 65, no. 2 (June 1996): 197–219.

———. *The Foundations of Mysticism: Origins to the Fifth Century*. Vol. 1 in *The Presence of God: A History of Western Christian Mysticism*. New York: Crossroad, 1994.

BIBLIOGRAPHY

———. *The Harvest of Mysticism in Medieval Germany*. Vol. 4 in *The Presence of God: A History of Western Christian Mysticism*. New York: Crossroad, 2005.

———. "The Last Judgment in Christian Tradition." In *The Encyclopedia of Apocalypticism in Western History and Culture*. Vol. 2, edited by Bernard McGinn, 394–95. New York: Continuum, 1998.

———. "Revelation." In *Literary Guide to the Bible*, edited by Robert Alter and Frank Kermode, 523–41. Cambridge, MA: Harvard Univ. Press, 1987.

Ozment, Steven. *Homo Spiritualis: A Comparative Study of the Anthropology of Johannes Tauler, Jean Gerson, and Martin Luther (1509–1516) in the Context of Their Theological Thought*. Leiden: Brill, 1969.

Patton, C. "Lyra's Commentary on Genesis." In *Nicholas of Lyra: The Senses of Scripture*, edited by Philip D. W. Krey and Lesley Smith, 19–43. Studies in the History of Christian Thought, edited by Heiko A. Oberman. Leiden: Brill, 2000.

Pelikan, Jaroslav. "Some Uses of the Apocalypse in the Magisterial Reformers." In *The Apocalypse in English Renaissance Thought and Literature*, edited by C. A. Patrides and Joseph Wittreich, 74–92. Ithaca, NY: Cornell Univ. Press, 1984.

Strohl, Jane. *Luther's Eschatology: The Last Times and the Last Things*. Ph.D. diss. Univ. of Chicago, 1989.

———. "Luther's Spiritual Journey." In *Cambridge Companion to Martin Luther*, edited by Donald K. McKim, 149–64. New York: Cambridge Univ. Press, 2003.

Tavard, George. "Medieval Piety in Luther's *Commentary on the Magnificat*." In *Ad fontes Lutheri: Toward the Recovery of the Real Luther: Essays in Honor of Kenneth Hagen's Sixty-fifth Birthday*, edited by Timothy Maschke, Franz Posset, and Joan Skocir, 300. Milwaukee: Marquette Univ. Press, 2002.

Tranvik, Mark D. "Luther on Baptism." In *Harvesting Martin Luther's Reflections on Theology, Ethics, and the Church*, edited by Timothy Wengert, 23–37. Lutheran Quarterly Books, edited by Paul Rorem. Grand Rapids, MI: William B. Eerdmans, 2004.

Wengert, Timothy. "Forming Faith Today through Luther's Catechisms." *Lutheran Quarterly* 11, no. 4 (1997): 383.

Wicks, Jared. "Living and Praying as Simul Iustus et Peccator: A Chapter in Luther's Spiritual Teaching." *Gregorianum* 70 (1989): 521–48.

———. "Luther (Martin)." In *Dictionnaire de Spiritualité*. Vol 9, 1206–43. Paris: Beauchesne, 1976.

Wingren, Gustaf. *Luther on Vocation*. Philadelphia: Muhlenberg, 1953.

General Bibliography

Althaus, Paul. *The Ethics of Martin Luther.* Translated by Robert C. Schultz. Philadelphia: Fortress Press, 1965.

———. *The Theology of Martin Luther.* Translated by Robert C. Schultz. Philadelphia: Fortress Press, 1966.

Altman, Walter. *Luther and Liberation: A Latin American Perspective.* Translated by Mary M. Solberg. Minneapolis: Fortress Press, 1992.

Bagchi, David V. N. *Luther's Earliest Opponents: Catholic Controversialists, 1518–1515.* Minneapolis: Fortress Press, 1989.

Blickle, Peter. *The Revolution of 1525.* Translated by Thomas A. Brady, Jr. Baltimore: Johns Hopkins Univ. Press, 1977, 1981.

Bornkamm, Heinrich. *Luther in Mid-Career, 1521–1530.* Philadelphia: Fortress Press, 1983.

Brady, Jr., Thomas A., Heiko A. Oberman, and James D. Tracy, eds. *Handbook of European History 1400–1600.* 2 vols. Leiden: Brill, 1995.

Brecht, Martin. *Martin Luther.* Translated by James L. Schaaf. 3 vols. Philadelphia: Fortress Press, 1985–92.

Chrisman, Miriam Usher. *Conflicting Visions of Reform: German Lay Propaganda Pamphlets, 1519–1530.* Studies in German Histories. Edited by Roger Chickering and Thomas A. Brady, Jr. Atlantic Highlands, NJ: Humanities Press, 1996.

Cranz, F. Edward. *An Essay on the Development of Luther's Thought on Justice, Law, and Society.* Harvard Theological Studies. Edited by Gerald Christianson and Thomas M. Izbicki, with introduction by Scott Hendrix. Mifflintown, PA: Sigler Press, 1998.

Dünnhaupt, Gerhard, ed. *The Martin Luther Quincentennial.* Detroit: Wayne State Univ. Press, 1984.

Edwards, Mark U., Jr. *Luther and the False Brethren.* Stanford, CA: Stanford Univ. Press, 1975.

———. *Luther's Last Battles: Politics and Polemics 1531–1546.* Ithaca, NY: Cornell Univ. Press, 1983.

———. *Printing, Propaganda, and Martin Luther.* Berkeley and Los Angeles: Univ. of California Press, 1994.

Eisenstein, Elizabeth L. *The Printing Press as an Agent of Change.* Cambridge: Cambridge Univ. Press, 1979.

Gerrish, B. A. *Continuing the Reformation: Essays on Modern Religious Thought.* Chicago: Univ. of Chicago Press, 1993.

———. *Grace and Reason: A Study in the Theology of Luther.* Oxford: Clarendon Press, 1962.

BIBLIOGRAPHY

Gritsch, Eric W. *Martin—God's Court Jester: Luther in Retrospect.* 2nd ed. Ramsey, NJ: Sigler Press, 1990.

Holl, Karl. *What Did Luther Understand by Religion?* Edited by James Luther Adams and Walter F. Bense. Translated by Fred W. Meuser and Walter R. Wietzke. Philadelphia: Fortress Press, 1977.

Huizinga, J. *The Waning of the Middle Ages.* Garden City, NY: Doubleday, 1954.

Janz, Denis R. *Luther on Thomas Aquinas: The Angelic Doctor in the Thought of the Reformer.* Stuttgart: Franz Steiner Verlag Wiesbaden GMBH, 1989.

Kirchner, Hubert. *Luther and the Peasants' War.* Translated by Darrell Jodock. Historical Series, edited by Charles S. Anderson. Vol. 22. Philadelphia: Fortress Press, 1972.

Köhler, Hans-Joachim, ed. *Flugschriften als Massenmedium der Reformationzeit: Beiträge zum Tübinger Symposion 1980.* Vol. 13. Stuttgart: Ernst Klett Verlag-J. G. Cotta'sche Buchhandlung, 1981.

Lazareth, William. *Luther on the Christian Home: An Application of the Social Ethics of the Reformation.* Philadelphia: Muhlenberg Press, 1960.

———. *A Theology of Politics.* New York: Lutheran Church in America Board of Social Ministry, 1965.

Lehmann, Hartmut. *Martin Luther in the American Imagination.* American Studies, a Monograph. Vol. 63. Munich: Wilhelm Fink Verlag, 1988.

Lindbeck, George. *The Nature of Doctrine.* Philadelphia· Westminister Press, 1984.

Lindberg, Carter. *Beyond Charity: Reformation Initiatives for the Poor.* Minneapolis: Fortress Press, 1993.

———. *The European Reformations.* Cambridge, MA: Blackwell Publishers, 1996.

———. *The Third Reformation? Charismatic Movements and the Lutheran Tradition.* Macon, GA: Mercer Univ. Press, 1983.

Loewenich, Walter von. *Luther's Theology of the Cross.* Translated by Herbert J. A. Bouman. 5th ed. Minneapolis: Augsburg Publishing House, 1976.

Löhse, Bernhard. *Martin Luther: An Introduction to His Life and Work.* Translated by Robert C. Schultz. Philadelphia: Fortress Press, 1986.

———. *Martin Luther's Theology: Its Historical and Systematic Development.* Translated by Roy A. Harrisville. Minneapolis: Augsburg Fortress, 1999.

Marius, Richard. *Martin Luther: The Christian between God and Death.* Cambridge, MA: Harvard Univ. Press, 1999.

289

Marty, Martin. *Martin Luther: A Penguin Life*. New York: A Lipper/Viking Book, 2004.

McGinn, Bernard. *The Mystical Thought of Meister Eckhart: The Man from Whom God Hid Nothing*. New York: Crossroad, 2001.

McGrath, Alister E. *Luther's Theology of the Cross*. Oxford: Basil Blackwell, 1985.

Oberman, Heiko A. *The Dawn of the Reformation: Essays in Late Medieval and Early Reformation Thought*. Edinburgh: T. and T. Clark, Ltd, 1986.

————. *The Harvest of Medieval Theology: Gabriel Biel and Late Medieval Nominalism*. Cambridge, MA: Harvard Univ. Press, 1963.

————. *The Masters of the Reformation:* Cambridge Univ. Press, 1981.

————. *Luther: Man* Between *God and the Devil*. Translated by Eileen Walliser-Schwarzbart. New Haven, CT: Yale Univ. Press, 1982, 1989.

————. "Luther contra Medieval Monasticism: Friar in the Lion's Den." In *Ad fontes Lutheri: Toward the Recovery of the Real Luther: Essays in Honor of Kenneth Hagen's Sixty-fifth Birthday*, edited by Timothy Maschke, Franz Posset, and Joan Skocir, 183–213. Milwaukee: Marquette Univ. Press, 2002.

Oberman, Heiko A., and Peter A. Dykema, eds. *Anticlericalism in Late Medieval and Early Modern Europe*. Leiden: Brill, 1993.

Ozment, Steven. *Age of the Reform: An Intellectual and Religious History of Late Medieval and Reformation Europe 1250–1550*. New Haven, CT: Yale Univ. Press, 1980.

————. *Protestants: The Birth of a Revolution*. New York: Doubleday, 1991.

————. *The Reformation in the Cities: The Appeal of Protestantism to Sixteenth Century Germany and Switzerland*. New Haven, CT: Yale Univ. Press, 1975.

————, ed. *Reformation Europe: A Guide to Research*. St. Louis: Center for Reformation Studies, 1982.

————. *When Fathers Ruled*. Cambridge, MA: Harvard Univ. Press, 1983.

Pelikan, Jaroslav. *Reformation of Church and Dogma (1300–1700)*. Vol. 4. Chicago: Univ. of Chicago Press, 1984.

Pero, Albert, and Ambrose Moyo, eds. *Theology and the Black Experience: The Lutheran Heritage Interpreted by African and African-American Theologians*. Minneapolis: Augsburg Publishing House, 1988.

Preus, James Samuel. *Carlstadt's Ordinationes and Luther's Liberty: A Study of the Wittenberg Movement 1521–22*. Harvard Theological Studies. Vol. 26. Cambridge, MA: Harvard Univ. Press, 1974.

BIBLIOGRAPHY

————. *From Shadow to Promise: Old Testament Interpretation from Augustine to the Young Luther.* Cambridge, MA: The Belknap Press of Harvard Univ. Press, 1969.

Prien, Hans-Jürgen. *Luthers Wirtschaftsethik.* Göttingen: Vandenhoeck and Ruprecht, 1992.

Robinson-Hammerstein, Helga, ed. *The Transmission of Ideas in the Lutheran Reformation.* Dublin: Irish Academic Press, 1989.

Scribner, R. W. *For the Sake of Simple Folk: Popular Propaganda for the German Reformation.* Oxford: Clarendon Press, 1981, 1994.

Searle, John R. "How Do Performatives Work." *Linguistics and Philosophy* 12 (1989): 535–58.

Shaull, Richard. *The Reformation and Liberation Theology.* Westminster: John Knox Press, 1991.

Stayer, James M. *Anabaptists and the Sword.* New edition including "Reflections and Retractions." Lawrence, KS: Coronado Press, 1976.

Steinmetz, David C. *Luther in Context.* Bloomington: Indiana Univ. Press, 1986.

————. *Luther and Staupitz: An Essay in the Intellectual Origins of the Protestant Reformation.* Durham, NC: Duke Univ. Press, 1980.

————. *Misericordia Dei: The Theology of Johannes von Staupitz in its Late Medieval Setting.* Leiden: Brill, 1968.

Stolt, Birgit. *Studien zu Luthers Freiheitstraktat mit besonderer Rücksicht auf das Verhältnis der lateinischen und der deutschen Fassung zueinander und die Stilmittel der Rhetorik.* Stockholm: Almqvist and Wiksell, 1969.

Tawney, R. H. *Religion and the Rise of Capitalism.* New York: Harcourt, Brace and World, 1926.

Thompson, W. D. J. Cargill. *Studies in the Reformation: Luther to Hooker.* Edited by C. W. Dugmore. London: Athlone Press, 1980.

Tonkin, John. *The Church and the Secular Order in Reformation Thought.* New York: Columbia Univ. Press, 1971.

Trinkaus, Charles, and Heiko Oberman, eds. *The Pursuit of Holiness in Late Medieval and Renaissance Religion: Papers from the University of Michigan Conference.* Leiden: Brill, 1974.

Vandiver, Elizabeth, Ralph Keen, and Thomas D. Frazel. *Luther Lives: Two Contemporary Accounts of Martin Luther.* New York: Manchester Univ. Press, 2002.

INDEX

Abraham, 112, 162, 163–64, 165, 177
Absolution, xxvii, xxviii, 183
Acedia, 129
Adam, xxv, 82, 113, 116
Adultery, 229–30
Agatho, Pope, 67
Alms, 34, 208
Ambrose, Saint, 40, 179
Anabaptists, 1, 149
Angels, 51–54, 172, 175, 181; evil angels, 51
Antichrist, 53; papacy as, 48–49, 121
Apocalypse, 46–47, 48–49; *see also* Judgment Day
Apocalypse of Saint John. *See* Revelation of Saint John
Aristotle, 169
Arians, 52
Augustine, Saint, 59, 149, 176

Backbiting, 26–27
Baptism, xxv, xxvii–xxviii, 57, 73, 133, 163, 192, 240–42; and Anabaptists, 149; as death of sin, 113–14; and priesthood of all believers, xxiv
Barnes, Robert, 48

Bernard, Saint, 149, 179, 180, 181
Bias, 93
Bible, xxii, xxiii, 119, 120, 121, 122; Old Testament, 73; *see also* specific topics, e.g.: Letter to the Galatians
Blasphemy, 213, 224
Bonaventure, Saint, 91, 180
Book of Revelation. *See* Revelation of Saint John

Canaanite woman, xxix
Cataphrygians, 51
Catechism: Large Catechism, xvii, xxv, 183, 185–202; Small Catechism, xxvi, 183
Cathars, 51
Celibacy, xxv
Christ, xv–xvi, xviii, 3–5, 70–80; second coming, xxi–xxii; theology of the cross, 91, 96, 125, 151–60
Christopher, Saint, xxix, 151, 155–57
Circumcision, 112
Commandments. *See* Ten Commandments
Confession, xxvii, xxviii, 183
Confession of Faith, 232–34; creation, 232–33;

redemption, 233–34;
 sanctification, 234
Contemplation, xiii, xiv
Contrition, 85–86
Covetousness, 73–74, 231–32
Creation, 232–33
Cross, theology of the, xvii, 91,
 96, 125, 151–60
Cruciger, Caspar, xviii

David, xiii, 17, 122, 123, 140,
 196, 211, 224; faith, 98,
 112; praising God, 102
Death, 212
Devil, 8–10, 12, 16–17, 53, 119,
 129–30, 138–40, 142–43,
 147, 180–81, 196, 212,
 220
Donatists, 51

Egran, John, 70
Encratites, 51
Epistle to the Romans, xvii, 57,
 104–18
Eschatology, xvi, xxi–xxiii, xxvii;
 see also Judgment Day
Eucharist. See Lord's Supper

Faith, xiv, xxii, 69–70, 73,
 74–78, 85–86, 101, 104–5,
 107, 109–10, 161, 162–67;
 and baptism, xxviii;
 centralization of, xvii; in
 the heart, 73, 167;
 justification by, xvi, xxiii,
 xxv, 73, 74–75, 76, 81, 87,
 104, 113; practices of,
 xxvi–xxix; prayer as

enactment of, xxvii; and
 reason, 56, 58, 163–64;
 and righteousness, 73, 77,
 83–84, 109–10; unbelief,
 73, 75, 84, 85, 104, 108,
 166
False witness, 231
Family life. See Parents and
 children
Forde, Gerhard, xv
Franciscans, 34, 49
Frederick, abbot of St. Giles of
 Nuremberg, 203
Frederick the Wise, elector of
 Saxony, xv–xvi, 6–7
"Freedom of a Christian, The"
 (Luther), xvii, 57, 69; text,
 70–90

Galatians, Letter to the. See
 Letter to the Galatians
Genesis, xvii
Good works, xxiv, xxv, 62–63,
 76–77, 80, 81–86, 105,
 110, 113; evil angels and,
 51; of prince, 29–30; and
 righteousness, 83
Grace, xiv, xxi, 108, 138,
 139–40, 141–42
Greed, 40–45
Gregory, Saint, 149, 176
Gritsch, Eric, xxx

Heresy, 51, 52, 55, 136, 142,
 147
Hess, Eoban, 184
Hilary, Saint, 67
Holiness, 99, 173–74

Hope, xvii, 59–68
Humanism, xv

Idolatry, 193–97; greed as, 40
Illumination, xiii, xiv
Interest. *See* Usury

Jacob's ladder, 172–81
Jerome, Saint, 47, 121, 143, 146, 217
Jesus Christ. *See* Christ
Jews, xxiii, 131
Joachites, 49
John Chrysostom, Saint, 59
John the Apostle, Saint, 50
John Frederick of Saxony, xvii, 91, 92
Judas Iscariot, xxix
Judgment Day, xxi–xxii, 46, 55
Justice, 28–29, 32–33
Justification by faith, xvi, xxiii, xxv, 73, 74–75, 76, 81, 87, 104, 113; *see also* Good works

Killing, 227–29

Laity, 79
Large Catechism, xvii, xxv, 183, 185–202
Last Judgment. *See* Judgment Day
Leo X, Pope, 69
Letter to the Galatians, xvii, 58, 161–71
Leupold, Ulrich, 184
Lindberg, Carter, 34
Lord's Prayer, xxviii, 64, 130, 174, 198–202, 218–21, 222–23, 224, 238–39
Lord's Supper, 57, 163, 183, 191, 192
Luther, Hans, 13–15
Luther, Martin, xiii–xxx; *see also* specific headings, e.g.: Justification by faith; Ten Commandments
Luther: Man Between God and the Devil (Oberman), xvi

Magnificat, xvii, 57, 91, 92–103
Manichaeans, 41
Marcion, 51
Marty, Martin, 69
Mary, xvii, 91–103; purification, 87–88
Meditation, xiii, xiv, xv, xvi, 119, 122–23
Merseburg, Elizabeth von, xviii–xix
Mohammed, 52, 53
Monastic life, xxiv–xxv, 125
Montanists, 51
Moses, 21, 22, 99
Mülphordt, Hermann, 70
Müntzer, Thomas, 51, 126
Murder, 227–29
Mysticism, xv

Nicholas of Lyra, 48–49, 175
Nominalism, xv
Novatian, 51

Oberman, Heiko, 1
Origen, 51, 146

Papacy, xv, 52–53, 54; as Antichrist, 48–49, 121

Parents and children, xxv, xxvi; honoring parents, 226–27

Paul, Saint, 11, 54, 78, 79, 84, 95, 98, 100, 108, 141, 148, 152, 158, 187, 199–200, 207–8, 220; *acedia*, 129; Antichrist, 53; Christ, 70, 76, 77, 149–50, 163, 169; Christian life, 86, 87; circumcision, 88; diligence, 91, 93; Epistle to the Romans, xvii, 18, 104–18; faith, 73, 75, 107, 112, 165; flesh and spirit distinguished, 104; good works, 112; greed as idolatry, 40; holiness, 99; Jews, 106; law, 81, 107, 115, 134, 135, 136; Letter to the Galatians, 161–71, 216; prayer, 227; righteousness, 72–73; scripture, 146; share in Christ's future glory, 14; sin, 62, 111, 113, 170–71; suffering, 154, 157, 159, 208; temporal government, 22, 88, 131

Pelagians, 51

Pelikan, Jaroslav, 49

Penance, 51, 143

Peter, Saint, 21, 77, 95, 110, 134, 142, 144; devil, 8; payment of tax, 88; penitence, xxix; prophecy, 49; suffering, 16, 154

Poor: alms, 34, 208; usury and, xvi, 34–35

Prayer, xiii, xiv–xv, xvi, xvii, xxiii, xxvii, 119, 122, 183–84, 198–202; Lord's Prayer, 191, 224, 238–39; for Master Peter the Barber, 217–34; of thanksgiving, 203–16

Predestination, 116, 252

Priesthood of all believers, xxiv, 78, 79

Prophecy, 49–50, 130, 146; kinds of, 49

Psalm 5, xvii, 59–68

Psalm 44, 96

Psalm 82, xvi, 1; commentary on, 19–33

Psalm 91, 14

Psalm 117, xvii, 125–50; admonition, 143–50; commentary on, 125–50; instruction, 135–43; prophecy, 130; revelation, 131–35, 146

Psalm 118, xvii, 58, 183–84, 203–16

Psalm 119, xiii, xiv, 72, 122, 123

Reason, 51, 55, 56, 165, 166, 169; faith and, 56, 58, 163–64

Redemption, xxii, 233–34

Revelation of Saint John, xvi, 46–56

Romans, Epistle to the. *See* Epistle to the Romans

Sabbath, 224–25
Sacraments, xxvii; *see also*
    Baptism; Lord's Supper
Salvation. *See* Eschatology
Sanctification, xxv, 234
Saracens, 52, 53
Satan. *See* Devil
Scholasticism, 59
Scripture. *See* Bible
Sin, xxvii, 76, 107–8, 110–12,
    138–40, 167, 169, 170–71;
    baptism as death of,
    113–14; freedom from, 76,
    105, 113–14; and grace,
    xxvii; hope and, 59, 60,
    62–63, 64–67; and mercy,
    59; and unbelief, 108, 110;
    see also Devil
Small Catechism, xxvi, 183
Sophists, 54, 121, 136, 137–38,
    144, 163, 165, 167, 168,
    169
Spenlein, George, xv, 3–5
Stealing, 230–31
Sternberg, Hans von, 125, 126
Stiefel, Michael, xxi
Struggle. *See* Trial
Suffering, 151–60; *see also*
    Cross, theology of

Tappert, Theodore, xvi
Tatian, 51
Tavard, George, 91
Temptation, xxiii, xxvii, 8–10;
    see also Devil; Trial
Ten Commandments, xxv, 18,
    74, 183, 188, 190, 223,
    224–32, 235–37; First
    Commandment, 183,
    193–97; long version,
    235–36; short version, 237
Tentatio. See Trial
Thanksgiving, xvii, 203–16
Trial, xiv, xv, xxiii, xxviii, 122,
    123; *see also* Devil;
    Temptation

Unbelief. *See* Faith
Usury, xvi, 34–45

Vocation, xxiv–xxv

Weller, Jerome, 8–10, 16–17
Weller, Matthias, 11–12
Where God Meets Man (Forde),
    xv
Works. *See* Good works
Wyclif, John, 48

Other Volumes in This Series

Abraham Isaac Kook • THE LIGHTS OF PENITENCE, LIGHTS OF HOLINESS, THE MORAL PRINCIPLES, ESSAYS, LETTERS, AND POEMS

Abraham Miguel Cardozo • SELECTED WRITINGS

Albert and Thomas • SELECTED WRITINGS

Alphonsus de Liguori • SELECTED WRITINGS

Anchoritic Spirituality •ANCRENE WISSE AND ASSOCIATED WORKS

Angela of Foligno • COMPLETE WORKS

Angelic Spirituality • MEDIEVAL PERSPECTIVES ON THE WAYS OF ANGELS

Angelus Silesius • THE CHERUBINIC WANDERER

Anglo-Saxon Spirituality • SELECTED WRITINGS

Apocalyptic Spirituality • TREATISES AND LETTERS OF LACTANTIUS, ADSO OF MONTIER-EN-DER, JOACHIM OF FIORE, THE FRANCISCAN SPIRITUALS, SAVONAROLA

Athanasius • THE LIFE OF ANTONY, AND THE LETTER TO MARCELLINUS

Augustine of Hippo • SELECTED WRITINGS

Bernard of Clairvaux • SELECTED WORKS

Bérulle and the French School • SELECTED WRITINGS

Birgitta of Sweden • LIFE AND SELECTED REVELATIONS

Bonaventure • THE SOUL'S JOURNEY INTO GOD, THE TREE OF LIFE, THE LIFE OF ST. FRANCIS

Cambridge Platonist Spirituality •

Carthusian Spirituality • THE WRITINGS OF HUGH OF BALMA AND GUIGO DE PONTE

Catherine of Genoa • PURGATION AND PURGATORY, THE SPIRITUAL DIALOGUE

Catherine of Siena • THE DIALOGUE

Celtic Spirituality •

Classic Midrash, The • TANNAITIC COMMENTARIES ON THE BIBLE

Cloud of Unknowing, The •

Devotio Moderna • BASIC WRITINGS

Dominican Penitent Women •

Early Anabaptist Spirituality • SELECTED WRITINGS

Early Dominicans • SELECTED WRITINGS

Early Islamic Mysticism • SUFI, QUR'AN, MI'RAJ, POETIC AND THEOLOGICAL WRITINGS

Early Kabbalah, The •

Elijah Benamozegh • ISRAEL AND HUMANITY

Elisabeth Leseur • SELECTED WRITINGS

Elisabeth of Schönau • THE COMPLETE WORKS

Emanuel Swedenborg • THE UNIVERSAL HUMAN AND SOUL-BODY INTERACTION

Other Volumes in This Series

Ephrem the Syrian • HYMNS

Fakhruddin 'Iraqi • DIVINE FLASHES

Fénelon • SELECTED WRITINGS

Francis and Clare • THE COMPLETE WORKS

Francis de Sales, Jane de Chantal • LETTERS OF SPIRITUAL DIRECTION

Francisco de Osuna • THE THIRD SPIRITUAL ALPHABET

George Herbert • THE COUNTRY PARSON, THE TEMPLE

Gertrude of Helfta • THE HERALD OF DIVINE LOVE

Gregory of Nyssa • THE LIFE OF MOSES

Gregory Palamas • THE TRIADS

Hadewijch • THE COMPLETE WORKS

Henry Suso • THE EXEMPLAR, WITH TWO GERMAN SERMONS

Hildegard of Bingen • SCIVIAS

Ibn 'Abbād of Ronda • LETTERS ON THE ŞŪFĪ PATH

Ibn Al'-Arabī • THE BEZELS OF WISDOM

Ibn 'Ata' Illah • THE BOOK OF WISDOM AND KWAJA ABDULLAH ANSARI: INTIMATE CONVERSATIONS

Ignatius of Loyola • SPIRITUAL EXERCISES AND SELECTED WORKS

Isaiah Horowitz • THE GENERATIONS OF ADAM

Jacob Boehme • THE WAY TO CHRIST

Jacopone da Todi • THE LAUDS

Jean Gerson • EARLY WORKS

Jeremy Taylor • SELECTED WORKS

Jewish Mystical Autobiographies • BOOK OF VISIONS AND BOOK OF SECRETS

Johann Arndt • TRUE CHRISTIANITY

Johannes Tauler • SERMONS

John Baptist de La Salle • THE SPIRITUALITY OF CHRISTIAN EDUCATION

John Calvin • WRITINGS ON PASTORAL PIETY

John Cassian • CONFERENCES

John and Charles Wesley • SELECTED WRITINGS AND HYMNS

John Climacus • THE LADDER OF DIVINE ASCENT

John Comenius • THE LABYRINTH OF THE WORLD AND THE PARADISE OF THE HEART

John of Avila • AUDI, FILIA

John of the Cross • SELECTED WRITINGS

John Donne • SELECTIONS FROM DIVINE POEMS, SERMONS, DEVOTIONS AND PRAYERS

John Henry Newman • SELECTED SERMONS

John Ruusbroec • THE SPIRITUAL ESPOUSALS AND OTHER WORKS

Julian of Norwich • SHOWINGS

Other Volumes in This Series

Knowledge of God in Classical Sufism • FOUNDATIONS OF ISLAMIC MYSTICAL THEOLOGY

Luis de León • THE NAMES OF CHRIST

Margaret Ebner • MAJOR WORKS

Marguerite Porete • THE MIRROR OF SIMPLE SOULS

Maria Maddalena de' Pazzi • SELECTED REVELATIONS

Martin Luther • THEOLOGIA GERMANICA

Maximus Confessor • SELECTED WRITINGS

Mechthild of Magdeburg • THE FLOWING LIGHT OF THE GODHEAD

Meister Eckhart • THE ESSENTIAL SERMONS, COMMENTARIES, TREATISES AND DEFENSE

Meister Eckhart • TEACHER AND PREACHER

Menahem Nahum of Chernobyl • UPRIGHT PRACTICES, THE LIGHT OF THE EYES

Nahman of Bratslav • THE TALES

Native Mesoamerican Spiritualit y • ANCIENT MYTHS, DISCOURSES, STORIES, DOCTRINES, HYMNS, POEMS FROM THE AZTEC, YUCATEC, QUICHE-MAYA AND OTHER SACRED TRADITIONS

Native North American Spirituality of the Eastern Woodlands • SACRED MYTHS, DREAMS, VISIONS, SPEECHES, HEALING FORMULAS, RITUALS AND CEREMONIALS

Nicholas of Cusa • SELECTED SPIRITUAL WRITINGS

Nicodemos of the Holy Mountain • A HANDBOOK OF SPIRITUAL COUNSEL

Nil Sorsky • THE COMPLETE WRITINGS

Nizam ad-din Awliya • MORALS FOR THE HEART

Origen • AN EXHORTATION TO MARTYRDOM, PRAYER AND SELECTED WORKS

Philo of Alexandria • THE CONTEMPLATIVE LIFE, THE GIANTS, AND SELECTIONS

Pietists • SELECTED WRITINGS

Pilgrim's Tale, The •

Pseudo-Dionysius • THE COMPLETE WORKS

Pseudo-Macarius • THE FIFTY SPIRITUAL HOMILIES AND THE GREAT LETTER

Pursuit of Wisdom, The • AND OTHER WORKS BY THE AUTHOR OF THE CLOUD OF UNKNOWING

Quaker Spirituality • SELECTED WRITINGS

Rabbinic Stories •

Richard Rolle • THE ENGLISH WRITINGS

Other Volumes in This Series

Richard of St. Victor • THE TWELVE PATRIARCHS, THE MYSTICAL ARK, BOOK THREE OF THE TRINITY

Robert Bellarmine • SPIRITUAL WRITINGS

Safed Spirituality • RULES OF MYSTICAL PIETY, THE BEGINNING OF WISDOM

Shakers, The • TWO CENTURIES OF SPIRITUAL REFLECTION

Sharafuddin Maneri • THE HUNDRED LETTERS

Spirituality of the German Awakening, The •

Symeon the New Theologian • THE DISCOURSES

Talmud, The • SELECTED WRITINGS

Teresa of Avila • THE INTERIOR CASTLE

Theatine Spirituality • SELECTED WRITINGS

'Umar Ibn al-Fāriḍ • SUFI VERSE, SAINTLY LIFE

Valentin Weigel • SELECTED SPIRITUAL WRITINGS

Vincent de Paul and Louise de Marillac • RULES, CONFERENCES, AND WRITINGS

Walter Hilton • THE SCALE OF PERFECTION

William Law • A SERIOUS CALL TO A DEVOUT AND HOLY LIFE, THE SPIRIT OF LOVE

Zohar • THE BOOK OF ENLIGHTENMENT

The Classics of Western Spirituality is a ground-breaking collection of the original writings of more than 100 universally acknowledged teachers within the Catholic, Protestant, Eastern Orthodox, Jewish, Islamic, and Native American Indian traditions.

To order any title, or to request a complete catalog, contact Paulist Press at 800-218-1903 or visit us on the Web at www.paulistpress.com